Praise for *Swallowing Clouds*

"Reading *Swallowing Clouds* is like sitting down to a richly orchestrated Chinese feast. As course after course is served, you not only enjoy its individual flavor, you also learn how the characters of its name are written and what early pictographs they derive from. You are entertained by folklore and tales from the author's life, each with its appropriate wine. And when you finally rise, satisfied, you realize that you have, in the words of a Chinese gourmet, been brought to 'understanding and tasting the meaning behind the food.' "

—John Espey,
Professor Emeritus of English, UCLA
and author of *Ezra Pound's "Mauberley"*

"*Swallowing Clouds* is one of the most interesting books I have ever read on Chinese food, culture, and language. I love the clever way in which A. Zee has meshed a highly informative text with a particularly wonderful touch of wit that makes reading his book such a pleasure!

—Ken Hom,
author of *The Taste of China*

"A charming and delightful book—I am glad to see an accurate book about Chinese food coming out."

—E. N. Anderson,
Professor of Anthropology,
U. C., Riverside
and author of *The Food of China*

Also by A. Zee

Fearful Symmetry

An Old Man's Toy

SWALLOWING
CLOUDS

A. ZEE

A TOUCHSTONE BOOK
Published by
Simon & Schuster
NEW YORK   LONDON   TORONTO
SYDNEY   TOKYO   SINGAPORE

TOUCHSTONE
Simon & Schuster Building
Rockefeller Center
1230 Avenue of the Americas
New York, New York 10020

10 9 8 7 6 5 4 3 2 1

10 9 8 7 6 5 4 3 2 1 Pbk.

Library of Congress Cataloging in Publication data
Zee, A.
    Swallowing clouds/A. Zee.
      p.   cm.
    Includes bibliographical references.
    1. China—Anecdotes.   I. Title.
DS736.Z44   1990
951—dc20   90-38670
                                               CIP
ISBN: 0-671-64665-6
ISBN: 0-671-74724-X Pbk.

Grateful acknowledgment is extended to the following for
permission to reprint copyrighted material:

Hong Kong University Press for ancient forms of the
Chinese character for fish from *The Etymologies of 3,000
Chinese Characters in Common Usage* by Chang Hsuan.
Hong Kong: Hong Kong University Press, © 1968.

Dover Publications, Inc. for ancient bronze inscriptions
from *Chinese Characters* by L. Wieger. New York: Dover,
© 1965.

To my parents

A map of China showing some places mentioned in the text.

CONTENTS

CONTENTS

PREFACE

MANY OF MY friends like Chinese food. Over a meal in a Chinese restaurant, the conversation will often turn to things Chinese—the culture and the language. Over the last decade or so, with tourism and commerce, Americans have become ever more interested in the Chinese language, particularly since it differs so totally from the languages of the West. The fascination with written Chinese goes back to the time when Europeans first came into contact with China and it has persisted ever since. What better place to chat a bit about the language than a Chinese restaurant, and what better way to illustrate some of the points made about the language than by pointing to the menu.

I invite you to come along for a chat. We will digress freely and wander down all the happy byways in a discussion about food and language. I can happily indulge my interest in etymology—the study of language. Over the years, I have learned the etymological origins of many Chinese characters, and in the course of writing this book, I have learned a great deal more. Incidentally, my interest in etymology is not restricted to Chinese; I find the etymology of English fascinating, with its wealth of vocabulary and its extensive borrowings from other languages. Chinese characters, however, present an additional etymological dimension since they are also pictographic. Many characters are derived from primitive pictures. With some imagination, you may be able to see cows mooing and fish swimming the next time you look at a Chinese menu.

At the same time that I am having fun with etymology, I am indulging, perhaps even more happily, in my interest in Chinese food. The pleasure is cerebral in one case, more visceral in the other. Writing this book has become a most enjoyable hobby for me, as I explore my interests in language and in food.

At a deeper level, the book is about Chinese culture. Much of Chinese living is devoted to the joys of the palate while the unique nature of the language has molded the civilization. I have tried to weave tidbits about Chinese culture into our exploration of language and food. One of my hopes is that even people who would normally not choose to learn much about China will find this book a pleasant way to obtain a glimpse of the civilization.

There are thus three leading characters in this book: the language, the food, and the culture of China. As I was writing, I often found myself drawn more and more into the food. At other times, it would be the other way around; I became absorbed in the etymology. Invariably, I would come back to one or the other. Meanwhile, the cultural framework is always there in the background. Is this book about food or language? Or is it really about culture? I will consider the book a success if I manage to confuse bookstore owners and librarians about where to put the book. The only solution, ladies and gentlemen, is to put it in all three sections—culture, language, and food.

A Chinese classic proposes that the well-rounded scholar should master the "six arts": rituals, music, archery, horsemanship, literature, and mathematics. In reality, the traditional Chinese scholar falls so far short of this ideal that it seems like a cruel joke. Still, the classic ideal is what I strive for. Of course, some modern equivalents have to be substituted: working on my tennis backhand appeals to me more than trying to become a Wilhelm Tell. But try as I may, I can't work up much of an interest in rituals; I submit my interest in food and cultural history instead.

THIS TIME LINE is meant to give you a rough overview of the chronology of Chinese dynasties. In the text, whenever I refer to a dynasty, I will always give its dates. There is no need to study this time line.

A complete table of Chinese dynasties is given on page 365. As you can see, only a professional historian can keep track of all the minor dynasties, many lasting only a few decades. To have a first acquaintance of Chinese dynasties, just remember the five "modern" dynasties: Tang, Song, Yuan, Ming, and Qing, in that order. A one-sentence summary of each of these dynasties will help you keep them straight. Chinese poetry reached its golden age in the Tang dynasty. Chinese cuisine, as we know it, was established and developed in the Song dynasty. As indicated on the time line, the Mongol Yuan dynasty, whose power was based on military might and rigid oppression, lasted a relatively short time. The Ming dynasty is perhaps best-known in the West for its vases. The Manchu Qing dynasty was pathetically weak and corrupt during the latter half of its rule.

In order not to clutter up the time line, I have indicated, in addition to the five modern dynasties, only the Han dynasty. During the expansionistic Han dynasty, Chinese influence was pushed far into Central Asia. The glory of the Han dynasty is such that to this very day some Chinese still refer to themselves as "Han people." Another important dynasty is the Qin, even though it lasted for an exceedingly short time. The building of the Great Wall and the compilation of the first dictionary both occurred during the Qin dynasty. Indeed, the Western name China was derived from the name of this dynasty, formerly transliterated as Ch'in. To keep the time line short, I have also omitted the earlier Xia dynasty (21st–16th century B.C.), Shang dynasty (16th–11th century B.C.), and Zhou dynasty (11th century– 221 B.C.).

The periodic fragmentation of China complicates the picture further. For instance, after 1127, the Song dynasty controlled only the southern half of China, while nomadic horsemen ruled over northern China and proclaimed in turn the Liao and Jin dynasties.

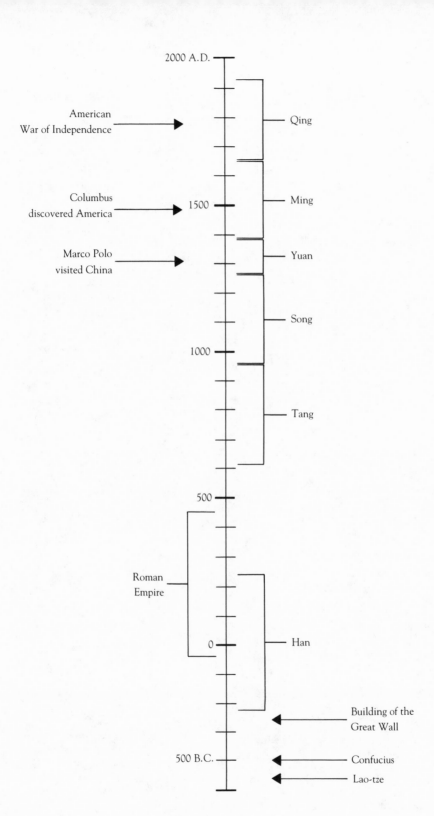

2000 A.D.

American
War of Independence

Qing

Columbus
discovered America — 1500

Ming

Marco Polo
visited China

Yuan

Song

1000

Tang

500

Roman
Empire

0

Han

Building of the
Great Wall

500 B.C.

Confucius

Lao-tze

A WORD
ABOUT
PRONUNCIATION

In this book I hope to teach you to recognize a few Chinese characters, so I will not even attempt to give you a guide to pronunciation. It would be foolish to learn pronunciation from a book anyway.

Occasionally, it is interesting and relevant to mention how a character is pronounced. I will not follow any particular system but will merely try my best to give you an approximate pronunciation.

In any book about China, there is the perennial problem of how Chinese characters are to be transliterated. For those of you who are interested, I will give you a brief description of the two main systems that have been used. You know there are two systems because surely you have noticed that Peking has become Beijing. If you are not that interested, you may want to just skim this note.

The earlier system was developed by Thomas Wade, a nineteenth century British army officer turned diplomat who spent most of his career in China. He devoted his later life to transliterating Chinese sounds. His system was further developed around 1912 by Herbert Giles, a professor at Cambridge University.

While the Wade-Giles system works fine for professional linguists who have been trained to know precisely what sounds to attach to each letter, it has caused a great deal of confusion for English-speaking Westerners. For instance, the name of the capital of China is pronounced in Mandarin with a *b* sound, not a *p* sound. Now a linguist can be trained to enunciate the *b* sound whenever he or she sees the letter *p*. But a casual reader who sees the *p* in Peking is going to pronounce it as if it is the first letter of an English word starting with *p*. As another example, the *tao* in Taoism is pronounced as *dao*. In general, the sounds represented by the letters *t*, *p*, and *k* in the Wade-Giles system are actually pronounced as *d*, *b*, and *g* respectively. *

If you talk to linguists, they will lecture you with great gusto, using such terms as aspirated and unaspirated, voiced and unvoiced, on-glide and off-glide, morphemes and words, aspect and tense, until your head starts to spin. It seems that the bottom line is that if I see a Chinese character transliterated with a *t* in Wade-Giles I should just pronounce it like a *d*.

Wade-Giles contains combinations of letters such as *ts*, *tz*, and *hs* that have long baffled Westerners. Another problem is that the same letters can represent distinctly different sounds. For example, *ch* actually represents four distinct sounds. That is why Chinese seems to the Westerner to be so full of words starting with *ch*. Wade-Giles tries to solve this problem of using *ch* to represent four distinct sounds by introducing additional marks, such as the apostrophe and the umlaut: there are ch and ch', u and ü. Since the casual English-speaking readers usually do not know what these marks mean, the result is more confusion.

This problem with *ch* is particularly confusing with regard to the names

---

* The shift of the *p*, *t*, and *k* sounds into the *b*, *d*, and *g* sounds, respectively, occurs in English after an *s*. Pronounce, for example, the words *stem*, *spin*, and *skin*.

of Chinese dynasties. Thus, with the Wade-Giles system we have the Chou dynasty (11th century–221 B.C.), the Ch'in Dynasty (221–207 B.C.), the Chin dynasty (256–420), and the Ch'ing dynasty (1644–1911). Good grief! Bravo for you if you can keep them apart. Some years ago, the government of the People's Republic of China introduced a system called pinyin for transliterating Chinese. In pinyin, the dynasties are known as the Zhou, the Qin, the Jin, and the Qing, respectively. (A table of the major dynasties is given on page 365.)

Pinyin is of course not perfect. After all, there are Chinese sounds that do not exist in English. Some letters have to be drafted more or less arbitrarily to serve. Thus for instance, you just have to know what sounds are represented by *q* and *zh* in pinyin.

Pinyin has its own peculiarities. The combination of letters *on* in *Song* dynasty is pronounced more or less like the *on* in the English word "bone." Of course, a casual reader is not going to know this and will speak of the Song dynasty as though it were the dynasty of song and dance. (In Wade-Giles, it is represented as the Sung dynasty, which is equally misleading.)

In this book, I have tried to use pinyin throughout. But I am faced with the problem that many terms of Chinese origin are now well known in their Wade-Giles transliteration. For instance, I hesitate to change Taoism to Daoism. I have also left such well-known names as Lao-tze alone.

While linguists can go on debating the relative merits of Wade-Giles versus pinyin, the rest of us are just devoutly hoping that a uniform system will be adopted, once and for all. In fact, pinyin is already widely used in the West; major Western publications such as *The New York Times* have all subscribed to this system. I am among those who hope that we will finally have one single undisputed system of transliteration, although, of course, there will still be confusion about words transliterated from a dialect other than Mandarin, like the Cantonese dish Moo Goo Gai Pan.

INTRODUCTION

CHINESE CHARACTERS FASCINATE many people. What secret messages do those mysterious pictographs convey? How does a language not based on an alphabet work? How can anyone possibly remember all those seemingly arbitrary patterns?

This fascination may reach deeper than we suspect. Symbols and signs have always carried talismanic and almost magical meanings for us humans. Consider the instantly recognizable peace symbol that aging hippies still wear or the corporate logos that define our society. Think of all those souvenirs made of Chinese characters that tourists pick up in garish Chinatown shops.

As is generally known, Chinese is not based on an alphabet. Rather, it consists of characters that evolved out of ancient pictures. Admittedly, languages based on alphabets are more efficient, and the idea of stringing letters together to form words is utterly clever. But I feel that if a computer were to design a language, it would use an alphabet. We humans would use pictures.

In this book, I will give you a taste of the language and culture of China by teaching you to read some of the Chinese characters found in menus.

Chinese restaurants are found in every corner of the world, or so it seems. In this country, Chinese restaurant menus are invariably printed in both Chinese and English. What better way to learn a few Chinese characters while you are waiting for your Moo-Shu Pork to arrive?

Next time you are in a Chinese restaurant, look at the Chinese side of the menu and try to pick out some characters. Perhaps you can have a contest with your dining companions. Children are notoriously enthusiastic about contests, and a contest to see who recognizes the most characters is an excellent way of keeping them from poking each other's eyes out with the chopsticks. Or perhaps you dine alone and simply need to pass the time while waiting.

Let me say right off that I am not writing a linguistic treatise. I do not want to make unrealistic promises. This book does not offer "Chinese in Twenty Easy Lessons." You will not master Chinese by reading this book. You will not even be able to read Chinese menus. Let's face it. If you want to learn any language, you will have to put in some hard work, and that can be painful. Instead, this book is meant to be fun. It is addressed to those who want to learn a few characters and have fun doing it. When you get through this book, you will be able to pick out a good fraction of the characters in menus. Perhaps you will even become more knowledgeable about Chinese food.

If, after reading this book, you want to go on and learn more Chinese, I would be overjoyed. Perhaps you have toyed with the thought of learning some Chinese, for one reason or another—you have always wanted to tour China, Taiwan, or Hong Kong, or you do business there—but are deterred by the magnitude of the task. This book offers you an easy and tasty way to start.

Don't just sit at home and read this book. Take it with you whenever you go to a Chinese restaurant. To help you remember, perhaps you should keep the book in the glove compartment of your car. Order some of the dishes mentioned. Try to picture the characters describing the dish you are eating. I hope to see your copy of this book stained with soy sauce.

Another motivation for me to write this book is to convince you that Chinese is in many ways an extraordinarily easy language to learn. Sure, if you already know English, French or German would be easier to learn. But try to compare learning Chinese with learning another language unrelated to the ones you know. I think that a Martian could very well find Chinese easier than English. Paradoxically, the very fact that Chinese is not based on an alphabet makes it easer to learn an entire group of words and to relate them to one another. After reading the next few pages, you will be able to recognize just about any character connected with cooking, for example.

So, let's start.

BEIJING MEN
BUILT A FIRE

IMAGINE YOURSELF AMONG a group of Beijing men. I mean real Beijing men. Darkness is falling and a chill wind is blowing down from the Mongolian steppes. You tug your skin wrap tighter around you. Suddenly the chief appears, growling, making strange guttural sounds. Ever since he was mauled by that bear in the throat, he has been impossible to understand. That he somehow survived has now endowed him with magical powers, particularly when he is wearing that full-length bearskin coat. As he approaches, you and your friends cower. The chief evidently wants you to do something, but you can't understand what. Frustrated, he suddenly picks up a rock. All of you jump away like jack rabbits, covering your heads in fright. But no, he doesn't throw the rock. Instead, he is scratching the earth. Curious, you approach cautiously. He is making lines in the earth with the sharp edge of the rock. He is drawing a picture:

What does it look like? Suddenly it dawns on you and you yell out "Fire! Fire!" (Your friends have always said that you are smart.) The chief throws you an approving glance as you tell your friends that the chief wants a big fire lit tonight.*

Chinese writing could really have started with a scene like this several thousand years ago. Naturally, over time, the pictures were simplified and modified. The next time the chief wanted a fire, he had only to draw 山 , and eventually, only 火 . The Chinese character for fire became

火

Now imagine sitting at your favorite Chinese restaurant. You pick up the menu. Some of the entries look like this:

牛肉炒麵 Beef Chow Mein

紅燒魚 Red-Cooked Fish

炸生蠔 Deep-Fried Oysters

烤羊肉 Roast Lamb

燻蝦 Smoked Shrimp

火鍋 Fire Pot

* Beijing man was unquestionably the earliest user of fire, around 500,000 B.C.

24

醬 爆 鶏 丁 Chicken Ding in Brown Sauce

鹽 焗 鶏 Salt-Baked Chicken

Test yourself on your pattern-recognition ability. How many occurrences of the fire character 火 can you find?

Here's a hint if you need help. Look at the third character on the first line: 炒 . Now I bet you can see the fire character 火 on the left. See it? Once you see it, you can easily discover the other seven appearances of 火 on the sample menu—one for each dish. Note that the first character in the sixth entry is fire itself, as in fire pot.

You guessed it! All eight characters containing the fire character are associated with some form of cooking. For example, 烤 means "to roast."

You have just learned a fundamental organizing principle of Chinese: characters related to one another share a common element. If you recognize 火 in an unfamiliar character, you would know immediately that the character has something to do with fire. The fire character 火 contained in a more complicated character such as 烤 is known as the fire "radical," or "root."

The same linguistic principle holds in English and other languages as well. We recognize the Greek word for fire in pyromania, pyralidid (a small moth attracted to fire), pyrargyrite (a sulfide-based mineral), pyretic (feverish), Pyrex (a heat-resistant glassware), pyritology (analyzing chemical compounds by using the blowpipe), pyromancy (foretelling the future by looking at flames), and finally, as is perhaps appropriate in a discussion of cooking, pyrosis (heartburn). The list goes on but I've made my point. Because of the convoluted history of the English language, you need some tutoring and a nodding acquaintance with Latin, Greek, and the modern Romance languages in order to recognize the etymological roots. Words containing recognizable roots often tend to be scholarly and polysyllabic. Few of us speak Anglo-Saxon and Middle English, but even if we do, we cannot see obvious relations between the words *fry* (Middle English, *frien*), *roast* (Middle English, *rosten*), *bake* (Anglo-Saxon, *bacan*), and *braise* (Germanic, *brasa*). In contrast, because Chinese has largely been insulated from foreign influences, the roots have not been obscured, and any Chinese who can read can easily pick out the roots.

Let us now go back and look at each of the dishes in turn.

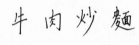

BEEF CHOW MEIN

"Hey, I know what this character 炒 means!" you say. Chow mein is Cantonese for fried noodles. Yes indeed, 炒 means "fry."

You even know how to pronounce it! "Chow" is pretty close to the Cantonese pronunciation. Not surprisingly, because of the size of China, numerous dialects flourished. Fortunately, unlike the situation in India, the written language has always been the same throughout China, thanks to a strong centralized government during much of Chinese history. Indeed, I am struck by how few major dialects there are. Furthermore, in most cases, pronunciations of the same character in different dialects are clearly related. Nevertheless, while the pronunciation for each character varies only somewhat from dialect to dialect, the cumulative effect in an entire spoken sentence is just enough to make speakers of different dialects mutually unintelligible. The difficulty is exacerbated by local idioms and slang. My father speaks a couple of European languages but claims that Cantonese is impossible to learn. In truth, it is considerably easier for the speaker of one dialect to learn another dialect than to learn an entirely foreign language.

Since the late 1940s, the governments on both the Mainland and Taiwan have designated Mandarin, the dialect spoken in and around Beijing, as the official language. While the younger generation now speaks Mandarin beautifully, the older generation has considerable difficulty. In the late seventies, I met Deng Xiaoping at a state occasion. I was eager to tell him how *I* would run China but alas, neither of us was able to understand a word of what the other said. An interpreter had to translate his Mandarin, heavily flavored with the twang of his native Sichuan dialect, into my Mandarin, which I learned while I was in graduate school in Boston. So much for that. Back to the food!

RED-COOKED FISH

The character 燒 means "burn" or "cook." This dish is also given on menus by the more descriptive name of soy-sauce fish. The fish is first lightly fried and then basted with a suitably seasoned soy sauce. The same idea can be applied to pork, chicken, and so on. The term "red-cooked" corresponds precisely to the Chinese characters 紅 燒 . (There, you have learned another character, 紅 , meaning "red," a very popular character in China, particularly since the revolution.)

Red-cooking is a style associated with the region around Shanghai, where my parents come from. The Shanghainese can be quite particular about the kind of soy sauce used. My wife Gretchen, who is of Irish-German descent, tells me that she would not think of using anything but what is known as "old" soy sauce for red-cooking. Around Shanghai, people like

their food sweet and in red-cooking they often add a dollop of sugar—
preferably brown sugar—to balance the salty taste of the soy sauce.

炸 生 蠔
DEEP-FRIED OYSTERS

The character 炸 is associated with explosive burning. Indeed, it is one
of the two characters in the word for "bomb." Many years ago, I lived in
New Jersey near a Howard Johnson's. Periodically, I would crave their deep-
fried oysters. After a few visits, I couldn't take their version anymore and
would have to drive to the Chinatown in New York, desperately seeking a
good seafood restaurant.

烤 羊 肉
ROAST LAMB

Old Beijing is remembered for its Moslem restaurants specializing in lamb.
Islam came to China through central Asia and most of its converts were the
nomadic tribesmen of the western part of the country. And since Moslems
do not eat pork, they excelled in the cooking of lamb. Some of them settled
in the capital and, quite naturally, ended up controlling the lamb trade. On
the first day of fall in the lunar calendar, these restaurants would display a
large mirror on which was written in red ink a single character 烤
meaning "roast."

Traditionally, the Chinese consider the summer as being harsh and
injurious to the body. Come fall, their thoughts turn to "repairing the body"
in preparation for winter. Lamb is considered just the thing. On the first day
of fall, those who could afford it flocked to the Moslem restaurants.

The Chinese do not roast much at home; they prefer to buy their roast meat at specialty shops that can be found in any Chinatown in this country. Roast pork and duck are among the most popular.

燻 蝦

SMOKED SHRIMP

This dish is not often found in Chinese restaurants in this country. Understandably, restaurateurs want to take the fast-and-easy stir-fry way out. Smoking as a form of cooking, however, is in fact fairly easy and leads to flavorful results. Gretchen makes a wonderful smoked chicken. She mixes together some grains of uncooked rice, a few tea leaves, and sugar in a wok and then sets the chicken in on a rack. She covers the wok and turns on the 火 (fire). That's about it. The same method may be applied to shrimp. By using different kinds of tea, you can obtain intriguingly different flavors.

火 鍋

FIRE POT

In recent years, fire pots have become increasingly popular. They can be purchased fairly inexpensively in the Chinatowns of major cities. On a chilly day, a leisurely meal built around the fire pot is just delightful. This is a do-it-yourself, group-participation meal reminiscent of the fondue. The host provides each diner with a mound of thinly sliced meat and seafood, vegetables, bean curd, and whatever else strikes the host's fancy. Chicken broth or some other soup stock is kept bubbling in the fire pot. With long serving chopsticks, each diner puts a piece of food into the boiling broth. The cooked morsel is then dipped into some sauce and eaten. The host would make a couple of different sauces, but part of the fun is that each diner may want to make his or her own, adding more or less of such ingredients as sesame oil, light soy sauce, vinegar, peanut butter, minced garlic, and so on. After all the food is eaten, the simmering liquid is then served as a soup. My favorite ingredient for the fire pot is lamb, sliced so thin as to be almost transparent.

For many years, Gretchen and I rarely used our fire pot because I could never get the charcoal briquets blazing. I would use lighter fluid and end up dripping it into the soup. I would stuff the chimney with newspaper and drop the briquets in but the briquets would refuse to catch. Once, my mother came to visit. After chuckling over my clumsy efforts, she simply placed the briquets on our electric stove and set it to medium. In no time at all, the briquets started glowing whereupon she picked them up with a pair of chopsticks and dropped them into the chimney. (The chopsticks are sacrificed in this method.) With this sure-fire, medium-tech method, it is now a breeze to use the fire pot.

醬 爆 鷄 丁

CHICKEN DING IN BROWN SAUCE

This dish is found in almost every Chinese restaurant, partly because it is easy to make: sauté bits of chicken in hot oil, then add sauce. If we put together the rather complicated-looking character for sautéing and the character for deep-frying, 爆 炸 we obtain a word meaning "explosion."

You have just learned another principle of Chinese: characters can be put together to form words with more complicated meaning.

Yes, the character 丁 is pronounced *ding* and means a small bit or sometimes an individual unit; I think it is both pictorially and phonetically rather apt.

鹽 焗 鷄

SALT-BAKED CHICKEN

I have rarely found this dish, one of my favorites, in a restaurant. You've guessed it—the dish requires some preparation. A large quantity of salt, roughly equal in weight to the chicken, is fried with anise pepper. The chicken, meanwhile, has been soaked in wine and subsequently hung out to dry. Wrapped in a muslin bag sewn tight, the poor bird is then buried in the toasted salt and sealed in a tightly covered earthenware pot. Finally, we are ready to stick the pot in the oven. A bit of work, yes, but the result can be finger-licking good!

Well then, we have met the character for fire and seven other characters, each associated with different modes of cooking and each containing the fire character as a root. Now you have to decide how much effort you want to put in.

I recommend that you take it easy. Just remember the character for fire and you are all set to identify all characters connected with cooking. And it is easy to remember 火 ! Look at the character and try to see the two logs and the three tongues of the leaping flame.

But if you are determined to master Chinese, you will want to go over the list of the seven characters describing seven different forms of cooking carefully: 炒 = fry, 烤 = roast, 炸 = deep-fry, and so on.

Perhaps I can suggest a compromise. Remember 炒 = fry; it's the simplest looking of the seven and also perhaps the most common. Astound your friends by picking out all the fried dishes on the menu!

The story of the character for fire is typical and illustrates two major principles about Chinese. First, the character is pictographic. Looking at characters today, we can still see in many cases the pictures from which the characters evolved. Second, once we master a character, we are immediately poised to make friends with a multitude of others. When the character we know appears in a more complicated character, it is called a radical. The radical gives us a hint of what that unknown character may be about.

There are radicals for characters associated with water, with the hand, with the foot, with the mouth, with the weather, with emotions, with illnesses, with metals, with earth, and so on. As we go on we will learn more and more radicals. * They are of enormous help in reading the written language. When you encounter a character you don't know, you can usually get a fairly good idea of what it means by recognizing its radical and by the context.

Chinese may be easier than you think.

---

* For your convenience, a table of some common radicals used in this book and a table of radicals and characters listed by chapter are given on page 366 and 367–376.

CHAPTER 2

SLICING
THROUGH WATER

AFTER FIRE COMES water. The character for water is just as easy to recognize as the character for fire. The earliest pictograph depicting flowing water looks like

$$\int\!\int\!\int \quad \text{or} \quad \int\!\int\!\int$$

The evolution of this character splits into two separate branches. Evolving from 氷 to 氷 and 氺 , the character for water eventually took on its modern-day form:

$$水$$

Meanwhile, the earliest form is retained as 川 . This character now means a small river and is pronounced *chuan*. Sichuan (or Szechuan) province, familiar to habitués of Chinese restaurants and written as 四 川 actually means "four rivers." (That's right, *si* or *sze*, depending on our dialect, means "four.")

By now, you are perhaps eager to look through a menu to see if you can find 水 or 川 . But if you do, you won't find many. That's because the character for water, when used as a radical, has undergone further changes. For example, soup is written as 湯 . The three strokes in the earliest pictograph for water have been compressed into 氵 , which can be seen on the left of the character for soup. 川 was rotated into 三 and then shortened into 三 . Later aesthetic considerations crafted the three horizontal bars into the more balanced-looking 氵 .

This combination of three strokes 氵 can no longer stand on its own as a character: in fact, it looks as if it would fall over to the right if unsupported. Thus, this combination only appears as part of a character and is always placed on the left, never on the right.

A graphic designer can readily understand the reason for this transformation. Consider writing soup as 𣱵昜 or 楊 . Neither of these characters exists, because they strike the Chinese calligraphic sensibility as unbalanced. The water root as written takes up too much room.

That characters have been shaped with aesthetic considerations in mind is an underlying theme in Chinese cultural life. One shudders to write a character that looks unbalanced. The same sensibility, perhaps with somewhat less intensity, existed in the West and has recently resurfaced. If I were a historian of pop culture, I could go on about calligraphy as a manifestation of cultural discipline. Is the decline of calligraphy and penmanship in the

West symptomatic of a breakdown in discipline, or in a positive light, of creative freedom? Perhaps people simply have better things to do.

Just as any character connected with fire and cooking contains the radical 火 , so any character connected with water, and by extension any liquid, contains the radical 氵 . I have already mentioned 湯 = soup.*

Traditionally, the Chinese believe that soup soothes the stomach and promotes good digestion. When I was growing up, we invariably had soup with dinner. In the realm of soup, the Cantonese excel. A few years ago, when I was telling my mother about all the different soups I had on a trip to Hong Kong, she replied, "Well, the Cantonese, they practically make a religion out of soup!"

Indeed, the Cantonese treat soup as one of the keys to good health. An elaborate system prescribes what kind of soup people should have according to their state of health. Are you feeling all dried up? Then you should have this soup. Are you feeling a bit tired? This soup would "repair" you. A bewildering variety of herbs, grains, dried fruits, roots, and so on are put in. For example, a soup to cool and clear your system contains pork, dried red dates, northern almonds, southern almonds (actually dried apricot kernels), and dried bok choy, among others.

How to keep all these ingredients straight? As you may expect, convenient soup packages are now available, with the various dried fruits, grains, and so on measured out in the recommended proportions. The soup is then

---

* Interestingly, the character for "forever" or "eternity" 永 contains the water radical. The idea clearly came from the ceaseless flow of water. In the original picture, the dot on top of the modern character represented a swirl in the flowing water.

a cinch to make: you just dump the contents of the package into a pot of water, add the appropriate meat, and simmer away. Some of these Cantonese soups have a pronounced medicinal flavor and are an acquired taste, but they are supposed to work if you have them day in and day out over a long time. A rather athletic friend of mine who happens to be a swimming champion swears by them. There is always a delicious-smelling pot of soup simmering ever so slowly in her kitchen. She taught me the regimen, but like all those regimens that are good for me, this one is just as hard to stick to as all the others. Oh well.

After coming to the United States, I learned from bitter experience not to order soup in Chinese restaurants. I am one of those unfortunates who suffer from the so-called Chinese restaurant syndrome triggered by the overuse of the flavoring agent monosodium glutamate (MSG). My ethnic pride compels me to add immediately that the syndrome is by no means restricted to Chinese restaurants. MSG manufacture and use in the United States is big business, and all kinds of restaurants use it routinely. An astonishing variety of prepared food is flavored with MSG; baby food manufacturers, however, removed it voluntarily from their products some time ago. Researchers have not agreed on how MSG works and why the syndrome affects only some people. Whatever the biochemical process may be, the syndrome is transitory, and the Food and Drug Administration has proclaimed it safe. In recent years, Chinese restaurants have become more sensitive to the problem and an increasing number of them now advertise on their menu "No MSG on request." I am pleased that this trend has caught on with Chinese restaurateurs, especially in the suburbs.

My reaction to MSG is immediate: my back tingles and my cheeks feel slightly numb. Why should soup be the worst offender? I used to think that it is because of the restaurateurs' laziness in making a decent stock. A more likely explanation is simply that the glutamates are more readily absorbed on an empty stomach. Have soup last or eat something before the soup, as in the French technique of eating a piece of buttered bread before any serious wine tasting.

This brings up that important question of when soup should be served. For the record, I was brought up with soup served at the end of the meal. The Chinese restaurants in this country invariably serve it first. In China, it appears to be a matter of regional preference: the Cantonese, for instance, have their soup first.

On my first visit to Japan, I was astonished to see the character for soup, 湯 , inscribed on the faucets in my hotel room. In a brilliant feat of deduction, I guessed that these faucets produced hot water. As you may know, written Japanese is an unwieldy mixture of three different scripts. One of the scripts, known as kanji, literally means Chinese characters, and uses them as such. In general, Chinese characters, when used by the Japanese, have the same meaning, but in many cases the meaning has shifted either in Chinese or in Japanese.

Another common menu character with the water radical is 油 , meaning "oil." Thus, sesame oil is 麻油 . The connotation of oil is rather liberally interpreted. Oyster sauce is 蠔油 and soy sauce is 醬油 .

I hardly expect you to memorize the rather complicated character that appears in soy sauce, but I want to tell you that it contains the interesting radical 酉 that evolved from the pictograph depicting an urn or a jar for fermenting liquid, of a type that can still be seen for instance in Chinatown grocery stores.

Actually, the character 將酉 is the general word for "sauce." Thus, soy sauce literally means "sauce oil." Two other popular sauces are hot (peppery) sauce and black bean sauce or black bean paste. If you are ever shopping for these sauces in a Chinese grocery store, just look for the urn 酉 with some complicated character on top.

The radical 酉 is associated with a number of characters all having something to do with fermentation. Two examples are 醋 meaning vinegar, and 酸 meaning sour. Incidentally, the term "sour grapes" has an analogy in Chinese. A person inflamed with jealousy, particularly in love, is said to have "drunk some vinegar."

Now think, what do humans regard as the most interesting fermented liquid? It is described by just about the simplest character you can form with the fermentation or urn radical: 酒 . On the left, we have the water or liquid radical just to emphasize that it is a liquid. Three guesses as to what it is? You're right, it means an alcoholic drink, a wine, or a spirit. On this universally beloved subject, more in the next chapter.

Now that we have learned all these water- and fermentation-related characters,

水 = water   醋 = vinegar

川 = a small river   酸 = sour

氵 = having to do with water 湯 = soup

油 = oil

let us look at a menu:

醬 爆 鷄 丁 Chicken Ding in Brown Sauce

鹽 水 蝦 Saltwater Shrimp

紅 燒 划 水 Red-Cooked Fish

蔥 油 淋 鷄 Chicken with Scallion Oil

四 川 泡 菜 Sichuan Pickled Salad

醋 溜 魚 Fish in Vinegar Sauce

酸 辣 湯 Hot and Sour Soup

Recognize some of the pertinent characters? Let us now go through each of the dishes in turn.

For the first dish, I purposely picked one that you already encountered in the last chapter. Look at the first two characters in the dish 醬 爆 鷄 丁 . See the fermentation urn radical 酉 in the first character and the fire radical 火 in the second? The dish is variously translated as chicken ding in brown sauce or diced chicken in dark sauce. Literally, the entry reads "sauce explosively stir-fried chicken ding."

The next two dishes feature the character for water. The first, 鹽 水 蝦 or saltwater shrimp, is simple to make: shrimp are quickly boiled in suitably seasoned water. The occurrence of the water radical in the third dish— 紅 燒 划 水 or red-cooked fish—calls for an explanation. The character 划 , as is almost suggested by the shape of 戈 , describes the action of oars as they slice through water. The combination 划 水 , literally "slicing through water," is then an alternative term for fish, an instance in which a living creature is represented by its action. Seeing this term on a menu, the Chinese can almost picture the tail of the fish slapping water.

This is the sort of linguistic term I like. Vivid and vigorous, it evokes for me childhood memories of going to restaurants with my parents. My father loves fish, and I remember the wonder of going up to the fish tank with him and looking at the fish swimming about as he picked one out. In fact, I seem to remember that all restaurants had fish tanks but that's surely a doubly selective effect of my memory, that my father liked to go to restaurants specializing in seafood and that visits to restaurants with fish tanks were more memorable. To children, the seemingly omnipotent act of picking out a live fish to eat must convey both terror and fascination.

The use of the term 划 水 rather than the standard character for fish in a restaurant menu has almost the power of subliminal suggestion to the reader on the freshness of the fish. And surely everyone knows that freshness is the sine qua non of fish eating. If the fish is truly fresh, though, I prefer not to have it red-cooked but lightly steamed, with ginger and scallion and a touch of wine. This mode of light steaming, known as 清 蒸 or literally "clear-steaming," is exceedingly popular with Chinese gourmets.

Note that the character 清 for "clear" is also water-based, literally meaning the clearness of fresh water. In menus, it suggests everything that is opposed to heavy sauces and grease. An upright official not tainted by corruption is called 清 高 or "clear and tall;" an innocent person is 清 白 , "clear and white." An honest restaurateur (and one who believes that happy customers make for good business) may even suggest red-cooking rather than clear steaming if his fish is not absolutely, positively fresh. Incidentally, did you recognize the fire radical 火 in "red-cooked fish" on the menu?

Chicken with scallion oil 蔥 油 淋 鷄 is an easy but

effective dish. See the water radical in the second and third characters? Perhaps you remember that the second character means oil. The third is a verb meaning "to pour liquid over something." Pieces of chicken are marinated in a wine sauce, steamed, and then covered with a mound of ginger and scallion strips. Smoking hot oil is then poured on top. As I write this, my mouth starts to water!

In 四 川 泡 菜 , Sichuan pickled salad, we see the two three-stroke combinations for water, one vertical and one horizontal, 川 and 氵 . 泡 means "to soak or to pickle."

In the next dish 醋 溜 魚 , fish in vinegar sauce, we again see the urn radical in the character for vinegar. The character 溜 , meaning "to marinate lightly in vinegar," does not appear often on menus. I consider it rather risky to order this dish because it often comes out much too vinegary and too gooey.

Finally, we come to 酸 辣 湯 , hot and sour soup. Recognizing the fermentation jar radical in the first character, you may have noticed that the Chinese characters for this soup are read sour and hot, not hot and sour. Does this curious reversal in English have any deep significance? Do the Chinese regard sourness as more of a defining characteristic of the soup than pepperiness? Surely here lies a doctoral thesis topic for someone. I can see it already, a dissertation entitled "On the Psychology of Food Nomenclature: A Comparative Study."

Perhaps interestingly, in spite of the bewildering variety of soups the Cantonese have, the most popular Chinese soup in this country is not Cantonese. Hot and sour soup is actually not an everyday menu item at home since it calls for rather exotic ingredients such as wood ears (a black fungus that grows on trees) and golden needles (dried tiger-lily buds). Lamentably, Chinese restaurants tend to skimp on ingredients since they can get away with it. More often than not, the hot and sour soup they serve is a travesty, a gooey concoction thickened with cornstarch. If you like hot and sour soup, you owe it to yourself to make it at home at least once, doing it right and seeing how good it actually can be.

One of the tastiest descriptions of soup I have ever read appears in a contemporary, fantasy martial-arts novel called *The Boy Who Shot the Hawk*. The novel follows the adventures of a teenaged boy and his sweetheart. At one point they meet a mysterious figure, whom the girl recognizes as one of the five premier martial-arts masters under heaven by noting that the man has only nine fingers. While Nine Fingers's skills in the martial arts have already become transcendental and zenlike, his great weakness is his taste for fine food. For not only is Nine Fingers a supreme martial-arts master, he also happens to be the finest gourmet in the world. In fact, he appears on the scene just as the teenagers are cooking a meal of beggar's chicken with a hen they have stolen. (More on beggar's chicken later.)

According to the ancient Chinese (and this is something I have never verified), when one's right index finger starts twitching, it's a sure sign that one's appetite is aroused. The right index finger is known as the eating finger in Chinese. Very strange. Anyway, Nine Fingers chopped off his own eating finger in a fit when he felt that his yearning for gourmet food was getting out of hand.

The girl, wanting Nine Fingers to stay and give them a few pointers in the martial arts and knowing his penchant for gourmet food, offers to cook him a meal. The next couple of pages describe how she proceeds to drive him crazy by refusing to tell him what she is cooking. Finally, she emerges from the kitchen of an inn where they are staying with a plate of beef strips and a bowl of soup. "In the emerald green soup were floating a hundred or so deep red cherries and underneath were tender morsels of bamboo shoots, the red mixed with the green and the white, the colors reflecting off each other: the soup was all subtle elegance." (Well, try ordering such a soup in your neighborhood Chinese restaurant.) The plate of beef strips looks quite ordinary by contrast.

Nine Fingers can hardly wait. Rinsing out his mouth with a swig of wine, he launches into the beef strips. As the juice from the tender morsels fills his mouth, he realizes that he is not eating any ordinary beef strips. A closer look reveals that each strip is made of several smaller strips. Nine Fingers closes his eyes and, chewing slowly, mutters, "Rump of lamb, breast of a suckling pig, leg of veal, and . . . and . . ." The girl chuckles. "And deer and breast of rabbit!" Nine Fingers exclaims triumphantly. The girl applauds while the boy gapes with amazement.

Nine Fingers turns happily to the soup. Spooning up a couple of cherries, he says smiling, "This is clearly

荷 葉 筍 尖 櫻 桃 湯

Water-lily leaves, bamboo-shoot, cherry soup!" The water-lily leaves, discarded upon serving, give the soup its clean fragrance and color. The subtle crispness of the bamboo shoots is complemented by the sweet softness of the cherries. Nine Fingers lets out a sigh as he bites into the cherries, for they have been hollowed out and stuffed with yet something else. "I am totally blown away. You are incredible as a cook!" Nine Fingers exclaims.

As Nine Fingers proceeds to recount to the teenagers how he had snuck into the imperial kitchen some years back and tasted the dishes there, the novelist never specifies what the cherries were stuffed with. What do you think, dear reader? My first thought was ham, particularly Chinese ham, to counterbalance the sweetness of the cherries.

As the story goes on, every day the girl entices Nine Fingers to stay an extra day and teach the boy by promising more remarkable dishes, much as Scheherazade, in the tales of Arabian nights, stayed her own execution by promising the king yet another tale. After several days, Nine Fingers says something loosely translatable as "Kiddos, no way I can hang around anymore. I am supposed to be a wandering master, and I just have to split and do my thing." Whereupon the girl nails Nine Fingers by replying, "But you haven't tasted my specialties yet."

"What? What?" he pants.

"I can't begin to list them all, but for example, stir-fried bok choy, slowly simmered bean curd, white-cut pork . . ." This of course has Nine Fingers completely hooked. As a true gourmet, he knows that it is in the most ordinary dishes that true cooks really show themselves. Incidentally, the girl cooks the bean curd by stuffing it into small holes she had hollowed out in a whole ham. She simmers the ham ever so slowly and after extracting the bean curd, she discards the ham. The procedure is reminiscent of a French haute cuisine recipe for cooking pheasant: a slice of pheasant meat is cooked between two pieces of veal which are then discarded.

I enjoyed this passage in the novel not only for its literary excellence which my sketchy translation cannot convey, but also for its illumination of some aspects of fine eating. * Consider the description of the soup. As in the haute cuisine of many cultures, color and aroma are very much prized in Chinese cooking, a fact that may not be apparent from some of the brown,

---

* The passage also shows how the Chinese love the challenge of trying to discern all the different flavors in a dish. This is in itself, of course, universal with all haute cuisines.

gooey dishes that I see only lamentably too often in Chinese restaurants. The Chinese are fond of saying that a great dish should embody 色 香 味 —color, fragrance, and taste. (We will not take time out to learn these three characters at this point but after all, this being a book partly about food, I have to call your attention to the obviously pictorial mouth radical 口 in the third character, meaning "taste." You will be encountering this radical again.) The use of water-lily leaves gives the soup not only its pleasing color but also what the Chinese call 清 香 , literally clear fragrance. It evokes the refreshing elegance of water lilies on a summer's day and in cooking embodies all that is subtle rather than heavy. Next time you are in a Chinese restaurant, ask them if they have heard of this basic principle of color, fragrance, and taste.

Once, when I was at a dinner with a well-known Chinese food critic and writer, someone mentioned this triad of food, fragrance, and taste. The elderly gentleman-gourmet responded that food writers, by constantly talking about these three characters, often miss the single character that summarizes the basic philosophy of Chinese cuisine. Naturally, we all wanted to know what that might be. He replied, to our surprise, that it was 意 , loosely translatable as "intention" or "meaning." Seeing that we were puzzled, he went on to say, "'When someone invites you to dinner, it is his intention that gives the food meaning. Only by understanding his intentions can you understand the taste you experience. This is what Chinese mean by 意 味 [loosely, understanding and tasting the meaning behind the food]."

Later, when I thought about it, it occurred to me that of the world's greatest cuisines, the Chinese is the only one you cannot enjoy by yourself.

PHONETICS, OR WHY SOME CHARACTERS LOOK HORRIBLY COMPLICATED

VERY EARLY ON, the ancients must have realized that the pictorial construction was not going to be nearly enough. You can't draw a picture for everything!

Imagine some poor scribe who had to write "roast." He knew how to say "roast," of course. "Kao," he said. As far as he knew, that was how "roast" was said since the beginning of time. The guy scratched his head until it occurred to him that the character for "examine" was also pronounced as *kao*. He knew how to write the character for "examine": 考 . The clever scribe put it next to 火 , the character for fire. And thus was the character 烤 for "roast" invented.

While the fire radical contained in 烤 tells us that the character has something to do with fire and cooking, the character for "examine" that it also contains does not contribute to the meaning at all, even though in contemporary English usage one might associate the notion of giving a student an exam with the notion of roasting the poor fellow. Rather, 考 plays a purely phonetic role. A Chinese familiar with the characters for "fire" and for "examine," encountering the character 烤 for the first time, would guess that it has something to do with fire and is pronounced something like "kao."

In fact, many characters look complicated merely because of the phonetic elements they contain. For instance, consider the rather frightening looking 燒 , meaning "to cook" or more generally "to burn," that we met in Chapter 1. The same phonetic element 堯 recurs in other characters and once you recognize it as a unit, then you will find numerous other characters less frightening.

Incidentally, in this case the phonetic element becomes easier to recognize if I tell you its pictographic origin, consisting of three earthenware containers 垚 piled high upon a stool or a table 兀 . (Incidentally, in the picture for the earth character 土 the two horizontal lines represent the surface soil and the subsoil; the vertical line is a plant growing out of the earth.) Thus, we find two logs, a fire, three earthenware containers, and a table. The earthenware containers probably hold offerings of food to an ancestor or a god.

燒 → the flame / the logs / the earthenware filled with food / the table

Once you've learned how to take Chinese characters apart, don't they seem a lot friendlier? To some extent, the same is true of English. Many really long words of the sort used in academia and with recognizable Greek roots—the ones most likely to frighten a Chinese first starting to learn English—are in fact the simplest, once you've learned how to take the word apart.

When we encounter a complicated-looking character, the chances are that it's phonetic. For example, remember 醬 , the character for sauce, with the urn radical 酉 ? All that complicated stuff on top of the urn is just a phonetic element.

The phonetic principle was in use by 800 B.C. or so and provided an efficient way of forming new characters. It is amusing to think that Chinese would have become a phonetic language based on an alphabet had this method dominated the purely pictorial method. That was precisely what happened in the development of purely phonetic languages. After all, the capital letter A came from a picture for an ox's head and B from a picture of a house. (Turn the A upside down to see the two horns on a head narrowing into a sharp chin. In Aramaic, *aleph* means *ox*.) At some point, the Phoenicians, the clever fellows who supposedly invented the alphabet, found it more convenient to use the twenty-six or so most commonly used symbols for their phonetic values and drop their pictographic content. Why didn't the same process occur in Chinese? I find it easy to theorize that, by 800 B.C. or whenever it was that the phonetic principle popped into someone's head, written Chinese was already so well developed by the method of combining the meanings of pictorial characters that it was impossible to discard all these characters.

It is obvious to me that all written languages must have started pictorially. Which path the language eventually followed depends on when the phonetic principle got invented. If at that point you have twenty or so pictorial characters, you may rather naturally use them as building blocks of a phonetic language. On the other hand, if you already have a rich repertoire of pictorial characters, the phonetic principle, though appealing, will necessarily play only a supplementary role.

It is erroneous to say, as we sometimes hear, that Chinese is entirely unphonetic. It is phonetic to a significant extent. Of those characters we have seen whose meaning is not derived from the meaning of the component characters, many, but not all, are constructed phonetically. Thus, 油 (oil) and 由 are pronounced the same, 醬 (sauce) and 將 the same, and so on.

What about the different dialects? It is in fact quite an impressive linguistic phenomenon that many phonetic characters remain phonetic as we go from dialect to dialect. In other words, if a character is phonetic in one dialect, it is usually also phonetic in another dialect. For example, the character 油 for oil is pronounced differently in Mandarin and Cantonese, but its phonetic element 由 (a common character meaning "reason" or "cause") is also pronounced differently in such a way that in both dialects the two characters 油 and 由 have the same pronunciations. This covariance in pronunciation, that as pronunciation shifts the pronunciations of characters shift in the same way, is of enormous help in learning a new dialect once one has learned one dialect.

As a memory aid the phonetic principle works in reverse in many cases. For example, all literate Chinese know how the character meaning "to burn" is pronounced, but few would know how the obscure and archaic character meaning "piling earthenware on a table as for a sacrifice" is pronounced. The character for "to burn" actually gives them a first clue on how that archaic character 堯 might sound.

Since the thrust of this book is to learn how to recognize written characters, we will not go into much further detail on the subject of phonetic construction.

CHAPTER 3

SLEEP
OF THE TRULY
INEBRIATED

WHEN WE PUT the water or liquid radical 冫 together with the urn or fermentation radical 酉 , we get 酒 , that universally beloved brew, the alcoholic beverage. In China 酒 , pronounced *jiu,* is fermented from a variety of grains, including rice, rather than from grapes. I will translate *jiu,* which covers an entire range of alcoholic beverages, loosely as wine. The Chinese classified *jiu* into white *jiu,* yellow *jiu,* and burning *jiu.* What is called liquor in the West is known to the Chinese as burning *jiu,* much like the firewater of the native Americans.

Rice wine is essential for Chinese cooking. So much so that it is virtually unthinkable to cook fish, for instance, without adding a tablespoon or so of wine to counteract the characteristic "fishy" taste. In general and almost as a matter of habit, a good cook will always add a sprinkling of wine, except to those dishes dominated by soy sauce.

Although wine is not used to create a rich, wine-based sauce as in French cooking, there are a number of dishes dominated by wine. Drunken chicken is probably the most common; in this dish the cooked chicken is marinated in wine for two days. Less common is drunken crab. Washed, raw pieces of unshelled crab are marinated in wine seasoned with shredded ginger for up to a week. The famed dish drunken shrimp requires fresh shrimp.

My mother recalls eating drunken shrimp on boat excursions in her youth. She told me that the fisherfolk would paddle their sampans up alongside and offer for sale freshly caught live shrimp. Wine was used to cook the shrimp on the spot: wine was poured into a rice bowl, a live shrimp dropped in, and the bowl immediately covered with another bowl; after the shrimp had thrashed about for a minute or two, it was ready to be eaten. I have always wanted to see how this dish actually works out for myself, but unfortunately I have yet to come across a supply of jumping jumbo shrimps in my local supermarkets.

Rice wine starts out as an almost colorless liquid that turns dark yellow with age. In many regions, wealthy families will seal off a large quantity of wine when a girl is born. The wine, known as "daughter's wine," is later drunk at the girl's wedding celebration.

Alcoholic drinks have always figured prominently in China; it could hardly have been otherwise in an agrarian society. The well-to-do drank wine at meals and in-between, at home and in various drinking establishments about town. In these establishments, singing and dancing girls would entertain the customers. The poor fermented their own drinks.

Of the numerous stories told about literati and their drinking habits, the following is among the more fantastic. But before I tell you the story let me teach you a couple more characters. Want to guess what 山 means? If you decide that it means mountains and comes from 山 , you have a good pictorial imagination indeed! You would have done well as a prehistoric caveman inventing characters! Another basic pictorial character is 人 for man or generally a human. Just as in the water radical, the character 人 when used as a radical is compressed into 亻 . As you can imagine, this radical appears in a multitude of words. An amusing example is 仙 , evidently a person dwelling in the mountains. But its actual meaning has shifted dramatically. Since hermits and alchemists went into the mountains to seek enlightenment and the elixir of immortality, the character gradually came to mean an immortal or a spirit that Chinese mythology is full of. There is no precise English equivalent, but perhaps one of the minor gods in Greek mythology embodies the concept of 仙 .

Now on to our story. During the Jin Dynasty (A.D. 256–420), a group of literati, fed up with society, formed what was known as the "Bamboo Grove Seven." Flaunting social conventions openly, they were forerunners of modern-day hippies. Our protagonist, the poet Liu Ling, was one of the infamous seven.* Liu was famed for his legendary ability to hold liquor. One day he passed by a drinking establishment. The fragrance instantly woke up the 酒 虫 (wine worm or wine insect) in his stomach. "Got to

---

* According to some sources, Liu Ling was actually a boy servant of the Celestial Queen Mother. While stealing a drink of celestial brew, he accidentally broke a glass and was thus banished to the human world by the Celestial Queen Mother.

check this joint out!" he said. As he started to enter, he noticed posted in front the two boastful lines:

> After one cup the ferocious tiger staggers drunk in the mountain,
>
> And after two bowls the ruthless dragon falls asleep deep in the sea!

Another sign proclaimed, "You don't get drunk, you don't pay!" Liu was provoked. "What an arrogant brewmaster making such outrageous claims! I'll show you!" he shouted.

The brewmaster, one Du Kang, came out and offered Liu a drink. Downing it in one gulp, Liu thought it had the subtle fragrance of the morning dew and started singing, "I, Liu Ling, have been to heaven sipping the brew of the Celestial Dragon, to the center of the earth drinking the cold spring water at its very source . . ." He hadn't finished the first verse before Du handed him the second cup. This time it tasted hot and fiery. Waving his hands and shaking his head, Liu chanted, "To the South Sea where the Buddhist goddess urges the holy dew on me, to the moon palace where the lunar maiden offers me a bottle of the gods' own brew . . ."

Du broke in, "Esteemed guest, you are drunk!" Liu was furious. Slamming his fist down on the table, he yelled: "I *am* boastful, I *am* arrogant, because I *am* the best drinker ever! I will drink your pitiful establishment dry so you can never post your sign again!" He snatched a drink from Du and downed it. He heard Du gently chiding him, "Time to go home, time to go home . . ."

"Yes, yes . . ." Liu found himself strangely complying. He climbed up on a cloud and floated home. His wife burst into tears at seeing him dead drunk. In fact, Liu was literally dead, drunk dead. But before he actually died, he instructed his wife: "No need to pray and to burn paper money and incense at my grave; just leave a jug of good wine on the first and fifteenth of every month on my grave. I have become a wine immortal 酒仙 !"

His wife did as she was told. On the first and fifteenth of every month, she would leave a jug of the best brew for her late husband. The next morning, she would find the wine gone.

Three years went by. One day, Du showed up at Liu's house asking for Liu. "What do you want? My husband has been dead for three years," Liu's wife replied. Du said, "I came to collect my money. Liu never did pay me." Liu's wife became furious. "You have the gall! My husband died from drinking your horrid stuff. I should have your arrested!" But Du replied, smiling, "Calm down, calm down. Your husband is not dead; he is just sleeping the sleep of the truly inebriated. You don't believe me? Take me to his grave."

Arriving at the grave, the brewmaster cried out, "Liu Ling, Liu Ling, quick, wake up! I have brought you an excellent wine." With a thunderous sound, the grave burst open. Rubbing his eyes and yawning, Liu Ling stood up, mumbling, "Where? Where is the excellent wine?" He grabbed the jug Du brought with him and gulped it all down.

Wiping his mouth, Liu said, "Fantastic, now I am really ready to become a wine immortal!" Laughing, Du held Liu's hand and the two floated up on a splendidly colored cloud.

The two friends, who really understood the power of drink, floated over the mountains of Honan. "What beautiful scenery! A wonderful place to set up a brewery," Du said.

"Yes, but to make a good brew, we need good spring water!" So saying, Liu splashed a jug of Du's wine over the landscape; and thus was born the famed Nine Springs Mountain 九泉山 of Honan province.

Recognize the water radical 水 in its original form in the second character? The character 白 means "white" or "pure," as we saw in Chapter 2. Thus, the second character, spring water, literally means "clear water." To this day, people and especially the natives of Honan say that the Du Kang wine and Liu Ling spirits (literally, "Liu Ling drunk;" that is, the spirits that made Liu Ling drunk) owe their excellence to the pristine mountain springs of the region.

I have vivid childhood memories of the drinking that went on during the banquets I attended. Unlike contemporary American society, when I was growing up, children attended almost all social functions. One of the men, rising to his feet, would "challenge" another man to a round of "fist guessing," a simple enough finger game but exceedingly effective in raising the level of conviviality. The respondent would rise, and both his and the challenger's cups would be filled. While the rest of the party cheered, the two men would swing their fists vigorously in the air as each man shouted out a number.* At the end of the third swing, each would extend some number of fingers, the object of the game being simply to guess the total number of fingers extended. The loser would then have to gulp his wine down, called 乾 杯 , pronounced something like gan-bay and meaning "drying out the cup"—the same idea as "bottoms up." As the evening wore on, both men, win or lose, would dry out their cups. The ladies generally did not participate. Rather, a man, rising to his feet, would "honor" some lady with a cup of wine. The lady, remaining seated, would be loudly urged by the company to dry her cup also. Most ladies would

---

* In the fist-guessing game, one does not yell out the plain numbers, of course. For instance, for eight, yell "Eight Immortals crossing the sea!" and for ten, "The entire family encounters good fortune!" Such references to folk culture as used in the fist guessing game are in danger of vanishing. In Appendix A, I describe the fist guessing game in detail.

demur and merely "wet their lips." Later in the evening, some man, feeling himself near his limit, would refuse to dry his cup, whereupon the party would loudly demand that his wife dry his cup for him. The vigorous fist-swinging and boisterous shouting do much to moderate the effects of the alcohol. At formal Western dinner parties, where one chitchats quietly with one's neighbors while sipping one's wine, I am always surprised at how fast the alcohol hits me.

Americans are generally under the impression that the Chinese are not particularly inclined toward alcohol. I think that natural selection accounts partly for that perception: those Chinese who immigrated to the United States are precisely those who are more apt to get their lives together. In the last few decades, many came as students or professionals. Certainly, there is a strong awareness within the overseas Chinese communities that alcohol is not conducive to bettering one's lot. As for the mainland Chinese, after a century of turmoil, war, and deprivation, people have generally come to regard alcohol as a dispensable luxury. In the 1980s, beer drinking increased rapidly in China, particularly among the younger generation. Tsingtao is the Chinese beer most familiar to Americans.*

* The characters 青島 for Tsingtao beer, meaning "green island," is the name of the once German colonial port city where the beer is brewed. See the character 山 for mountain in the character for island? It is used as a radical for characters having to do with geographical features on land. Incidentally, if you know Tsingtao beer then you also know how the character 清, meaning clear as in "clear-steamed fish," is pronounced since it contains 青 as a phonetic element. You probably know the last imperial dynasty of China to be the Ch'ing dynasty (or Qing dynasty in the pinyin system). Ch'ing is in fact the transliteration of the character 清 : that infamous last dynasty calls itself one of clarity. Here is an example of the confusion in transliterating Chinese: Ts'ing, Ch'ing, and Qing all represent the same sound. (In the map on page 6, Tsingtao is written in pinyin as Qingdao.)

Nevertheless the fact remains that the Chinese are less interested in consuming alcohol than many other people. They are certainly not in the same league as the Russians. At a wedding feast I attended in Soviet Georgia, the table was set with two bottles of vodka and two bottles of wine for each person. In fact, I find that wedding banquets provide marvelous occasions for sociological observation. Once, I was invited to a Chinese wedding banquet in New York given by people belonging to what can be described as the nouveau-riche merchant class, a class looked down on as ostentatious and uninformed by those better educated but less wealthy in the community. Set before every person was a bottle of an expensive brand of Scotch. Many of the guests were not sure what to do and so proceeded to gulp the whiskey down straight. The party got roaring in a hurry. But perhaps the most boisterous wedding party I ever attended was a totally nonalcoholic Moslem wedding in Cairo. Gallons of what tasted like Kool-Aid were served.

In ancient China, the oenophile could choose from a wide variety of flavors. In thirteenth-century Hangzhou, according to one contemporary account, fifty-four different kinds of rice wine were sold. The number of drinking establishments indicates the widespread use of alcohol. Various festivals and parties provided excuses for everyone to get drunk. In light of America's own disastrous experiment with prohibition, it is amusing to note that China's prohibition against alcoholic beverages was enacted and repealed no less than forty-one times during the twenty-four centuries between the Zhou (11th century–221 B.C.) and the Yuan (1271–1368) dynasties.

Of all the Chinese wines and spirits, mao-tai is probably the best known to Americans, partly because of Nixon's historic visit to China. The legend associated with the drink goes as follows. One winter's day in the village of Mao Tai (literally, something like "haystack"), where most inhabitants were engaged in wine brewing, it started to snow, and most unusual it was for this part of the country. In the midst of the snow, a barefoot maiden dressed in rags whom nobody had seen before appeared in the village. She went to the richest man's place and said to the brewery workers, "Oh please, give me a bowl of 酒 to make me warm. I am so cold." One of the workers reached into a barrel and offered a bowl to the poor maiden, saying, "Drink this and leave quickly before the boss sees you." But before the maiden could touch bowl to her lips, the rich man came out. Furious, he snatched the bowl from the maiden and barked, "Stealing my wine, eh. You filthy bitch! Scram!"

Walking through the village, the maiden came to a dilapidated hut where an old couple lived. Seeing the maiden, the old man cried out, "Come on in and have some 酒 to warm yourself. You shouldn't be walking around on a day like this!" After the maiden had a bowl and warmed herself by the fire, she got up to leave. "Where are you going?" the old woman said. "Where?" the maiden replied. "We homeless poor just go wherever we go." The old woman held the maiden's hands. "We are all poor, so no need to stand on ceremony. Please share our dinner and spend the night here."

That night, the old man dreamt of a beautiful celestial maiden 仙 女 , trailing two long red ribbons, dressed and bejewelled thus and thus (I spare you the details) and coming to the village holding a crystal goblet filled with a celestial wine from the palace in the sky. With a smile, she poured the wine onto Mao Tai village. The old man woke with a start and told his wife. A sunny new day was already dawning. The maiden was gone! Going outside, they were astonished to see a brook murmuring by their hut. The old woman said, "Let's try this water in our wine brewing." The 酒

thus made turned out to be terrific, with a subtle bouquet, full-bodied without being pretentious, as they say. Its fame spread far and wide, and was even served to a Republican president visiting from a beautiful country far, far away.

Meanwhile, guess what happened to the rich man? His wine turned sour. He tried various tricks but nothing worked. Nobody wanted to touch his stuff. He lost his advertising budget and soon squandered his whole fortune. To this day, a bottle of mao-tai always comes with two red ribbons attached, in remembrance of the celestial maiden.

In China, grape wine became known through military conquests during the expansionist Han dynasty (206 B.C.–A.D. 220). One such expedition was described by the Tang dynasty poet Wang Han:[*]

葡 萄 美 酒 夜 光 杯，

A lovely grape wine in a night-glow cup,

欲 飲 琵 琶 馬 上 催

As I am about to drink the cavalry-corps lutes hurry me on;

醉 臥 沙 場 君 莫 笑

Please do not mock me lying dead drunk on the battlefield,

古 來 征 戰 幾 人 回

How many have ever returned from war and conquest?

---

[*] I should say that much of Chinese poetry is devoted to praising the pleasures of the drink. By consensus the best poet ever is Li Po (李 白) of the Tang dynasty.

A resolute romantic, he out-Byroned Byron. Judging from his poems, his life appears to have been one continuous alcoholic haze.

In case you would like to drink wine from a cup that glows at night, I should explain that the cup came as a tribute from the West to a Zhou dynasty emperor. Made of a translucent white jade, it was said to glow in the dark. Perhaps it was coated with a phosphorescent substance. Tacky, eh?

In the poem, the warrior was trying to get drunk before going into battle. Evidently, they already had grape wine. Were they trying to get more —or perhaps—a better vintage? How could the wine from central Asia be any good? Did they import from Greece by caravan? Or perhaps from the Middle East? Manischewitz?

Look at the first line of the poem. Can you find the character for wine? Yes, there it is, the fourth character. Now look at the first character of the third line 醉 . Aha, see the urn or fermentation radical. It means drunk. The right half is a phonetic element.*

Chinese has a wealth of characters describing different states of inebri- ation and they all carry the fermentation radical 酉 : for example, 醺 means "giddy"; 酗 , "drunk and belligerent"; 酣 , "drunk and merry"; and 醒 , "drunk and feeling sick."

We see how the radical system can extend itself and branch off, as it were. The radical 酉 , which came from a picture of an urn, generates a series of characters having to do with fermentation. The most important

---

* Are you a budding linguist? Scanning the poem, you might also have noticed the character 沙 . Perhaps the water radical 氵 caught your eye. But the character means "sand," a sandy field being the poetic representation of a battlefield. What is going on? While sand does not appear often on menus (hopefully), the etymological origin of the word is of sufficient interest to warrant a comment here. What, you might ask, does sand have to do with water? The character 少 that appears in the right half of 沙 , means "less" or "lack of." When the tide recedes, you see sand. Get it?

of these characters, 酒 for alcoholic beverage, then allows the radical to be associated with another series of characters having to do with inebriation.

Incidentally, the intimate connection between wine 酒 and vinegar 醋 , made clear in Chinese by their sharing a radical, is obscured somewhat in English by a distorted spelling. Consider the corresponding French words: *vin* (wine) and *vinaigre* (vinegar). In French, *aigre* means "sour." Vinegar is wine gone sour. The two words share the same root.

It's amusing to see that the character for medical doctor, 醫 , also contains the 酉 radical. Presumably, early doctors gave their patients fermented drinks to revive them.

By the twelfth century, "very good wines" were widely imported from abroad, as was noted by Marco Polo. Grape wine had lost its novelty and was no longer worth dying for. In any case, the people preferred rice wine. Signor Polo gushed that the rice wine was made "so well and with such a flavor that it is better worth drinking than any other wine of grapes and men could not wish better." The modern-day nouveaux riches in the Chinese community in the United States apparently disagree with the Venetian's judgment. Incidentally, the Mongol Yuan-dynasty court that Marco Polo visited was exceptionally soaked with drink. Several Yuan emperors died of alcoholism.

Psychologists studying memory tell us that smell and taste are two of the most potent cues for retrieving past experiences: a particularly unusual smell or taste would often trigger a flood of vividly recollected childhood experiences. To the Western reader, perhaps the best-known description of this phenomenon is that given by Proust in his *Remembrance of Things Past*. For

Proust, the taste and smell of a "crumb of madeleine soaked in [a] concoction of lime flowers," which his aunt used to give him, immediately brought back the setting of his aunt's old gray house. (Next time I am in France, I've got to ask for crumbs of madeleine soaked in lime-flower tea and watch how the waiter reacts.) For me, the taste and smell of a lump of fermented glutinous rice, known as *jiu niang,* does the trick.

I must have been six or seven then; we lived in a second-floor apartment on a bustling street in Hong Kong. I would spend what seemed like hours watching the people walk by. Once a month or so, a *jiu niang* vendor would come by, balancing his wares on a bamboo pole. He would cry out in his peculiarly accented Shanghainese, "Madame, want some *jiu niang?*" To this day, I can hear in my mind the almost musical cadence of his cry. His use of Shanghainese was also distinctive, since Cantonese was and is the dialect of Hong Kong. He was probably in his forties, but at the time I thought of him as a wiry old man, dressed in a nondescript, dark-colored Chinese outfit. I particularly remember his severely crew-cut, almost bald, head. My mother would invariably buy some, often telling us children later, as a cautionary tale, how arduous and miserable the lives of such vendors were. The alcoholic content is fairly low. My mother declared that it was okay for us children to have some. No doubt, this taste of the otherwise forbidden further strengthened my memory of *jiu niang.* Such was my first introduction to the aroma and allure of alcohol, mixed with the taste of cold and wet glutinous rice.

Jiu niang is made by fermenting glutinous rice, also called sticky rice, with a mixture of "wine ball" and flour. You can purchase a wine ball just as you would purchase a starter yeast to make yogurt. Once made, *jiu niang* has to be refrigerated. Hardly anybody would actually make *jiu niang* since it

is available ready-made. In this country, you can ask for it as "brewed rice,"
or you can try the challenge of finding the two fermentation jar
radicals in 酒釀 (*jiu niang*) in the refrigerator section of a Chinese
grocery store.

SWALLOWING
CLOUDS

In old China, the streets were alive with peddlers selling a bewildering variety of snacks. The wonton seller was always one of the favorites, carrying his wares on a long bamboo pole. On one end hangs the stove with the pot of broth, on the other his supply of yet-to-be-cooked wonton. Setting up his business on a street corner, he would get the broth boiling and call out to the passersby to sample his delicious wonton. With big clouds of steam coming out of his pot and the enticing fragrance of the broth, few passersby could resist. When I was a young boy in Hong Kong, wonton were often sold from more-or-less permanent stands set up in the streets.

Alas, these street wonton were forbidden to me. When I had the chance, I would look at the customers sitting on tall stools, slurping their wonton with big clouds of steam swirling about them. And thus I developed an almost romantic fondness for wonton. To this day, in between mostly unsuccessful searches for a good bowl of wonton, I would bug Gretchen to make some.

Who among those who have tasted Chinese food would not know about wonton? It is perhaps the best-known of Chinese food items and rare is the Chinese restaurant in this country that does not offer wonton. But try to find a good bowl. Ha! As is often the case in gastronomy, the simplest of foods are often the most abused. As I go from restaurant to restaurant, my disappointment deepens. Whereas the skin should be thin, it is thick. Whereas the wrapping should be tight, it is loose. Whereas the broth should be clear and flavorful, it tastes like a solution of MSG. Whereas the filling should provoke curiosity in its variety, it tastes like Spam.

I give up and go home to Gretchen. Actually, homemade wonton easily taste better than any you are likely to find in a restaurant these days for two obvious reasons. First, at home we spare no expense in making the filling: the shrimp are fresh, the bamboo crisp, the pork succulent. The more variety in the filling, the more interesting the taste. And no MSG. For broth Gretchen just uses a standard chicken broth. Second, the handiwork in wrapping wonton is more precise at home. I like wonton wrapped tightly so that they wrinkle or pucker around the filling upon boiling. I must confess that some Cantonese restaurants achieve this effect extremely well. Since no great culinary finesse is involved in cooking wonton, why should home-made wonton taste anything but terrific?

It is also great family fun; I recommend it highly. Get some friends and relatives together and go to work wrapping up a mountain of wonton. Wrapping wonton is traditionally a group activity; it would be tedious for one person. The kids can participate. Even my three-year-old son can wrap a wonton, though he may not make it especially tight and orthodox in shape. One problem we have is that Gretchen and the kids like to eat the wonton skins raw. When done, the wonton rise to the top and are dished out to everyone's bowl, and the kids have fun trying to identify the authorship of each wonton. (Wonton skins are now widely sold, but then of course the trick is to find the right brand. The ideal skin should be thin but not so thin as to tear. That makes for another frustrating search altogether.)

I suspect that in many run-of-the-mill restaurants the wonton have sat all too long in some freezer. Another malpractice is to cook a large batch of wonton all at once. The cooked wonton are then fished out and allowed to sit on a strainer, whereupon they become soft and dissolute waiting for a customer.

Of course, it is possible to find good commercial wonton. From my experience, the best bet is a modest Cantonese restaurant in Chinatown specializing in wonton, noodles, and similar snacks. The key is a heavy traffic in orders of wonton. The wonton could be very good indeed because a really good restaurant broth cannot be easily matched at home. In restaurants, they keep a stock of soup bones on a perpetual simmer. The ideal for the broth is said to be 湯 清 味 厚 or "broth clear, taste thick": that is, a clear broth with lots of taste. Would that they never invented MSG!

Notice that you have already met the first three characters of this phrase in chapter 2: we have soup, clear, and taste. The first two characters have the water radical 氵 ; the third, the mouth radical 口 .

Obviously, an enormous variety of fillings is possible, as long as the filling is crisp and clear to the taste. Gretchen usually makes one of the many types popular in the Shanghai region, using chopped shrimp, minced pork, chopped bamboo, lard, sesame oil, cornstarch, and a beaten egg. You can take away and add ingredients according to whatever is available. Chopped-up mushrooms, for example, are good. There are regional variations, as one might expect. In the orthodox Cantonese wonton, for example, a whole small shrimp is used. Pork and fish are also often used instead of shrimp. One gourmet claims that in using pork as a filling, the ideal ratio of fat to lean should be 3 to 7.

As Gretchen brings the broth to a boil and drops the wonton in, I love to watch the billowing clouds of steam, and I wait in anticipation. Wonton, like a number of Chinese foods, should not be eaten in polite company. They must be served piping hot and slurped down. The smoothness of the wonton skin as it slides down the throat must be savored. As I write these words, bad memories well up of sitting in a restaurant staring at two thick-skinned wonton containing some unidentifiable substance and about to come loose on their own, floating pitifully about in a lukewarm soup.

I know, I know, wonton are not all that great. It is partly my romantic attachment. It is a mood food: as a midnight snack it is unbeatable. Perhaps there are some left over from the day.

Wonton is commonly written as 雲 吞 . The first character contains the rain radical 雨 or 乑 . Can you see the four raindrops? The horizontal bar ⼀ is supposed to represent the sky, the inverted U, the cloud. I am puzzled by the vertical bar | . Some linguists say that it emphasizes the raindrops falling. The rain radical appears in a group of characters having to do with the weather. When combined with the phonetic element 云 , the rain radical gives rise to the character 雲 , meaning "cloud" and pronounced *won*. Amusingly, the rain radical on top already contains an abstract representation of a cloud. The second character in wonton, 吞 , contains the mouth radical 口 and means "to swallow." Thus, wonton 雲 吞 means "swallowing clouds."

This is one of my favorite food names: I find it picturesque and apt. When I look into a piping hot bowl of wonton, I see billowing clouds. To Joni Mitchell, clouds are "ice-cream castles in the air." To me, clouds are wonton in the sky. The Chinese restaurant advertising wonton is inviting you to swallow some clouds.

Incidentally, while 雲 吞 is how wonton is usually written on restaurant menus, some pedants have insisted on writing wonton as 餛 飩 , a term I do not like. The two characters are simply made up to be pronounced as wonton, each consisting of the radical "to eat" 食 with some appropriate phonetic element. Another theory, advanced by a Song dynasty chronicler, is that wonton were invented by a person named Wonton. I find that highly implausible. Most likely, wonton was called wonton for reasons now long lost. The characters 餛 飩 were then constructed phonetically to reproduce the commonly used name. Some wit might then have hit upon the descriptive transliteration 雲 吞 .

The character 食 ("to eat") is derived from the picture 𰎩 showing a bowl ∪ containing rice ⋇ and placed next to a spoon ∠ , probably once ◡ .* The bowl with the rice is simplified to ⊖

* The modern character for spoon is 匙 , with 是 a phonetic element.

and then to 白 . The archaic symbol △ or 亼 , meaning "union" or "bringing together," is then added on top, presumably to suggest the notion of bringing the spoon together with the bowl of rice, thus finally forming 食 .

If you wander around a Chinatown or the Far East looking for a restaurant you will see the character 食 fairly often. It serves as the radical for a whole group of characters associated with food. One character that you will certainly find on your menu is 飯 , meaning "boiled rice." (The right half is merely a phonetic element.) Restaurants are often referred to as 飯 店 , literally "boiled-rice shop." Sometimes the more pretentious names 酒 樓 or "wine pavilion" and 酒 家 , "wine home," are used.

I find it intriguing that the ancient symbol for union is a triangle △ . The character now used to describe union 合 has a mouth added, possibly to suggest the concordance among three persons speaking.

I consider the fried wonton offered by some Chinese restaurants an atrocity. I read that it can be good if properly done, but I have never tasted a decent sample.

Related to the wonton are 水 餃 or "water dumpling," that is, boiled or steamed dumplings, and 鍋 貼 or literally "pot stickers," that is, fried dumplings. Notice the "eat" radical in the character for dumpling.

The cultivation of rice requires warm climate, and thus until recent times, northern Chinese ate mostly grains. The staples consist of wheat, millet, corn, and sorghum (called kaoliang or *gaoliang* in pinyin). Wheat is consumed in the form of noodles, buns, dumplings, and various regional forms of bread and pancake. I often joke with Gretchen that she must be a northern Chinese since she prefers noodles, dumplings, and the like to rice.

A village saying of North China has it that

Let the language lesson start!

The first character 好 means "good." Its etymology is particularly interesting. The left half 女 is a character meaning "woman." It clearly suggests some sort of pictograph 妛 . I think it looks like a pregnant woman. The right half 子 is a character meaning "child" or "children," or sometimes more specifically "son" or "sons." The character is based on the picture of a swaddled infant 孒 so that only the arms, but not the legs, are visible. (When I first showed Gretchen this explanation, she said no, no, it is obviously a woman rocking an infant to sleep.) Now we put woman and child together to form the character 好 .

According to one authority, 好 represents one's wife and children, that is, one's loved ones, and by extension, all that is good. A more plausible interpretation, but less pleasing to contemporary feminists, supposes that a woman bearing a son is the personification of goodness. Since 女 can also be used to indicate daughter or daughters, and since the two characters 子 and 女 used together does mean children, yet another interpretation is that the word just derived from children. It was good to have lots of children. Ideology can shape etymology.

The second character 吃 with its mouth radical means "to eat." Together, the combination 好 吃 , "good to eat," is a commonly used expression meaning tasty. You can compliment your favorite Chinese restaurant by saying that their food is 好 吃 , pronounced roughly as "how chi." The expression "How chic!" is close enough that you may want to use it as a mnemonic.

The next character 不 is a negation, meaning "not" or "no." The fourth character contains a radical 辶 which comes from a rather distorted picture of the foot walking and is now associated with all sorts of characters having to do with movement. It reminds me of some of the symbols printed on popular brands of running shoes. Anyhow, the character 過 means "to pass by," and hence "to surpass."

Next, we have the character 餃 for dumpling, followed by the character 子 which we just met and which means a child. No, the combination 餃 子 does not mean "son of dumpling," but rather a "child dumpling." The character 子 is often used as a diminutive ending in an affectionate sense. It does not suggest that the dumplings are small, but rather that they are cute.

So what do we have? Good to eat does not surpass dumplings. You see these northerners like dumplings.

On to the second line! The first two characters together mean "comfort." The next two have already appeared in the first line. Finally, the last two characters mean "lying down."

Thus, we have here a humble country saying expressing the simple pleasures of living: For tastiness you can't beat dumplings, and for comfort you can't do better than lying down.

The notion of filling pouches of dough with bits of meat is so natural that it appeared in several cultures. It is not true that Marco Polo brought the wonton and pot sticker back to Italy as agnolotti and ravioli. Ravioli, in particular, was already popular during the Roman Empire. China and Rome, however, were not isolated from each other but connected by the Silk Route. Supposedly, when American Jews first had wonton, they exclaimed that the soup was full of kreplachs.

An interesting folktale about "water dumplings" involves the folk pictures that people would buy and paste on their walls on festive occasions like New Year's Eve. These pictures were printed by woodblock in the tens of thousands. Traditionally, the job of coloring them was contracted out to illiterate peasant women, who were taught little songs indicating which colors to use for which parts of the picture.

Once upon a time, there was an artist whose portrayals were so vivid that folks believed that of the thousands of reproductions of his work, one would actually come to life. There was a young couple whose fields were ruined one year by a summer flood. Feeling sorry for them but hardly able to help, their friends gave them a picture showing a pot of dumplings being cooked. Boy, it was so realistic you could practically feel the steam!

On New Year's Eve the unfortunate couple decided to boil some water for a frugal meal of plain noodles. A miracle! When they lifted the cover, they found the pot full of dumplings!

From this day on, the couple merely had to boil some water to get a pot full of dumplings. They neglected their field work, spent their days lying around, and grew into lumps. In fact, guess what, they almost looked like couch dumplings. They were so lazy that they didn't even maintain their house. Why bother?

Came fall and one night the rain leaked through the roof. Neither husband nor wife could bestir themselves to climb out of bed. The next day at mealtime they did their usual thing. Surprise! No dumplings, only plain water. Only then did they notice that their picture was soaked through and the ink had washed off!

It doesn't take a Ph.D. to analyze why such folktales were widespread and popular. My question is: didn't they get tired of the same food day after day?

Making pot stickers takes a bit of skill, but it is not that difficult either. You put the dumplings into a pan of hot oil to brown them on one side. The dumplings should be densely packed in the pan. After about a minute, when their bottoms turn golden brown, pour in some water and immediately cover the pan. The dumplings are thus half-fried and half-steamed. When the water is all gone, shake the pan so that the pot stickers, in spite of their name, do not stick to the pan. Then turn the pan over onto a plate.

A good pot sticker should be juicy when bit into. The fried side should be golden brown without being greasy, crisp without being hard. I find that most restaurant pot stickers are much too thick-skinned.

The linguistically precise among you would have noticed that since "cloud" in Chinese is "won" 雲 , wonton literally means "cloud swallowing," not "swallowing cloud," as I had it. Herein lies an interesting linguistic twist. Chinese and English are both examples of what linguists call subject-verb-object languages, or SVO languages for short. In contrast, in Japanese and German, to cite two examples, the verb often comes at the end of a sentence. That Chinese and English have the same word order is sometimes cited as one of the reasons why it is easier for a Chinese to learn English than for a Japanese. For the same reason, English-speaking people generally find it far easier to learn Chinese than to learn Japanese. Anyhow, the sentence "When I eat wonton, I imagine that I am swallowing clouds" would be translated into Chinese with almost exactly the same word order:

當我食雲吞時，我想像我在吞雲

Never mind all the other characters; just focus on the fourth and fifth characters, 雲 吞 (wonton), and on the twelfth and thirteenth characters, 吞 雲 (swallowing clouds).

Allow me to play grammarian for a moment more. Both constructions, "swallowing cloud" and "cloud swallowing," are allowed in English. "We enjoy swallowing cloud" and "Cloud swallowing is best enjoyed with a friend" are both acceptable sentences. As the second sentence shows, "cloud swallowing" may be used as a noun describing the act of swallowing clouds. On the other hand, we can also use "cloud swallowing" with "cloud" as a subject; for example, "I saw the cloud swallowing up the small plane." Again, this sentence can be written in Chinese with the same word order.

While "cloud swallowing" and "swallowing cloud" are essentially equivalent in English, the phrase "swallowing cloud" in Chinese has acquired an idiomatic meaning as part of the expression 吞 雲 吐 霧 , literally "swallowing cloud (and) exhaling fog." Before I explain what the expression means, let's take a moment to appreciate the orderliness of the language. The first and third characters, for "swallowing" and for "exhaling," share the radical 口 for mouth, while the second and fourth characters, for "cloud" and for "fog," share the radical 雨 for rain and, by extension, any meteorological phenomena. Again, Chinese may not be as hard to learn as you may think! Consider a Chinese learning English. There is no apparent connection between swallowing and exhaling, between rain and fog.

Can you guess what the expression might mean? It describes a person smoking opium or other illicit substances. As an abbreviation, the Chinese phrase "swallowing cloud" may also have the connotation of doing drugs.

Perhaps nothing else will make the Chinese more livid with anger than for the uninformed to suppose opium to be of Chinese origin. Arab traders first brought opium to China as a cure for dysentery during the Tang dynasty. After the introduction of tobacco into China from the New World in the seventeenth century, the practice of smoking opium also developed. But addiction to opium became a widespread problem as a direct result of England's attempt to solve her trade deficit problem.

By the late eighteenth century, England was facing an enormous deficit in its trade with China. While the demand for tea, porcelain, and silk exploded in England, the Chinese showed little interest in English goods. To solve the problem, the English started pushing opium forcibly on China. By then, England—the biggest pusher ever in the history of drugs—was in control of the major opium-growing regions of the world. Alarmed by the tragic consequences of opium smoking, China protested but to no avail. Finally, in 1839 China banned the import of opium and burned the opium stockpiled by the English in Canton. This gave the English the pretext for war they had long been waiting for. The pitifully feeble Manchu Qing dynasty government was no match militarily for the English. The Opium War, surely the most sordidly motivated and tragically named war in history, ended in the treaty of Nanjing (1842) whereby China was forced to open its ports to English trade and to cede the village of Hong Kong to England. An already weak China was pushed farther down the road of decay and disintegration, the consequences of which are still reverberating with us today.

CHAPTER 5

CHINESE PIGS
STAND

ONCE AGAIN, IMAGINE that you are the caveperson that you were in Chapter 1. Ever since you figured out what the chief wanted, everyone thinks that you are so smart. Needless to say, scratching out pictures on the ground with sharp rocks is now *the* chic pastime. Everyone is doing it, but you are the first to think of decorating the cave walls with pictures of the animals you see around you.

It is a good guess that the first pictures made by man were of animals. Not surprisingly, the Chinese characters for animals are among the most pictorial. For those who can see, a Chinese menu is full of animals leaping or swimming across the page.

Let us begin with the goat or lamb, written in modern Chinese as 羊 and derived from 羊 .

It does not take much imagination to see the two horns, the large head, the four legs, and the tail of a goat, as seen flattened out from above. Mutton is widely consumed in northern and western China. *The Book of Songs* (namely the *Shi Jing*), a collection of ballads compiled around 600 B.C. supposedly by Confucius himself, describes a lamb roast held almost three thousand years ago. The lamb was seasoned with garlic before being cooked on a bed of fragrant southernwood, whatever that is. The people sang:

> High we load the stands,
>
> The stands of wood and earthenware.
>
> As soon as the smell rises
>
> God on high is very pleased:
>
> "What smell is this, so strong and good?"

The ancients must have really liked lamb as is evidenced by the character 美 , meaning "beautiful." You may have noticed that this character is formed by putting the character for lamb on top of the character 大 . Recall from Chapter 3 that 人 means man or more generally a human. When the man stretches out his arms, as in the famous Da Vinci picture, he becomes bigger. Thus, 大 means "big." By the way, you probably didn't realize that you already know how to pronounce 大 . The character appears in the Chinese originals of words such as typhoon ("big wind") and tycoon ("big official"). Unfortunately, there is a slight complication. In Cantonese, for example, 大 is pronounced as "dye" rather than "tye." In Beijing's Mandarin, it is produced as *dar* (rhyming with the word bar). I have already mentioned in "A Word About Pronunciation"

Peter Zee demonstrating the characters for "big," "medium," and "small." In Peter's Chinese school, children are taught to form Chinese characters with their bodies. A couple of years ago, when we taught Peter to swim, he wouldn't put his head under water. Finally, I said, "I bet you can't form Chinese characters under water!" He rose to the challenge, and that cured him of his fear of being under water.

that the Chinese *d* sounds traditionally got transliterated as *t* sounds. (It is not merely a question of differences between dialects as we see here.) We will see more examples of this *d* to *t* shift.

So the ancient Chinese combined the characters for lamb and big to invent the character for beauty. They associated a fat lamb with beauty!

Talking about beauty, I should tell you that in Chinese the United States is 美 國 , literally "beautiful country." When the major European powers first came to China, the Chinese would find a single character that most closely approximates the name of their country phonetically. 美 is pronounced as *mei* and echoes the "mer" in America. Of all the characters with an *m* sound, the one most complimentary in meaning was chosen. What about the song "America the Beautiful"? In Chinese, it would be beautiful Beautiful Country. Notice also how the character for country, with its enclosing square box 囗 , expresses the notion of territorial boundary. With the same construction, England is called the "country of heroes"; France, the "country of law"; and Germany, the "country of virtue." China is 中 國 , the "middle country." The ancient Chinese thought that they were at the center of the world. The etymology of the character for middle is obvious: it shows an arrow going through the center of some target. The character for small is 小 . This came from an idea that a stick ∣ is being cut into small bits like the two bits ヽ ノ shown.

The bull has two horns, four legs, and a tail, just like a goat. But you can't very well have a top view of the bull and so the pictograph for the bull 朱 or 半 from 肖 is said to be a rear view of the animal. We can see the horns and the tail hanging down between the hind legs. The modern character is 牛 .

In modern usage, the character 牛 stands for both the bull and the cow. In fact, separate characters exist for the bull and the cow but they have fallen into disuse. This phenomenon is typical: most Chinese characters for animals are now unisex. Mature and baby animals are also generally not distinguished. If a distinction must be made, the Chinese say "male 牛 " for the bull, "female 牛 " for the cow, and "small 牛 " for the calf.

The character for pig presents some interesting lessons in Chinese etymology. The original character for pig 豕 looks to me like a pig standing up. I would have thought that a pig looks more like 豕 .

I read somewhere that in some pig farms in this country the feeding trough was raised on purpose so that the poor pigs had to feed standing up. Supposedly, the farmer got a leaner grade of pork as a result. I doubt that the ancient Chinese knew about such advanced agribusiness techniques. Of course, in ancient times, people actually wanted their pigs to be fat. Instead, since in classical Chinese a line of text is written vertically, characters that were too wide were often rotated by 90 degrees. An interesting example of this phenomenon is the character for eye 目 . Its ancient form looks something like ⊙ or ⊙ , later evolving into ▥ .* A 90-degree rotation then takes it into the modern form. Anyhow, Chinese pigs stand.

Somehow, the pig's tail got an extra stroke so the relevant character is now written as 豕 . Chinese pigs not only stand but they also have two tails.

At some point, someone fooled around with the character some more. A phonetic element was added to the existing character for pig to form the

---

* According to some scholars, the ancient form for eye is actually ▱ representing the eyelids and the pupil. The pupil is later suppressed to give ▱ . Wieger, page 323.

more complicated character 豬 . You can recognize the original character on the left. The phonetic element on the right, 者 , is a bona-fide
character capable of standing on its own. It serves as a mnemonic, indicating
that the character 豬 is to be pronounced more or less like 者 .
The original character for pig 豕 is now seldom used by itself. And thus
it happens that the modern character for pig looks considerably more complicated than its counterparts for lamb and cow.

While pork is a mainstay of Chinese cuisine, one prominent character
in folk culture does not eat pork. While the educated class has always been
agnostic about the afterlife and skeptical about religion, the common people
in traditional China worshiped an assortment of deities, immortals, and
spirits that would vary from region to region. People would offer up things
like food, and pray for whatever the deity could influence. One of the most
popular deities, not surprisingly, is the god of wealth. He does not eat pork.

Why? The god of wealth is a Moslem. It turns out that this tradition
goes back to the Tang dynasty (618–907), when trade with the West over
the Silk Route was booming and many Persian and Arab merchants lived in
China. These traders were enormously wealthy and quite naturally metamorphosed into the god of wealth. Indeed, he is usually pictured as wearing
a strange hat which later scholars have identified as in the style of ancient
Persia.

It is amusing to note that in Chinese mythology gods are divided into
those with responsibilities, known as 神 , and those without any responsibilities, known as 仙 . With responsibilities goes power and thus 神
have influence over various human activities. The god of wealth is a
神 . On the other hand, the Liu Ling who slept the sleep of the truly
inebriated is definitely a 仙 : all he has to do is go around and have a

good time. Thus, while vintners would admire a 酒仙 they would worship a 酒神 , asking him to insure that the vintage would turn out well. Incidentally, it is possible for a human being to turn into either a 神 or 仙 . Me, I would rather be a 仙 , for sure.

The original character for pig illustrates how more abstract characters were constructed. Put a roof 宀 on a pig 豕 and what do you have? The character 家 . As in all ancient agrarian societies, pigs lived around and often even inside human dwellings. Thus, this character has come to mean home or family. Home is where pigs are sheltered. *

In menus, you encounter 家 in connection with home-style cooking. In small, unpretentious restaurants in Chinatown, sometimes it is worth taking a chance on dishes marked as home-style. Look for the pig under the roof. Much more rarely, the character can also appear in connection with Hakka cuisine, a cuisine yet to become fashionable in this country. In Cantonese restaurants, I have occasionally encountered the dish Hakka bean curd, in which pieces of bean curd are stuffed with pork or shrimp.

In the Hakka dialect, 家 is pronounced as "kka" and Hakka is written as 客家 . You may have noticed that the character 客 also contains the roof radical. It means "guest." The original pictograph

appears to represent an extra person next to the hearth. This shows that the dot on the roof radical 宀 was once a chimney. If you have ever visited south China or Hong Kong, you may have seen the Hakka Chinese. The

---

* One ancient form of the character for home actually has a man, a woman, and a child under a roof. Another interpretation is that home is the place where the pig was readied to be sacrificed as an offering to the ancestral spirits.

women are dressed in black from head to toe. The origin of the Hakka Chinese presents something of a mystery for historians. Although they have settled in south China for ages, their name "guest home" appears to describe a wandering gypsylike people.

Want to try your hand at etymological sleuthing? What do you think the character 牢 depicting a roof over a bull means? Three guesses. A hint: this character evokes feelings far different from those evoked by the character for home.

Cattle are kept in corrals and so the character 牢 has come to mean "prison." Another amusing character 安 has the roof radical over 女 the character for woman. A guess as to what it means? A woman under one's roof brings contentment. The character means "contentment"; in contemporary usage it also carries the connotation of safety, as in safe and sound, and of peacefulness.

Indeed, if I tell you that 安 is pronounced as "an," you may realize that it appears in the name for Tiananmen Square in Beijing, often translated as the Gate of Heavenly Peace. The three characters 天 安 門 mean literally "heaven/sky peace gate." (Notice that the character for sky 天 consists of a horizontal stroke representing the sky over a man with an outstretched arm, and that the character for gate or door 門 is clearly pictorial.) The name Tiananmen will now forever bear bitter irony after that outrage to all humanity, the infamous Tiananmen Square massacre of 1989.

Don't bother to learn the complicated modern character for pig. If you recognize 豕 as pig, you are in good shape. You can identify all the pork dishes, and if you also see a roof 宀 , all the home-style dishes.

The Harvard Faculty Club is the only establishment I know of in this country that serves horse meat, and even that tradition, if it was ever a tradition, has fallen by the wayside. Thus, there is no point for you to learn the character for horse if you are to stick to menus. But I can't resist giving you the character anyway because it gives such a vivid image of spirited horsiness. Indeed, the character for horse is often given as an outstanding example of Chinese characters as pictographs. In the ancient form

we see a prancing horse suddenly turning his head, causing his luxuriant mane to flutter in the wind.

Something of this sense of movement is retained in the modern version 馬 . In their treatise *The Chinese Written Character as a Medium for Poetry*, Ernest Fenollosa and the poet Ezra Pound were very much impressed by precisely this sort of imagery. But more on Chinese characters and poetry later.

Horse meat does not generally figure in Chinese cuisine (although the region around Kweilin or Guilin in pinyin is known for a dish of rice noodles cooked with horse meat). The horse was much honored in China and appeared extensively in paintings and in sculpture. Ancient chronicles recorded how fortunes were given in exchange for thoroughbreds from the West, that is, Arabia. The military importance of horsemanship was appreciated early on and further emphasized by the horse-riding Mongols who invaded China in the thirteenth century. This respect for horses shows up in a number of Chinese expressions. For instance, to compliment a person for his or her energy and drive, the Chinese say that the person has "the spirit of the dragon and of the horse."

As you stroll through Chinatown, you might notice racks of roasted or smoked meat hanging from hooks. The character for "meat" (or "flesh" in general) 肉 is strikingly pictorial: 肉 . Doesn't it remind you of the upper torso shown in anatomical texts? Thus, 牛 肉 is beef, 豬 肉 is pork, and so on. When 肉 appears in a menu unspecified, you may assume that it refers to pork. Incidentally, a sexy woman is described sometimes as 肉 感 , meaning "flesh feel." The term is somewhat derogatory and is typically applied to starlets.

A pork dish, Tung-po pork, is named after one of the greatest poets in Chinese history, Su Tung-po or Su Dongbo in pinyin (1036–1101), who also happens to be one of the most notable characters in the annals of food. His writing is full of references to eating. As the governor of the Hangzhou region, Su embarked on important water works that directly benefited the populace. Partly because of this, and partly because his love of food and life made him appear less removed from the common man, he was well liked. At the completion of the water works, the grateful people, knowing Su's interest in food, presented him with a large quantity of pork, whereupon he invented a new pork dish. Basically, pork pieces, including the fat and the skin, are slowly simmered in a marinade of wine, soy sauce, ginger, scallion, and garlic. When properly done, the pork is so tender that it is said to practically melt in one's mouth. As the story goes, Su then presented his new dish to the laborers that worked on the dam. The people liked the dish so well that it soon became one of the specialties of the region.

A folk story of this type has to be understood in the feudal class structure of ancient China. To the common people, it is not so important that Su is a great poet and an efficient administrator, but that he shared with them a love and enjoyment of food.

Chinese emperors were supposed to send out an emissary periodically to check on local governors. In practice and more often than not, the visit would allow two corrupt officials, the emissary and the governor, to have a great time at the expense of the people. The imperial emissary would exact a fat bribe for a good report to the emperor.

In any case, the story goes that an imperial emissary arrived to visit Su Tung-po and noticed that the local restaurants all featured Tung-po pork. Here you will recall that, as mentioned earlier, 肉 means flesh in general, but if left unspecified usually means the pig's flesh. Thus, Tung-po 肉 can be taken to mean Tung-po's flesh. (Possessives are often omitted in Chinese.) The imperial emissary concluded that the people hated Su Tung-po so much that they practically wanted to devour his flesh. Upon hearing this, the enraged emperor banished Su Tung-po to the far south.

This story sounds apocryphal to me: more likely, Su was too "clean" to be into bribery and so got a bad report from the emissary. It does reflect, however, the puzzlement the population must have felt when a beloved official was suddenly banished only to be replaced by a corrupt incompetent.

The story also reminds me that many famous pork dishes, to be done correctly, require the use of really fatty pork to remain juicy. The classic description of Tung-po pork is just cholesterol city itself. Once when I complained to a Chinese restaurateur whom I also know to be a gourmet herself, she agreed that many of my complaints were justified but she also insists that given our concern for health many classic dishes just can't be prepared properly. Chinese cuisine, no less than French cuisine, has also suffered from the "nouvelle" trend toward healthier food.

THE
APPALLING
IGNORANCE
OF SOME
SCRIBES

CHINESE COULD HAVE been really simple if it had adhered strictly to the basic phonetic and pictorial principles. But as you have already seen in many examples, the original pictographs have been distorted over the centuries. This distortion is unfortunate, but inevitable: unfortunate because it makes learning Chinese all that much harder, but inevitable because the same corrupting process occurs in all living languages. Besides, the pictogaphs had to be simplified to be useful.

The bright side is that in Chinese the major distortions occurred fairly early on, toward the end of the Zhou dynasty (11th century–221 B.C.). As a result, even in rather ancient documents, the characters were written in exactly the same form as they are now. In English, one would have a tough time with the spelling even in documents only a few centuries old. English spelling became erratic and often nonphonetic after the Norman Conquest. The Normans forbade the use of English as a written language. Centuries later, when writers such as Chaucer started writing again in English, they essentially made up the spelling as they went along and English became less phonetic than the romance languages.

As an example of a distorted character, consider 友 meaning "friend." Rare is the modern-day reader who knows that it derives from the hand.

Let's start with the modern character for hand 手 . It was originally written as 凵 and later as 屮 . Some etymologists think that ⌒⌒ was supposed to be the lines of the palm.

Used as a radical, the character for hand was simplified to 才 , or it may well have been derived independently from a pictograph of an arm with a three-fingered hand, presumably five-fingered in some even earlier form. The radical was further straightened out and acquired an additional stroke to become 扌 , or as you can see, it could have come directly from 屮 .

The full, modern character for hand is also sometimes used as a radical, for example 看 , meaning "to look at" or "to watch." Remember the Chinese eye 目 rotated by 90 degrees from ⟨D ? The hand 手 is shading the eye 目 from the sun, so that you can look more comfortably.

What about the character for friend? The original pictograph depicts two hands pointed in the same direction 屮屮 . Over time, one hand was distorted to ⼇ and then to ⼃ , the other to X and then to ⼜ , and hence the modern character 友 for friend, deriving from two hands working together. It would take quite a feat of pictorial imagination to recognize the two hands.

Some distortions can be understood as the result of newfangled writing instruments. The ancients carved their writings on tortoise shells, animal bones, and bamboo. Scholars refer to this early script as "shell-bone script." Later, people wrote on smooth bamboo or wooden tablets with a sort of fountain pen pictured on ancient bronzes as

 .

We see that the ink was held in a reservoir on top and flowed through a bamboo tube. Around 200 B.C. one Cheng Miao invented a wooden pencil ending in a fibrous point which he dipped in ink and wrote with on cloth. This was a significant change: it became much harder to make curved lines. At this point, the rounded characters of the ancients became more squarish and curved lines were broken at right angles. Soon came the brush, a bamboo tube with animal hair attached. Generally speaking, with the brush held the Chinese way, it is much easier to make downstrokes than upstrokes.

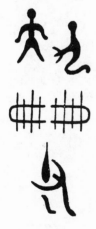

In this bronze inscription dating from about 1500 B.C., we see the kneeling man making offerings to his ancestor, whose spirit is present in the inner sanctum of the temple, represented by the "fence." In the foreground, we see the hand (discussed on page 92) offering up a teardrop-shaped object that etymologists say represents the smell of meat rising. The squiggle beneath the hand represents wine being splashed on the ground— that's how wine is traditionally offered to the spirits.

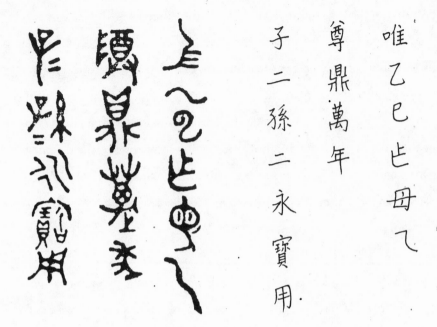

This inscription, taken from a bronze vessel, says, "On this day, in the presence of the deceased grandfather, the grandmother offers, with wine duly splashed on the ground, a bronze vessel that will last for ten thousand years, and which the sons and grandsons will treasure forever." Chinese is written in columns moving from right to left. Thus, the fifth character in the far-right column means "mother" or "grandmother." See the nursing breasts of the mother? Following this character is the squiggle representing the offered wine being splashed on the ground. (See the caption to the figure on page 93). In the far-left column, we see the character for "son" (discussed on page 73), the character for "grandson," the character for "forever" (discussed on page 35), and the character for "treasure" (discussed on page 303). It's fun to compare the modern script, shown on the right, with the ancient script. Notice that the character for "grandson" consists of the character for "son" next to the spool of thread that appears in the modern "silk" radical. The idea of lineage is conveyed.

Ancient bronze inscription and modern Chinese translation taken from Chinese Characters by L. Wieger.

The difference due to different writing instruments is best experienced. If you have a Chinese writing brush or an artist's brush, you will find it difficult to make rounded curves such as $\smile$ and $\frown$. (Remember that the Chinese hold the brush vertically.) Thus, $\smile$ became $\vdash$ (or $\vdash$ as written with the brush) and $\frown$ became simply — (or — as written with the brush). Now we can understand how the character for bull or cattle went from 朱 to the modern form 牛 .

Most distortions, however, came from outright errors. As the Zhou dynasty decayed, universities were not what they once were and the ignorance of some scribes was appalling. Sounds familiar, eh? College graduates who can't spell and scribes who don't know their characters. Tsk, tsk. When some of these scribes got stuck with some characters they didn't know how to write, they would often just invent something on the spot. Confucius once complained, "When I was young, the scribes, if ignorant, at least had the honor and decency of leaving a blank for a character they didn't know how to write. Nowadays, we don't even have such ignorant but honorable types!" Ignorance combined with dishonor, sounds familiar also. Such arbitrarily invented characters became known as "strange characters". They keep etymologists employed.

CHAPTER 6

A DELICACY FOR AGING MEN

IN 1972 THE University of California offered a course on *gallus domesticus,* the household chicken, in response to students' demand at that time for a "more relevant and less traditional" curriculum. Mind you, the chicken, if you really think about it, has been practically one of the building blocks of human civilization. The professors, historian Page Smith and biologist Charles Daniel, have since published the material in what surely ranks as one of the most amusingly offbeat books in recent times. According to them, the rise and fall of the chicken has mirrored the rise and fall of human civilization itself.

The chicken was considered magical in many cultures. In ancient Greece, cocks were kept in the temple of Hercules and hens in the temple of Hebe. (In case you forgot, Hebe was Hercules's last wife.) The two temples were separated by a river which the cocks, "stimulated with lust, would fly across" from time to time. Afterwards, "purged by the river, they would return to their god and to their purified dwellings." Perhaps the Greeks still have some hang-ups in connection with the chicken: compared with other people, they consume relatively little chicken. In the 1950s, the Greek government had to conduct a campaign urging the population to eat more chicken.

Or try to picture, on the day of kapparah, orthodox Jews reciting hymns while holding a chicken, the men holding cocks, the women hens. The chicken is circled around the head nine times and then slaughtered. This is supposed to lead to a long and healthy life. (The nutritional use of the chicken in Jewish life is of course well-known, from chicken soup to the awesome exploitation of chicken fat.)

The Chinese, on the other hand, basically just eat the critters.

The character for bird 鳥 presents almost as vivid an image as the character for horse. We can see the head, the long tail, the wings, and the feet. If you can't, look at an older form 鳥 .

If you see any character containing this basic character for bird, you can safely bet that character would have something to do with birds. In particular, the character for chicken is 鷄 and for duck, 鴨 . In both characters, the stuff besides the bird radical are phonetic elements.

Next time you look at a Chinese menu, look for the character for chicken. Some of you will find it immediately, others among you will fail, but not for any shortcoming on your part. Herein lies a linguistic curiosity.

In ancient times the character 鳥 refers specifically to long-tailed birds. (You can sort of see the long tail from the stroke ㇉ in the character.) Short-tailed birds were known as 佳 , evolving from something like 𨾨 . This character is now rarely used by itself but appears as a radical in characters describing various short-tailed birds. In particular, the character 雞 also means chicken, or strictly speaking, a short-tailed chicken.

I wonder if Chinese is the only language that distinguishes between long-tailed and short-tailed chickens. That distinction has long been lost, however, and most Chinese are not aware of the difference between the characters 鷄 and 雞 . They are used interchangeably. If you want to be a pain, ask your waiter if the restaurant is serving long-tailed or short-tailed chicken. He will surely be puzzled. You may then wish to point out to him which variety the menu is actually advertising.

It is an interesting linguistic phenomenon that 鳥 eventually beat out 佳 to become the generic term for birds. Quite naturally, the need to distinguish between long-tailed and short-tailed birds gradually became lost on the city-dwelling literate population.

The Chinese supposedly mastered the technique for incubating large numbers of eggs in order to feed the labor force employed to build the Great Wall. Now even more so than ever, the chicken and her egg provide a relatively inexpensive source of protein for a hungry world. (Remember that it was not that long ago that "a chicken in every pot" was a slogan in an American presidential campaign.) Incidentally, until the 1920s, before the American poultry industry was established, much of the chicken eggs and other poultry products consumed in this country were imported from China.

The outcry of the fledgling poultry industry led to the erection of high tariffs for the import of chicken eggs under the Fordney-McCumber Bill, a bill regarded by some historians as contributing to the onset of the Depression. *

Of the vast multitude of chicken dishes in Chinese cuisine, 叫 化 鷄 or beggar's chicken, enjoys a certain romantic air. The story goes that a beggar once stole a chicken and, having no utensils to cook with, went down to the river and encased the chicken, feathers and all, in mud. He tossed the whole thing into a fire. After some time, he took it out. Cracking the whole thing open, he found the feathers came off easily with the clay. The chicken, so it's said, was juicily delicious. These days of course, affluent ladies in Hong Kong instruct their cooks to reproduce the legendary tastiness of beggar's chicken and gourmets contribute articles on the best kinds of clay to use, and so on.

The term 叫 化 for beggar, a relatively modern term dating from the Yuan dynasty (1271–1368), was originally associated with mendicant Buddhist monks. See the mouth radical 口 in the first character? The character means "calling out." The etymology of the second character 化 is interestingly abstract. Perhaps you recognize the man radical 亻 . Remember that it came from the character 人 for man. Now, consider a man upside down Y . Well, what does that mean? He is a dead man, of course. In time, the pictograph for the upside-down, dead man was distorted to ㄥ or ㄨ . Finally, we have the

---

* Living in a society where we can basically have as much animal protein as we want, we tend to forget how critical the chicken was once to the well-being of nations. Consider that when the British forced China to open its ports to trade in 1834, among the first cargoes they brought back to England was chicken. This breed, known as the Shanghai, was solemnly presented to the young Queen Victoria. For some years, a breeding trio (defined by poultrymen as a cock and two hens) of the Shanghai, considered superior to the native European breeds, was said to be worth more than a title.

character 化 , showing a live man becoming a dead man. This character eventually took on the meaning of "transformation" or "change." When you give alms to a mendicant monk, you are doing such a good deed that your fate in the next life may be changed for the better. In Buddhism, almsgiving is known as "changing one's fate in the next life." Thus, the begging monks call out for you to change your fate. The term 叫 化 , literally "call change," came to mean beggar. Well, nowadays, if you don't give alms, beggars in our big cities are ready to change your fate in this life!

While for the American supermarket shopper ducks are practically unknown compared to chicken, they figure prominently in Chinese cuisine. Beijing Duck is perhaps the most celebrated. In this classic dish, the skin, rather than the meat of the duck, is the prize. Cooked to just the right fragrant crispness, the skin is separated from the meat and eaten between thin pancakes with a sauce and the white parts of scallions. The duck meat is considered to be inferior and is either discarded or used to make a separate dish.

The secret of making Beijing Duck is dry weather. The recipe calls for hanging the duck up to air-dry for a day or so. One Christmas when we were living in Princeton, New Jersey, Gretchen decided to serve Beijing Duck. The day before, it drizzled interminably—living in Princeton was sometimes like living in a swamp. The relative humidity hit 100. Crisis time! We dragged out all the electric fans we owned and for hours, blew on the duck from all sides. It didn't work.

The other secret is to get really fat ducks. In old China, the ducks used for Beijing Duck were force-fed. Did you know that the ducks eaten in this country are the descendants of the famed Long Island ducklings, first brought to New York from China by a Yankee Clipper captain in 1873? In Beijing, be sure to visit a restaurant specializing in Beijing Duck. This delectable dish, as served in the Chinese restaurants in this country, seems to have gotten worse over the years. They doubtless take shortcuts, such as blowing on the duck rapidly with a powerful fan. Also, the proper preparation of the sauce, which is to be brushed on the duck skin, is neglected. The sauce often tastes too sugary and, for all I know, probably comes straight out of a bottle.

To Westerners visiting Chinatown grocery stores, one of the strangest sights is that of preserved ducks pressed in the shape of a disk. Just thinking about these almost transparent, golden yellow ducks makes my saliva flow. The pressed duck is a specialty that dates from the Western Wei dynasty (A.D. 535–556) when Nanjing, the imperial capital at that time, fell under a prolonged siege during some war or another. The preserved ducks were made by the peasants for the soldiers. Why pressed? They took up less room and were easier to transport under battle conditions.

Duck eggs are invariably used to make the "thousand-year-old eggs" that hold such terror and fascination for Westerners. They are firmer than chicken eggs and thus better-suited for preserving. Also, since ducks were confined to villages with water and since in old China transportation was so inadequate, duck eggs (and ducks) had to be preserved in order to get them to markets far away from water.

As to how thousand-year-old eggs came to be, there is a folktale. A long time ago, by the banks of Dong Ting Lake (in Hunan province), lived a poor young duck driver named Shui Ge ("water brother"). Although one hundred ducks were all that he had to his name, he wandered through the countryside happily, driving his flocks here and there. As you know, rice grows in watery fields. After the rice is harvested, a rice field is rich with aquatic life attractive to ducks. Thus, much as cowboys drove herds of cattle in the Wild West, duckboys (I suppose that's what you would call them) would drive flocks from field to field as the rice was harvested.

One evening, as he was resting in his shelter (by the nature of their profession, the duckboys had to camp out all over the countryside), a pretty maiden came holding a duck in each hand, saying, "You must have lost these. I found them in my vegetable garden." The youth quickly counted his ducks and, sure enough, there were only ninety-eight in the pen. But he asked the maiden, "Are you sure? These two ducks appear to have been just fed." The maiden replied, "Well, not wanting them to starve and stop laying eggs, I just fed them a handful of grain." The youth was most thankful; after all, most people would just have gladly eaten his ducks and his livelihood. The maiden, whose name was Song Mei ("pine sister"), pointed to the house where she lived down the road by the pine trees.

As the maiden was about to leave, the youth said, "Wait. How do I know that these two ducks belong to me, and not to some other duckboy?" "Oh, don't worry," the maiden replied, "no duckboy has passed by in the last couple of days." Yet the youth insisted. "I will bring these two ducks next to my pen and see if my ducks respond to their quacking," he said, and indeed, as soon as the two ducks quacked, you heard a chorus of quacking. The ducks were happy that their lost friends were back. "As the next test, we will see if my ducks accept these two," he said as he put the ducks into the pen, and sure enough, the two merged into the crowd without being chased. The maiden was so pleased that she clapped her hands. Would you know it, she had fallen in love with the honest youth!

The next morning, the grateful youth took thirty duck eggs to the maiden's house, but no matter what he said, the maiden and her parents would not accept the gift.

That evening, as the youth drove his ducks homeward from the field, he noticed those same two ducks sneaking off into the maiden's garden again. He had a bright idea. "Why not leave the two ducks," he thought, "and let Pine Sister have the pleasure of finding the eggs. Since she won't accept my gift directly, I can repay her this way." Early next morning, as he passed by the maiden's garden, the two ducks came out to join their quacking companions on their walk down to the field. This went on day after day. After several days, the youth was puzzled that the maiden never mentioned the eggs in their now twice daily chats.

Half a month went by until one day while cleaning out trash from her garden, the maiden came across some thirty duck eggs lying in a lime pit. As it was the rainy season, the eggs had been soaking in limey, muddy water. She took the eggs to the youth, but he insisted they were hers. A budding lawyer, he demanded, "How can you prove beyond a reasonable doubt that they are from my ducks?"

After some discussion, they decided to have a feast. Opening the eggs, they were dismayed to find the eggs all black and rotten-looking. What a pity! What a waste! But then the youth tasted one and discovered to his delight that these black eggs had a deliciously unusual flavor. Everyone in the village thought the flavor was strange but marvelous.

Soon the youth, the maiden, and her parents were making and selling preserved duck eggs or what Americans call "thousand-year-old eggs." (Funny, these Westerners always exaggerate, since it only takes about a month in the summer to preserve duck eggs; in the spring and fall, about two months.) Water Brother and Pine Sister gradually refined their technique, adding brine and sometimes tea. The egg white, if you can still call it that, turned into a soft, dark green mush, while pretty crystalline patterns appeared in the dark brown skin encasing the yolk. The crystal patterns looked like pine needles. Water Brother referred to these delicate patterns as "pine blossoms" in honor of his beloved Pine Sister. Thus what the Chinese call "pine-blossom skin egg" was born. The youth and the maiden got married, became fabulously rich, and lived happily ever after. I suppose he was even given an honorary degree for discovering chemical osmosis.

Thousand-year-old eggs are now readily available in Oriental grocery stores, even in the medium-sized town I live in. Crack and peel them as you would any egg. You should then rinse them under a running faucet before slicing them into bite-size pieces. I like to sprinkle some sesame oil on them. The eggs used to come encrusted with lime and other foreign matter such as straw. Nowadays, they come individually wrapped in a six-pack plastic carton. I have noticed that the wrapping paper says in Chinese and English "Guaranteed no lead oxide." I gather that there used to be a problem.

I remember as a kid liking to hold the dark skin of the preserved egg up to a light, the better to see the pine blossoms. I regret to say that the eggs I have been buying these days rarely show any pine blossoms even though the wrappings quite explicitly promise pine blossoms.

Thousand-year-old eggs are definitely an acquired taste, much like blue cheese for the Chinese. Gretchen never did take to them. The darkish green color turns many people off. To see whether those who do not like the thousand-year-old egg dislike it because of its flavor or because of its color, I have given the egg to children of various ages. The young ones really like it. Our three-year-old son Peter adores it. Not surprising, says Gretchen, since the yolk has the texture of baby food.

Most Chinese restaurants in this country do not want to mess with any other birds. Seldom have I seen goose 鵝 and squab 鴿 offered. If you recognize the character for bird, you are almost halfway to identifying the dish in question.

One famous story in Chinese art history involves a goose and the Jin dynasty (256–420) calligrapher Wang Xizhi. In the millennia of Chinese calligraphy, Wang is regarded as the greatest of the great. Anything written by him would be considered priceless even during his lifetime. Anyhow, Wang was inordinately fond of eating goose. The story goes that a literatus went to visit Wang, carrying with him the plumpest and juiciest goose he could find. Wang was totally smitten with the bird. It was love at first sight! Without a word, he took out a piece of paper, picked up his brush, and scrawled a single character 鵝 "goose" on the paper. He handed the paper over to the literatus in exchange for the goose. Talk about power of the word!

As for squab, its flesh is considered by gourmets to be leaner and more delicate than that of other birds. Once it learns to be a pigeon and starts to fly, it then becomes, of course, too tough to eat. Incidentally, the variety most prized by the Chinese gourmet is the American squab.

The real value of the squab on the Chinese table is its supposed embodiment of licentiousness. Among the domestic birds, pigeons are said to be the most sexually active. And contrary to other birds, the female chases after the male for sexual favors. Having observed this, the Ming dynasty (1368–1644) doctor Li Shizhen declared that eating squab could improve sexual potency in the male. You can take it or leave it, as you like! Incidentally, because of a massive book he compiled in 1593, Li has had an enormous influence on Chinese eating habits. For more than three hundred years, his words were quoted as the venerable voice of authority.

And thus the squab, whether *it* likes it or not, has become a favorite delicacy of aging men. Personally, I just find squab an interesting change from chicken. The one I had in San Francisco recently was so poorly cooked as to be inedible. In folk practices, squab are also often fed to adolescents during puberty and to convalescents.

The sage Kao-tze, who lived during the Warring-States period (475– 221 B.C.) asserted that 食 色 性 也 —"Food and sex are intrinsic to human nature." Needless to say, of all of Kao-tze's thoughts, this is the one line that is best remembered over the centuries. Ask the average Chinese. If he knows only one line of classical philosophy, this is the one he would know. And he would probably attribute it to Confucius. Poor Kao-tze!*

We have already met in our discussion of dumplings the first character 食 in this saying. Remember the spoon and the bowl of rice? It means to eat. The second character we have also met as the first member of the triad 色 香 味 —color, fragrance, and taste—used in discussing fine food. The second character means color? Yes, color is used as a euphemism for sex. Evidently, black-and-white movies were not considered sexy. The third character means human nature. Finally, the fourth is an exclamation used in classical Chinese. By sheer coincidence, it is pronounced much like "yeah" and carries almost the same connotation.

To be sure, all human cultures engage in the ingestion of food and the

---

* The remark of Kao-tze actually appeared in a debate with the philosopher Mencius. Having said that, he went on to say that benevolence is intrinsic while righteousness is extrinsic. Nobody remembers that remark!

procreation of children. It is how these basic acts are regarded within the collective consciousness that varies from culture to culture. That the Chinese have such a saying known to practically anyone—as well-known as, say, "A rolling stone gathers no moss"—is sometimes held to be significant.

Quite naturally, a sensual appreciation of food resonates with a sensual appreciation of sex. It is certainly no accident that within our Western perspective, when we think of the great cuisines of Europe—the Italian and French—we think of cultures also given to the sexual experience.

The intertwining of food and sex has been much explored in Chinese novels, most explicitly in the late sixteenth-century work *Jin Ping Mei (The Golden Lotus)*. In the most notorious scene, the leading man of the novel makes love with his two concubines in a grape arbor on a hot summer's day. The lovemaking alternates with the eating of various delicacies. The American sinologist Frederick Mote observed that the "calculated, leisurely experiencing of all the sensations of taste, color, fragrance, temperature, form, and action" is a sharp contrast to the frantic orgies of similar scenes in Western literature. He claims that the novel's expression of sensuality, particularly in its use of food, was "unlikely to take place in any other civilization."

Aha, I see that Mote uses the same color-fragrance-taste triad in his description of sex that we talked about in Chapter 2 in describing food.

So in eating squab, it would seem, the aging man is expressing both of his basic needs. Interestingly, the noted American gourmet Craig Claiborne has written that the French and the Chinese are both very fond of squab. Perhaps these two know something others don't.

CHAPTER 7

NO CONTEST
BETWEEN FISH
AND A BEAR
WITH EIGHT LEGS

IN DESCRIBING A difficult choice, Mencius (circa 371–288 B.C.) said, "How am I to choose between fish and the bear's paw?" This phrase, "fish and bear's paw" is now a common idiomatic expression that has exercised gourmets for centuries. Learned gastronomes would hold forth, denigrating or extolling the bear's paw. Special arrangements would be made for a panel of judges to taste the bear's paw. In recent years, the consensus has been overwhelmingly in favor of the fish, but periodically a grumbly voice would be raised in print charging that those who pooh-poohed the bear's paw simply hadn't found a cook who knows how to cook it. (There is perhaps some culinary basis for suspecting that the bear's paw may be tasty: it is heavily padded. But as a result, it is also difficult to cook well. Chinese gourmets regard the Germans and Russians as experts at cooking bear's paw.) *

In any case, the fish has long won the affection of the Chinese gourmet. In no other cuisine is the fish prepared in so many different ways. In coastal regions, fish are abundant and often form the mainstay of the diet. However, in the western provinces such as Gansu, on the edge of the great Gobi desert, fish are hard to come by. At dinner parties, a fish carved out of wood is sometimes presented on the table to express the host's regret that fresh fish is not available.

My father was from Ningbo, a coastal city near Shanghai. He was exceedingly fond of fish, and I grew up with fish almost every day. I spoke earlier about my childhood memories of going with my father to select a live fish. Another childhood memory I have is that of eels. One famed Ningbo dish is deep-fried eels. In season, eels were bought live. The cook would prepare a wok full of hot oil. We children, overcoming our fear of killing and titillated by our fascination with death, would sneak into the kitchen to watch the cook, holding the eel in one hand, slit it with one smooth motion. Chopped rapidly into pieces, the eel was cooked in an instant in the hot oil. The dish would arrive at the table with the pieces of eels still twitching.

Gretchen has an enormous fondness for this dish which, needless to

---

* Incidentally, Mencius chose the bear's paw in answer to his own question. He also went on to say that he loved both life and righteousness but if he couldn't have both, he would choose righteousness. Even educated Chinese these days mostly remember that Mencius had to choose between fish and the bear's paw, and not the part about life and righteousness.

say, we are not going to prepare at home, even setting aside the difficulty of obtaining live eels. For the same reason, our neighborhood Chinese restaurant is not going to serve it. They say that you can get anything in New York and we did find a restaurant there that specializes in Ningbo cuisine. Another favorite of Gretchen's at this Ningbo restaurant is the fish casserole with a slippery type of bean skin called fenpi that gives the dish an interesting texture. We are rather fond of casseroles in general. The Chinese word for casserole means literally "sand pot." You may have seen these traditional sand-colored casserole pots with dark brown covers.

Do you have any political enemies? If so, then beware of a whole fish steamed or braised in a Chinese restaurant. A whole fish is ideal for hiding a thin, flat dagger. In the early years of the Spring-Autumn period (770–476 B.C.), an emperor was so heavily guarded that his enemies were unable to get at him. Finally, he was killed at a banquet by an assassin disguised as a waiter who had concealed his dagger inside the fish. They didn't have metal detectors back then. This famous story, recorded in *The Chronicles of the Assassins,* gave rise to an expression about daggers concealed in fish and to a popular Beijing opera.

The character for fish is strikingly representational. Look at the form of this character as it evolved

When you see the modern character 魚 on a menu, try to see how closely it resembles the 魚 that may appear shortly on your plate. The tail has become the four dots; the scaly body, the central crossed area; and the head, the two strokes on top.

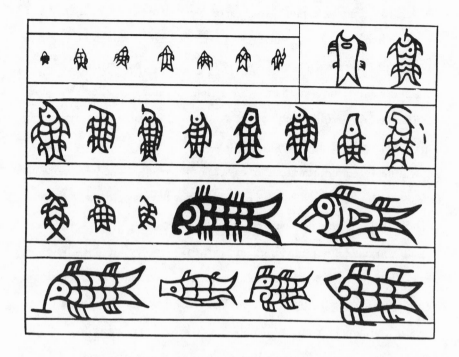

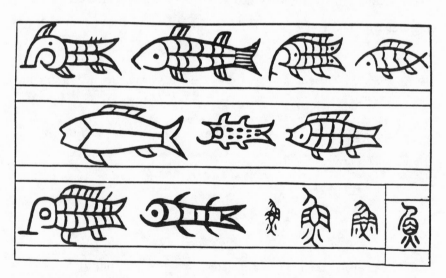

For each character, there are many ancient forms known. Here is the character for "fish" as it appeared in ancient times.

In China, when you talk fish, you talk about the carp 鯉 (notice the fish character used as a radical), which is so often represented in Chinese painting and decorative art. And when you talk carp, you talk about the carp of the Yellow River of North China. Around the city of Kaifeng, the Yellow River descends from the highlands into its flood plain with a torrent of water. The carp tries to jump the torrent and for its vitality is thus held in the same esteem as the salmon of the Pacific Northwest. At a place called the Dragon Gate, the rush of water is particularly spectacular and it is said that a carp that successfully jumps over this drop will immediately turn into a dragon and fly into the sky. This gave rise to a local folk superstition: those families whose sons were to prepare for the imperial examination to become a scholar-mandarin, or whose sons had successfully passed the imperial examination, would not eat carp out of respect for the carp spirit. The supposed transformation of the carp into a dragon was likened to the transformation of the student into a mandarin. The carp was thus thought of as a kind of patron saint of the student.

While I pride myself on being an adventurous eater I do draw the line at risking death in order to taste some delicacy or another. You may have heard of the fish the Chinese call 鯸鮐 or 河豚 (among many other names); the Japanese call it *fugu*. The fish contains in its liver and ovaries a deadly toxin that causes paralysis and death within minutes. While the existence of this fish was recorded in ancient chronicles, it was not till the Song dynasty that people figured out that the fish could be eaten if the liver and ovaries were removed. Utmost care had to be exercised to prevent the toxin from spilling out.

To describe an exceedingly risky adventure, the Chinese sometimes say "risking death to eat 河豚 ." In a similar vein, the Japanese have a saying, "I would love to eat fugu, but I would also like to live." The Song dynasty poet and self-proclaimed gourmet Su Tung-po, whom we met before in connection with the pork dish named after him, was certainly not afraid. Once, when he was visiting a region known for its 河 豚 , a merchant invited him to sample the fish. Excited that such a famous poet was coming to dinner, the whole family hid behind a screen when the fish was served, eager to hear whether Su liked it. As they waited with bated breath, Su put his chopsticks to the fish and ate without saying a word. Finally, after he had finished, he exclaimed, "Indeed, it's worth dying for!"

The mystique of a thrill with every bite has made this fish the ultimate gourmet item in the Far East. Song dynasty poets, including Su, tried to outdo each other singing the praise of 河 豚 . It was even said that after tasting this fish, all else would seem to be without taste. Still another reason not to try it, I say. If you must, then Japan is the place to go. To put an end to the spectacle of diners keeling over after eating fugu, the Japanese government has stepped in and licensed specialized fugu chefs. The chefs are held strictly responsible for any deaths, and their license and picture are prominently displayed in fugu restaurants to reassure the diners. For an extra kick, some people even like a slight numbness in the mouth caused by a trace of the toxin.

The mystique of this fish is such that it is called by many names, including "round-ball fish" after its shape. Notice that while the official name of this fish contains the fish radical, its common name 河 豚 has the pig character 豕 . The left half of 豚 is actually the character for flesh 肉 compressed for lack of room, thus 肉 → 月 . The ribs have become just two short horizontal strokes. The character 河

contains the water radical and means "river." The name of the fish, "river pig," was probably coined to suggest its tastiness.

The West Lake in Hangzhou is among the best-known scenic spots in China. The region boasts two celebrated fish dishes, both supposed to have been invented about a thousand years ago by a woman known as 宋 嫂 . The second character contains the woman radical and means "an older brother's wife." If ever language reflects culture, the abundance of terms in Chinese specifying various familial relationships tells us clearly how important these relations are. The Chinese are appalled by the totally imprecise generic terms used in English. Your sister-in-law? Do you mean your older or younger brother's wife, or do you mean your husband's or your wife's older or younger sister? For each of these possibilities the Chinese have a term. This drives the translators of Chinese novels crazy. Some of them resort to footnotes to explain how different characters are related to one another even while the relations would be obvious to a Chinese reader.

To complicate matters, the Chinese would also address a good friend's wife as 嫂 , a term of respect and endearment. Further, a woman worthy of respect but clearly not of an older generation is often also addressed by this term. Thus, the woman who invented those fish dishes was known as 宋 嫂 in the village. (Her last name 宋 Song, happens to be the same as the "Song" in Song dynasty.)

All right then, on to the story. Let's call the female lead simply Woman Song. Woman Song's husband had a younger brother. (These family relations are always spelled out.) When she was widowed, she vowed to bring up the little boy. They lived by the lake and fished for their livelihood. One day, the boy fell ill. In nursing him back to health, the Woman Song hit upon the idea of taking the bones out of a cooked fish and, since the lotus grew in profusion in the West Lake, combined it with ground lotus roots to make a thick broth. Thus was the first dish 宋 嫂 魚 羹 or "Woman Song's Fish Broth" invented!

You may recognize the third character as fish. The fourth character would appear once in a while on menus and means a thick broth of some sort. The etymology of this awkward-looking character is interesting. Let's first take it apart into a top half 羔 and a bottom half 美 . Aha, the top half is almost the lamb from Chapter 5, but not quite! It has those four dots: they represent four legs. The emphasis on legs suggests a lamb that has just begun to walk and hence a baby lamb. As a linguist, you are probably already chuckling over the curious pictorial redundancy since, as you may recall, the two lower horizontal strokes in 羊 already account for the legs of the lamb. Thus, the character-maker of old was like a child who draws a lamb complete with four legs and then adds four tiny legs to indicate that the lamb is a baby!

Now to the bottom half 美 . Do you remember it? It is formed by combining the characters for lamb and for big and means "beautiful": the ancients loved a big, fat lamb!

Talk about pictorial redundancy. The character for thick broth 羹 is composed of a baby lamb with eight legs and a big fat lamb with four legs! It assumes its meaning of thick broth from a beautifully fat baby lamb. Evidently, lamb broth was so popular that it became associated with the very idea of thick broth.

This Woman Song was sure inventive. After her brother-in-law (that is, her husband's younger brother) regained his health, he got tired of Woman Song's Fish Broth and longed for something else. What an ingrate! The Woman Song then had the idea of making a sauce with sugar and vinegar to put on a whole cooked fish. Thus was invented 西 湖 醋 魚、 or "West Lake Vinegar Fish." You probably notice the water radical in the second character for lake. What about the third character? Did you recognize the fermentation jar 酉 ? Yes, it is vinegar.

These two dishes were so tasty that Woman Song soon decided to open a small restaurant serving them. The fame of these dishes spread far and wide and eventually reached the court. The emperor ordered that Woman Song be brought to the imperial palace to cook these dishes for him. The Woman Song, however, regarded this emperor as a tyrant. And so one night, while the imperial messenger was waiting for her to go to the capital, she simply disappeared with her brother-in-law, never to be seen again.

Folktales such as this one—and there are many—illuminate food history as well as tell us something about Chinese folk culture. In contrast to the stories about wine I told in Chapter 3, which have a certain mythic flavor, this story specifies the time and place. I could well believe that the Woman Song really existed. Details, such as the fact that her husband was the fifth child in his family, further suggest that such stories were not invented arbitrarily. Many Chinese dishes, much like Peach Melba or Beef Wellington, were invented by actual people in historical times. The story also shows that the appearance of a new dish is an event worthy of even the emperor's notice.

For such a tale to have come down to us through a thousand years, it must have a strong folk appeal. The story emphasizes that a widowed woman could be independent and even bring up a young relative on her own, and that an inventive person, using readily available and modest local resources, could create something that even the emperor would covet. She wasn't a famous person like an opera star or a general. But probably the most appealing feature to the folks telling and retelling the story is how a common person can snub an unpopular emperor.

The ancient Chinese had looked westward, through the Silk Route, towards India, Central Asia, and beyond. Dynastic capitals until the Song dynasty (960–1127) were all located in the region around Xian, where tourists now go to see the unearthed terra-cotta army of the Qin emperor. But starting with the sixth century or so, the Yangtze river delta region (the region around present-day Shanghai), with its rich soil and network of canals and rivers, had been developing and prospering. Meanwhile, trade over the Silk Route became less and less significant to the national economy. By the end of the Tang dynasty (618–907) and the beginning of the Song dynasty (960–1279), the center of gravity of China had moved east, to the Yangtze river delta and the surrounding coastal provinces.

A nouveau riche merchant class emerged. Trade over the Silk Route had required large investments with no profits to be seen until the camel caravan had made its long trek back. Military escorts had to be provided through the barren and unpacified regions. In contrast, in coastal East China, anybody with enough capital for a few boats could realize large profits in a short time.

With wealth came demand for the finer things. Art and culture flourished, and a more refined cuisine was developed. Much of what we now know as Chinese cuisine originated from the Song dynasty.

The Cantonese are famous for their 魚生粥 , literally "fish raw porridge." Raw fish is sliced as thin as possible. Boiling hot rice porridge is then poured over the fish slices. (Incidentally, did you know the

English word "porridge" came from the old French and Latin word for "leek" and that leeks are known as *poireaux* in French and *porri* in Italian?) Scallions, the Chinese equivalent of leek I suppose, and perhaps some other condiments are often added.

The character 生 means "to give birth," "to grow," "to live." It came from a picture of a growing plant 坐 emerging from the ground. Notice the same distortion that occurred in the evolution of the character for cattle operates here to produce the modern character. It also means "alive" and hence, by extension, "raw" in cooking.

The character for porridge 粥 contains the rice radical 米 . The character for rice comes from the pictograph 米 which shows rice (the four dots) growing in the fields (the cross). The two wriggly lines around the rice radical in 粥 depict the steam rising up around the rice. Very pictorial, yes?

When I was a kid in Hong Kong, I would walk by street vendors selling raw fish porridge and literally salivate. I was salivating not only because of the aroma but also because raw fish porridge, just as street wonton, was strictly forbidden to me. My father felt that the fish might be unfresh and full of parasites.

Needless to say, there's no raw fish porridge in the average Chinese restaurants in the United States, but it is certainly available in the China-towns of the major cities. Try it if you appreciate bland but subtly flavored food.

Raw fish porridge recalls a Chinese culinary tradition now preserved in the Japanese sashimi. Numerous texts, starting with the Zhou dynasty (11th century–221 B.C.), attest to the ancients' fondness for raw fish. The popularity of raw fish sliced thin reached its zenith during the Ming dynasty

(1368–1644) but suffered a precipitous decline after the same venerable doctor Li who extolled the sexual potency of squab warned of the dangers of eating raw fish. And thus, a particularly delicious culinary tradition died at the hands of the good doctor. Indeed, with population pressure the lakes and rivers were getting more and more polluted, and people were dying from eating infected raw fish. By contrast, Japan was a small island, with fresh fish from the ocean never far away.

In China the eating of raw fish lingered on in coastal regions. It even took on a poetic and nostalgic aura. A Qing dynasty (1644–1911) poet wrote of the pleasure of eating, on a cold winter's day, raw fish sliced thin and translucent, "delicate like slivers of jade." In the last two lines of the poem, he falls into remembering the good old days of the preceding Ming dynasty: "A glass of warmed wine keeping the chill away/Eating sliced raw fish as was fashionable in the ancien régime."

These two lines of innocuous poetry could very well have landed the poet in hot water. The rulers of China have traditionally been suspicious of intellectuals writing hidden messages criticizing the government, and throughout history wrathful emperors have put to death writers who dared extol the virtues of the preceding dynasty.

The collective memory of a race can be quite short. Most Chinese have forgotten that sashimi was much enjoyed in ancient China; some even chide the Japanese for eating raw fish. My first encounter with sashimi was at the New Jersey home of a Japanese friend. I almost gagged. What do you expect from someone who grew up indoctrinated into thinking that all kinds of dreaded diseases could result from eating raw fish porridge? Curiously enough, some years later during a visit to Japan, I acquired an instant fondness for sashimi.

The character 生 , meaning "raw" in connection with food and "to be born" or "to be alive" in general, appears in 先 生 , the Chinese equivalent of the term of address for "mister" (obviously derived from "master"). The first character means "earlier" or "before." Thus, the term of address means literally "you were born before me" and hence more worthy of respect. Age was venerated. In Japanese 先 生 is pronounced *sensei* and is used to mean a venerable teacher.

Let us end by going back to the bear. Interestingly enough, the ancient character for bear 能 has now become one of the most common words meaning "can" as in "I can do it." The ancients were in awe of the bear's power.

To avoid confusion, some scribe eventually invented a new character 熊 for "bear" by adding ⺍ four legs to the old character. But the old character was derived from the pictograph

能 .

Can you picture the crouching grizzly with his massive front paws? Thus, in the modern character for "can do" 能 the right half represents the two hind legs and the bottom portion of the left half are the front legs. The modern character for bear 熊 depicts then a bear with eight legs. That should make some gourmets happy!

All right, here is a question for all you true gourmets out there. Of the four paws of the bear, which would you prefer?

According to one opinion, the left front paw is preferred because the bear licks his left front paw as he hibernates.

CHAPTER 8

COURTESANS
DO NOT
EAT CRABS

THE CRAB OCCUPIES a special place in the pantheon of Chinese gastronomy.
A Jin dynasty (A.D. 256–420) poet wrote:

右手持酒杯

Holding a glass of wine in the right hand,

左手持蟹螯

Grasping a crab claw in the left hand,

拍浮酒船中

And drifting along in a boat filled with wine,

便足了一生矣

Ah, my life is totally satisfied!

The romantic imagery associated with a crab feast extends to the present. To the Chinese, crab eating evokes images of sitting in front of chrysanthemums, of the clean taste of vinegar, ginger, and wine, and of a moonlit autumn night. The wine is indispensable: one folk saying has it that to have crab but no wine is one of the great tragedies of life.

The reference to chrysanthemum and the moonlight autumn night comes from the crab season in the fall. A folk saying among crab lovers has it that

九 月 圓 臍 十 月 尖

or "Ninth month round abdomen, tenth month sharp." The saying originates from the fact that the crab's reproductive season occurs during the ninth month of the lunar calendar, at which time the female crabs are particularly plump and delicious. The saying also serves as a mnemonic to distinguish the female crab from the male: the part of the shell that corresponds to the abdomen is round in the female and sharp or pointed in the male. The saying is a mnemonic because the female is preferred and thus, by the tenth month the catch consists of mostly male crabs. It is said that the males are exhausted from copulation and hence less tasty. There are, however, some gourmets who prefer the male, saying that by the same token it is leaner and more digestible. You tell me.

In Chinese gastronomy the female is preferred because the eggs often found in females are rated as a high delicacy. The eggs, known as 蟹黄, can be preserved in sauce form and used as a flavoring agent in soups and noodles. The character 黄 means "yellow": the color and firmness of the eggs are much discussed by epicures specializing in crabs.

This saying contains several points of etymology. The third character,

meaning round, contains the enclosure or encircling radical 囗 associated with the character for country that we discussed in connection with
the word for the United States. It is interesting to note that this radical,
drawn as a circle in ancient times, has become a square but nevertheless is
still associated with roundness.

Notice the seventh character; it contains the character 大 for big
and the character for small 小 which we met in Chapter 5. Put the
character for small on top of the character for big and what do you get? You
get a sharp point at which big tapers into small! The seventh character 尖
means "sharp" or "pointed."

From my translation of the saying, you can guess that the second and
sixth character 月 means "moon" or in this context "month" in the
lunar calendar. Evidently, it came from 𝄡 , the same moon as in the
West, except for the two dots. I leave it to you to make your own theory
about what the two dots mean. Etymologists don't really know.

Curiously, the fourth character, which evidently means abdomen, appears to contain the moon as a radical. In fact, it isn't the moon but the
flesh radical compressed from the character for meat or flesh as I explained
in connection with the "death fish." This is the etymological version of
what biologists called convergent evolution: two characters with rather different pictographic origins may, with distortion and simplification, evolve
into apparently the same character or radical.

Let us go back to that Jin dynasty poem. You may be surprised but it is
full of radicals and characters you have seen before. Can you pick out the
two instances where the character for wine appear? Can you see the water
radical in the character 浮 , meaning "to float," "to drift along"? See
the two occurrences of the character for hand 手 ? Also, notice the

hand radical 才 in the character for "to hold" in the first and second line, and in the character 拍 (meaning "to hit lightly," that is, in the context of the poem, to move the oar slightly once in a while) in the third line. You may also have recognized the character 生 for "alive" or "raw" that we met in the last chapter. Here it means "life." Also, as you may have guessed, 一 means "one," so that 一 生 means a "lifetime."

See how much you already know!

But what about the character for crab? It looks rather complicated 蟹. See it in the second line of the poem? The key is to recognize that it contains the radical for insect and crawling creatures 虫, which in turn comes from the picture 〇. In fact, most of the goodies from the sea, shrimp 蝦, oysters 蠔, and clams 蜆 all contain the insect radical. Notice that the character for insect appears on the left except in the character for crab. These characters are all constructed out of 虫 and a phonetic element. For example, the phonetic element 解 appearing in the character for crab is itself a character meaning "to untie," "to explain," or "to analyze."

None of this is going to help you, however. Instead, just remember the character for insect 虫 and you will be able to pick out the shellfish dishes on the menus of your local restaurant. Linguistically, the Chinese lump the shellfish with insects.

What! I can hear the taxonomists howling. For those of you curious about taxonomy, the ancient Chinese were actually half right. You no doubt remember from high school biology that the class Insecta and the class Crustacea, which contains shrimp, crabs, and lobsters, belong together in the phylum Arthropoda. Clams and oysters, however, are in an entirely different phylum. But wasn't it William James who told us about how the crab protested being classified as a crustacean? "Whyyy, me tough guy, come and go as Aah please, Aah ain't gonna belong to no group!" grumbled the indignant crab. So perhaps we shouldn't worry too much about calling the crab an insect. *

Talking about the indignant crab, I am reminded that the Chinese describe the behavior of a bully as "walking sideways," figuratively from the association of a crab as an armored bully with claws. In a curious linguistic resonance, we call an ill-tempered person "crabby." William James's remark conveys the same imagery.

In the autumn, the sideways-walking bullies come out to wander around the water-flooded paddies and are thus easily caught. Indeed, rice paddies support a host of delicacies from fish to frogs. Crabs are also caught from streams and lakes. Sea crabs, though larger and fatter, are said to be less flavorful. One Chinese gourmet, having traveled the world sampling crabs, concluded that the Dungeness is the best sea crab anywhere.

A curious folk belief is that in the reincarnation cycle prostitutes or courtesans become crabs (presumably female crabs) in the next life. Some courtesans do not eat crabs as a result.

In fact, courtesans are very much associated with the eating of crabs. But please, if you think of courtesans, don't think of the ladies walking

---

* An interesting dish in which the insect radical appears is 螞 蟻 上 樹 , literally "ants climbing up a tree." The first two characters both contain the insect radical and are constructed phonetically. Taken together, they mean "ants." Notice that the character for horse is used as a phonetic element in the first character. If you see this dish on your menu, don't be alarmed! It involves neither insects nor horse meat. It is merely a common household dish consisting of ground beef (or pork) with vermicelli. The bits of ground beef evidently reminded somebody of ants.

around Times Square! A courtesan was someone who could play you a classical tune on a lute on a moonlit night if you so desired. If in contemplating the eternal futility of existence you should sigh and utter the first line of a Tang dynasty poem in infinite sadness, she could, without an instant of hesitation and in the voice of a nightingale, respond by murmuring the second line. And then, of course, she was exquisitely skilled in all the ancient ways of love. Ah, such were the famous courtesans of ancient China, many of them immortalized in songs and poems for all posterity.

The tradition has long died out in China, of course, but lingers on in Japan embodied in the geishas. In fact, the word "geisha" comes from the Chinese word 藝 妓 "art courtesan," a high-class courtesan skilled in the arts. (See the woman radical in the second character?) Some years ago, when I visited Japan, a friend took me to see a geisha he had known for many years. I was instructed beforehand to admire the refined way she would turn her wrist while pouring tea.

Alas, such a cultured way of life is doomed to disappear as our civilization marches on. In any case, I wanted to explain how courtesans are associated with the eating of crabs, and for that matter, with the annals of gastronomy. When the literate, the wealthy, and the elegant visited the courtesans who were high-class enough to be immortalized by history, what could these bored and jaded people do besides playing the lute and humming poetry? They ate fine food of course.

In the treatises on the firmness of crab eggs, a Ming dynasty (1368–1644) courtesan is celebrated for having made a decisive contribution. To have the best crab eggs, she said, you must separate the males from the females. The courtesan's observation is remembered in a triplet that rhymes in Chinese: "Let the females not bother the males, let the males not bother the females, then long will the eggs stay firm."

Neither you nor I were born yesterday. Come on, surely the folks who catch crabs have known this long before the Ming dynasty. They just weren't surrounded by a flock of adoring literati who would write down anything they said! The courtesan's remark must also have tickled the literati's sense of humor, given the setting. I can picture them roaring with laughter and asking for another round of drinks.

This brings me to a point mentioned earlier, that wine is indispensable while eating crabs. This has a sound gastronomic basis: rice wine just goes well with crab, what more can I say? But the intimate association of crab with wine is also firmly established as a matter of medical balance.

In Chinese medicine, the balance of opposing tendencies is considered tantamount to good health. This balance can easily go out of whack by being too hot or too cold, for instance. As a result, all foods are classified according to whether their intrinsic essences are hot or cold. Well, crabs turn out to be the epitome of coldness and thus must be balanced with some heated Chinese wine or spirit.

The notion of balance of food echoes one of the ideals of Chinese civilization, or perhaps more precisely, of the Confucian world view, namely the quest for harmony. Extremes are abhorred. Moderation and balance reign supreme. This sense of harmony also underscores the importance of the surroundings in fine Chinese dining: the moonlit night in autumn, the chrysanthemums, all these play a role in one's sense of harmony with nature.

While a number of classic dishes use crabmeat, such as crabmeat with bean curd, crab fanciers universally prefer to eat crabs steamed in their shells. On this East and West agree. The whole point, as detailed in numerous Chinese gastronomic writings, is that it takes time to crack open the shells. Be leisurely, have plenty of wine around, and make a mess! The preferred dip is a sauce made of shredded ginger and *good* vinegar. I like melted butter, too, but Gretchen feels that crabmeat is already rich enough. Incidentally, the taste in eating crab may have evolved since ancient texts speak of sugared and honeyed crabs, a practice now uncommon.

My mother is extremely fond of crabs and eating crabs was very much a gastronomic event in my family as I was growing up. In this country, one of my pet peeves is the general unavailability of live crabs. Even as great a market as the Pike Place Market in Seattle normally only has boiled crabs available. In one of his books, Calvin Trillin describes his travels across country in search of the crab. I have had similarly discouraging experiences. Gretchen and I once made a pilgrimage to the previously mentioned Dungeness, a tiny town on the tip of a coastal spit on the Olympic peninsula in Washington state. When we got there we asked several likely-looking locals and ended up at a restaurant with the word crab in its name that was situated at the end of a lonely road overlooking some coastal water. Well, it is surely one of the great paradoxes of the universe that restaurateurs in Dungeness appear not to understand what fresh crabs are. When we lived on the East Coast, we made a similar trip, visiting the little towns along Chesapeake Bay. In most of the towns, the closest thing we could find to fresh crabs were crab cakes. Gretchen expressed it best when she said that the food we had on that miserable trip was like the kind of food she had in her high school cafeteria. I personally think that crab cakes are an abomination. I sometimes imagine that in the afterlife those responsible for them will be called to justice and face a tribunal of crabby crabs.

Time to move on to shrimp. Dried shrimp are often used in home-style cooking to give many dishes their characteristic flavor. If you have ever visited a Chinese grocery store, you must have been struck by the large variety of seafood available in dried form. In the past, drying was of course a universal method of preserving food, but nowadays, even when the fresh form is available the dried form is often used for its more concentrated taste. In the same way, we eat raisins even when grapes are available. In Chinese cuisine, fresh shrimp and dried shrimp are in effect two different food items, just as grapes and raisins are different.

Similarly, scallops are great both fresh and dried. (Think of fresh scallops and think of scallop seviche in Mexican cuisine, yum.) Dried scallop is prized by Chinese gourmets both for its taste and for its texture. It can be torn into shreds by hand and used to flavor a number of classic dishes.

Lobsters are known as "dragon shrimp," written as 龍蝦 . See the insect radical in the character for shrimp? The complicated-looking character 龍 means "dragon." Actually, it is not that complicated if you can imagine seeing the right half as a picture for its wing. On the left hand side, we see the compressed flesh radical on the bottom, as it often appears in characters describing wild animals such as the bear.

The government of the People's Republic of China has undertaken a campaign to simplify Chinese characters. All publications in mainland China are now printed with simplified characters. As an example, the character for dragon is simplified rather drastically to 龙 .

While no one can deny the importance of the simplification campaign in boosting literacy, it has also often done violence to the etymology of various characters, particularly those of pictorial origin. The poor dragon has lost its wings. Indeed, we can't even tell on first encounter whether 龙

is beast or plant, wood or liquid: more important than its wings, it has lost its radical.

If you are a tea connoisseur, you may know of oolong tea, meaning "black dragon" tea. The character for dragon is pronounced something like "*long*," or more accurately like "lone" as in the word *alone*.

Another possible appearance of the character dragon on menus is in the fruit longan, served in some restaurants as a dessert alongside the fruit lichee. When peeled, longan is round and white, about the size of a large strawberry and its texture is not unlike that of a grape. Longan is written as 龍眼 , literally meaning "dragon eyes," the name deriving from the round, black fruit. See the rotated character for "eye" on the left in the second character? The right half is a phonetic element. Incidentally, canned longan is readily available in Oriental grocery stores. It is a big hit with little kids. Try it with vanilla ice cream and tell them that they are eating dragon eyes. You can buy dried longans at Chinese markets in this country. The Cantonese use them to flavor certain soups.

All the goodies from the sea are referred to collectively as 海鮮 meaning seafood.

You may recognize the telltale water radical 氵 in the first character meaning "sea." Walking around Chinatown looking for a restaurant? Then keep an eye out for this character and you can be sure you're on the trail of some delicious seafood. However, once in a while you will probably go astray because the port city Shanghai, written as 上海 , means "on the sea." Now you even know how "sea" is pronounced—*hai*.

The character 上 , which your brilliantly deductive mind tells you is pronounced *shang*, means "up" or "on." You will understand its pictorial origin immediately if I show you the character for "down" or "under": 下 . Thus, 上 = up and 下 = down.

A friend of mine who went to the Orient was pleased that he could readily distinguish the up 上 and down 下 buttons in elevators. If you remember that 上 looks like it is pointing up, you will be able to distinguish the seafood dishes from the Shanghai-style dishes. Next time you walk around Chinatown, see if you can distinguish the seafood restaurants from the Shanghainese restaurants.

The second character in seafood, 鲜 , meaning "fresh" in this context and transliterated in pinyin as *xian* (pronounced something like "shien"), practically cries out for some etymological sleuthing. Look at it for a moment and separate it into its left and right halves: 鱼 and 羊 .

Think of all the animal words you have learned. Aha, this character is composed of fish on the left and of lamb on the right. The character means "fresh" because the ancients discovered that fish and lamb were best eaten fresh.

Used in connection with food, the character has taken on the connotation of flavorful. Indeed, it is a key character used in discourses on Chinese gastronomy and one that has resisted a precise translation. In these discussions, the character is used to describe a dish in which the natural flavors of the ingredients have been brought out and accentuated. Perhaps I can convey a rough notion of what the character means by saying that the Chinese often think of a well-prepared stock as 鲜 . Dried scallops are also considered the essence of flavor or *xian*.

In connection with this character, I can tell a story about a certain scholar-gentleman of some renown who lived towards the end of the Qing dynasty (1644–1911). He complained to his wife constantly that her food was not *xian*. Finally, she blew up and demanded that he produce something that tasted *xian*, or else. Terrified by her wrath, the scholar wandered about despondently, racking his brain trying to think of a new dish guaranteed to be *xian*. Being a scholar, he finally realized the etymology of 鮮 and produced a soup of fish and lamb! I am afraid that this particular soup, although duly recorded in the annals of Chinese gastronomy, does not enjoy a strong following.

Coming back to seafood then, we see how appropriate the notion of fresh and flavorful are in the Chinese word for seafood 海鮮 , pronounced "hai shien" (*haixian* in pinyin) and literally "the fresh and flavorful food from the sea."

If you are reading this book, you probably love Chinese food. And if you love Chinese food, you may be familiar with hoisin sauce. Beijing duck, for instance, is usually eaten with hoisin sauce. Now, consider hoisin and *haixian*. Sound similar? Yes, indeed, hoisin is *haixian* pronounced in Cantonese. The "hoi" in hoisin sauce and the "hai" in Shanghai refer to the same character. You know more than you think—the trick is to tie the bits and pieces together! Actually, hoisin sauce has a fruity—not sea—flavor. It was apparently invented and named by people who did not live near the sea and who tried to imagine what fresh seafood tasted like.

The generic Chinese restaurant in this country serves a pathetically narrow range of seafood. Consider the marine animal 海參 , known as sea cucumber in this country. Gretchen loves sea cucumbers, but try to find a restaurant which serves them! When we lived in Seattle we did find one. The proprietor, fearing that his customers would not know what a sea cucumber was, listed the dish by its French term as braised bêche-de-mer. This dish became a favorite of my son Andrew, who was about three years old at the time. Whenever we went to that restaurant, Andrew would clamor for bêche-de-mer. Once, when asked by a family friend what his favorite food was, he astonished the matron by replying that it was bêche-de-mer. She was impressed that he spoke French.

Once Gretchen went up to Vancouver and brought back some sea cucumbers in a rock-hard, dried form, the only way it is sold in Chinese grocery stores. The U.S. customs inspector, incidentally, was curious but perfectly sympathetic.

When Gretchen got home, she had to learn the drill: the sea cucumbers are to be soaked in a bowl of clear water for several days, with the water replaced twice a day. It was sort of fun to see the sea cucumbers growing bigger and softer every day. Now you understand why your neighborhood Chinese restaurant is not going to bother.

Sea cucumber is a texture food. That gooey yet crisp feel has to be experienced to be appreciated. Red-cooked sea cucumber 紅燒海參 is prized as a banquet dish. The trick is to make sure the sea cucumbers are cooked just right, that is, without disintegrating completely while retaining a hint of crispness. By the way, if you are ever presented with the dish and you don't want to appear gauche, remember that the correct etiquette calls for a spoon instead of chopsticks. If you use chopsticks on the slippery, gelatinous sea cucumber, you will be sure to make a fool of yourself and be branded as lacking in savoir faire.

Sea cucumber makes also for a favorite summer dish 涼拌海參, Cool-Mix Sea Cucumber. The water-based, first character 涼 means "cool." You may also have noticed the hand radical 扌 in the second character, meaning "to stir" or "to toss" (as in a salad, for example). Sea cucumbers are cooled after cooking, cut into strips, and refrigerated until serving. A sauce made by mixing soy sauce, sesame sauce, vinegar, sesame paste, and garlic paste is poured over the cold sea cucumber shreds when served. That's it.

Things are improving for seafood lovers in this country. Seafood no longer just means breaded shrimp, and it is not only due to the influence of East Asian cuisines. Americans have seen what the Italians and French eat. Calamari is now a commonplace. Even my local supermarket carries squid. While I do not expect it to carry bêche-de-mer anytime soon, I can always be hopeful. May the situation continue to improve!

TO ALL
YOU
CARNIVORES

Now THERE! You, the bloodthirsty carnivore and blood relative of the caveperson who scratched out the first characters in the dirt, have learned a whole smattering of meaty characters. So let's just see:

羋 → 羊 = lamb

𤘻 → 牛 = bull

豕 → 豖 = pig 豬

鳥 → 鳥 = bird

鷄 = chicken

雞 = chicken (short-tailed)

鴨 = duck

鵝 = goose

鴿 = squab

肉 → 肉 = flesh, meat in general

魚 → 魚 = fish

虫 → 虫 = insect or crawling

creature, but in fact usually

shellfish

蟹 = crab

蝦 = shrimp

蠔 = oyster

蜆 = clam

If you like, perhaps you can go back and look at all the dishes listed in the preceding chapters. See if you can now identify whether they are fish or fowl, beef or pork.

Now we'd better go on and give the vegetarians their due.

THE SWEET FRAGRANCE OF CROPS RIPENING

FOR FUN, TRY this word game when you are "dining Chinese." Ask your dining companion, or your children, or yourself for that matter, what character ought to describe something as basic and common as vegetation or plants. Imagine yourself once again to be the smart caveman who invented the character for fire.

How about 丫 ? Reasonable enough. See the central stalk, see the two growing leaves, see the generic plant?

Since plants are rarely seen in isolation, the ancient Chinese took to writing the basic character twice, 丫丫 , to suggest lots of plants. Thus was born the character 艸 meaning "luxuriant vegetation."

This linguistic device of expressing abundance by writing the same character twice occurs often. For instance, two fires 炎 makes a blaze.

As another example, consider the obviously pictographic character for tree 木 . (You can probably picture the original form 米 , with the upward reaching branches and the downward reaching roots.) Write tree twice and you have 林 , a forest. Go one step further: write 森 and you have a jungle. In fact you might as well go all out. The two-character combination 森 林 (wow, five trees!) is now used to describe a real jungle like the Amazon. Can you still say that Chinese is not an easy language to learn?

Incidentally, 木 has gradually acquired the meaning of "wood" at the expense of tree. (As an interesting sidelight, we call a forest "woods" in English.) Virtually all characters that contain 木 as a radical have something to do with wood or a woody plant. *

Back to plants and vegetation in general. Eventually, vegetation 艸 was used more as a radical to construct more complicated characters than as an isolated character. As a radical it was simplified somewhat to 艹 , or economizing on strokes, to 艹 . The upward thrust of the leaves disappeared. Thus, the modern character for vegetable is 菜 .

See the radical 艹 on top? It is referred to as the "grass" radical since it appears in the character for grass. When you browse through a Chinese menu, if you spot the grass radical, then you can be fairly sure that

---

* If you look back at the poem in Chapter 3 about the wine cup that glowed in the dark, you will see the word for cup 杯 has a wood radical. Does this mean cups were made of wood in ancient times? It is possible but some scholars don't think so. The character for cup might have contained four strokes that got distorted into the wood radical. This is an instance in which relying on radicals for meaning may lead you astray.

the associated character has something to do with vegetables or plants of some sort.

The pictographic content of the character for vegetable is quite amusing. As a sharp-eyed, budding linguist, you may have noticed the character for tree 木 on the bottom. In fact, if we take away the grass radical from the character for vegetable, we have 采 .

See the hand or paw 爪 reaching down on the tree, picking fruit off the tree? We have thus the character 采 , meaning "to pick." In modern Chinese, the hand radical 扌 is added for good measure, giving rise to 採 , meaning "to pick." The older, and more correct, 采 has fallen into disuse. (Incidentally, the character 爪 is nowadays used exclusively to mean the "hand" or "paw" of animals. An insult is implied if it is used in reference to a person.)

When the grass radical is added to the character "to pick," we have the notion of harvesting or picking vegetation and hence by extension, vegetables.

By the way, you may already know how to pronounce this character for vegetable 菜 . If you live in a large city, your supermarket probably sells bok choy 白菜 . I live in a medium-sized town in California, and my neighborhood supermarket certainly does. Bok choy, sometimes referred to as Chinese cabbage, is transliterated from the Cantonese pronunciation; the Mandarin pronunciation is similar. The character pronounced as "bok," 白 , means "white." (We met this character already in Chapters 2 and 3.) If you know what bok choy looks like, then you know why the Chinese call it "white vegetable."

Another interesting character is 花 , meaning "flower." Perhaps you remember the character 化 meaning "transformation" (As in a live man transformed into a dead man in Chapter 6, remember?). Here 化 serves as a phonetic element but it also suggests the transformation of bud to flower. *

The basic character 屮 has given rise to many characters that most Chinese no longer realize have anything to do with plants: for example, 出 "to emerge" or "to exit." It came from the idea of a plant emerging from the soil 出 . If you are ever in a public building in China, you will want to learn to recognize 出 口 as the sign for exit, literally "exit mouth," with the character for mouth 口 . Perhaps you will remember from our discussion on raw fish porridge that a plant growing particularly well is pictured as 坐 and later 生 , giving rise to the character for "alive" and hence "raw" or "uncooked."

I went and looked at the menu of my neighborhood Chinese restaurant. Here are some entries involving the grass radical that I found.

1. 四 川 泡 菜
2. 芝 麻 牛 肉
3. 蔥 爆 羊 肉
4. 冬 菇 蒸 鷄
5. 魚 香 茄 子
6. 奶 油 菜 心

* Remember how we looked for pine blossoms in thousand-year-old eggs? Look for the words 松 花 on the package. The first character, with its wood radical, means "pine."

If you are the sort that relishes a challenge, now is the chance to test yourself on what you have already learned. I have purposely left out the English translations.

First of all, four of the dishes contain meat or flesh of some sort. Can you pick out the beef, mutton, chicken, and fish dish? A quick look back at Interlude 3 may help.

Next, look for the fire radical. See it in the third dish? I don't expect you to remember what type of cooking it describes. (Let me remind you, though, that it describes "explosive frying" as was discussed in Chapter 1.)

Finally, can you locate all the places where the water radical appears? It occurs twice in the first dish. If you said that the first dish has something to do with Sichuan, you have a good memory, indeed.

To come back to the main topic of discussion here, you may also have noticed that every dish contains a character with the grass radical. In fact, the fourth dish contains two such characters. In the first and last dishes, the character in question is just 菜 or vegetable. Let us now name each dish in English, at least as my neighborhood restaurant describes it.

四 川 泡 菜

1.SICHUAN PICKLED VEGETABLE

I was somewhat sneaky in including this entry since I had already mentioned it in the chapter on the water radical, explaining that 泡 means "to pickle." Now you know every character in this dish. I have been in a few Chinese restaurants where a small dish of Sichuan Pickled Vegetable was given out as a complimentary appetizer. I hope the trend continues and spreads.

芝麻牛肉

2. SESAME BEEF

Not long ago, I watched a television quiz show in which the contestants were totally stumped by a question involving Ali Baba and the Forty Thieves. The contestants continued to look blank even after the host of the show prompted them by mentioning the tales of the Arabian Nights. It was even a show in which the contestants were noted for their remarkable knowledge of assorted facts. Lately, there has been a great deal of talk about cultural literacy in this country, and I realized with some sadness that *A Thousand and One Nights* had just passed out of our culture. The command "Open sesame!" no longer holds the magical spell that it had for generations of children.

The sesame plant originated in Persia and from there spread westward into the Middle East and Europe and eastward into China and beyond. Sesame and a whole host of exotic "Western" food came into China during the expansionist Han dynasty (206 B.C.–A.D. 220). The list of food brought back by one early Han envoy includes grape, alfalfa, walnut, onion, peas, coriander, cucumber, and, last but not least, sesame. Remember the poem about the military expedition to get grapes and wine? (Somehow, poets would rather write about the grape than sesame.) If you go back to that poem now, I bet you can pick out the two Chinese characters for grape. (Hint: look for the grass radical 艹 .) The two characters, pronounced "poo tao," represent a phonetic transliteration of the Persian word for grape.

Sesame seeds are highly prized for their oil content and as a flavorful addition to breads. If you know Middle Eastern food, you may know that the confection called halvah, with its distinctive and exotic flavor, is based on a sesame paste. Sesame oil was important to Middle Eastern cultures. It takes 12,000 seeds to make one ounce of sesame oil. Incidentally, while writing this passage, I was tempted to bet, given the importance of sesame oil, that the boiling oil the clever slave girl Morgiana poured on the thirty-seven thieves hiding in oil jars had to be sesame oil. But in fact, if you read the story carefully, you might remember that earlier on the captain of the thieves had purchased mustard oil. (Ever since I was a kid, I have wondered why the thieves did not scream out and thus alert the others as they were being scalded to death one by one. If you know, tell me.)

Several cultures regard the sesame plant as having medicinal value and, by association, magical powers. That is probably why "Open sesame!" was the incantation to open the secret portal rather than, say, "Open barley!", as Ali Baba's greedy brother tried in his desperation. I understand that sesame also appears in cabalistic texts.

In Chinese cooking, sesame oil with its distinctive fragrance is used in stir-fry cooking and in making Chinese salads, a whole class of dishes ignored by Chinese restaurants. For a quick salad, Gretchen chops up some celery, mixes it with bits of dried shrimp, and sprinkles sesame oil on top. The Chinese like these dishes particularly on hot summer days.

葱爆羊肉

3. LAMB SAUTÉED WITH SCALLIONS

This dish is now customarily rendered as Mongolian Lamb on Chinese menus in the United States, although the Mongolian Lamb I have eaten is a much more elaborate affair. Each diner is given a two-foot-long pair of chopsticks that he uses to cook narrow strips of lamb to his own liking on a central grill. The lamb is then dipped in a bowl in which the diner has mixed a raw egg with soy sauce, scallions, and ginger shreds. Traditionally, Mongolian Lamb or Beef is eaten with the diners standing on one foot while resting the other foot on a bench. This curious stance is supposedly a compromise between the Mongols' custom of eating while sitting on the ground and the Chinese custom of eating while sitting on chairs. The eating of Mongolian Lamb or Beef was also traditionally an all-male affair, held outdoors in winter and with much alcohol consumed. I remember how pleased I was, when as a teenager, my father asked me to go with him to one such gathering.

Incidentally, in ancient times, the Chinese ate sitting cross-legged on the floor, each with an individual portion of food placed on something like a modern coffee table. Indeed, this is more or less how the more traditional Japanese still eat, sitting on a tatami mat with individual portions to eat. The widespread use of chairs in the Song dynasty is said to be another contributing factor to the development of Chinese cuisine.

If you know Chinese food at all, you know that scallions are almost indispensable. In this country, scallions are sometimes called green onions, indicating that the onion is more important than the scallion. The Chinese on the other hand call the onion　洋葱、, literally "ocean scallion," really meaning "foreign scallion." You might have already figured from the presence of the water radical　氵　that the character for "ocean"　洋 has something to do with water. (The character for "lamb"　羊　appears as a phonetic element here.) The character is often used to indicate that the object in question came from overseas and is of foreign origin. In this context, the figurative meaning of "foreign" is dominant so that the character is used even though the onion came to China by land.

冬菇蒸鷄

4. CHICKEN STEAMED WITH MUSHROOMS

Here the budding linguist may get confused. There are two characters with the grass radical, and so quite logically you may assume that together they mean "mushroom." But no, only the second character means "mushroom." The third character means "to steam."

But where is the fire radical 火 , you say? Indeed, it is there but well-disguised. The character for "to steam" was once written as 菱 . The flame underneath the steamer is clearly visible. The grass radical must indicate that the steamer was made from the fiber of plants. Indeed, the original pictograph looks like

All this is fine and dandy, but don't you think the character, as written in this form, looks rather awkward? The fire radical takes up too much room, making the character too high. And so for aesthetic reasons, the component strokes of the fire radical were taken apart and abbreviated as four dots all lined up.

It is the same simplifying principle that applies in turning the water radical 水 into 氵 .

Thus, the fire radical is present but disguised in the character for "to steam." A number of characters associated with cooking contain this disguised fire radical. In Chapter 1, we were just beginning to explore Chinese characters, and I didn't want to mention all this to confuse you.

In fact, most Chinese have long forgotten that a number of characters that apparently have nothing to do with cooking actually originated in the kitchen. A good example is 黑 , meaning "black." It came from the pictograph 羕 , with two fires, that is, a big fire burning underneath a chimney hole ⊙ . The character acquired its meaning from the soot left by big fires in the chimney. Notice that while one of the fire radicals is now disguised as ⼩ the other has been distorted and absorbed into the main stem of the character as 火 → 大 → 土 .

A related character is 熏 , meaning "to smoke." You may notice that it is formed by adding the strokes 千 on top of the character for black. These strokes were distortions of 〻 and later 屮 ; they represented smoke coming out of the chimney. More often than not, you will see this character written as 燻 on menus, as we saw in the chapter about fire.

You, the linguist, can chuckle at the redundancy of the extra fire radical on the left, introduced by people who have forgotten that two fire characters are already contained in 熏 . This is like giving the bear four extra legs, not to mention the two lambs with twelve legs in the character for thick broth.

After this digression on fire let us go back and look at the four characters 冬 菇 蒸 鶏 for the dish under discussion, Chicken Steamed with Mushrooms. Remembering the bird radical, you identify the last character as chicken. Good. That leaves the first character. It means "winter." Winter? Apparently, certain types of mushrooms are gathered in the cold, damp winter. Mushrooms are usually written in the combination 冬 菇 , literally "winter mushroom."

魚 香 茄 子

5. EGGPLANT WITH FISH FLAVOR

The character for eggplant is easy to pick out here. Look for the grass radical. Because of a somewhat convoluted history, you may actually know how to pronounce this character, more or less. As you probably know, the tomato was introduced into Europe from Central America, where the Aztecs apparently regarded it as a weed in their maize fields. Europeans, perhaps misinformed by the Aztecs, initially thought the tomatoes (derived, by the way, from the Nahuatl word *tomatl*) were poisonous. Upon seeing this strange fruit, the Chinese, not knowing what to make of it, simply called it the "foreign eggplant" and proceeded to make a sauce out of it, known as "eggplant sauce" 茄 汁 . Note the water radical in 氵汁 , a character meaning "sauce" or "juice." In Cantonese 茄 is pronounced something like the *ca* in "care" and 汁 like "dzup." The English liked the concoction and adopted the sauce, name and all. Hence, ketchup or catsup. The sauce is popular throughout East Asia and figures prominently in the cuisines of such people as the Malays and the Thais. The tomato, and its derivatives, from ketchup to tomato sauce, have spread throughout the world and rank as one of the greatest poor boy-turned-success stories in the history of food.

There, you now know that eggplant is pronounced in Cantonese as "kare" (as in "care").

Notice a curious symmetry in the story. Just from the name, it is clear that the English also didn't know what to make of the eggplant, a fruit that originated in tropical Asia and spread to Europe via Syria.

In the fourth character, we have 子 for child, which we encountered earlier, and here used as a diminutive ending: little eggplant, as it were.

The second character 香 in our menu entry is interesting. The top half came from 禾 , a character meaning "grain" or "crops." It is formed from the character for tree or plant with a ripe ear of grain hanging from the top: 禾

禾 = 木 with ／ on top. The bottom half is derived from a pictograph for a jar or barrel ⊟ . Incidentally, this bottom half is often erroneously identified as the character for the sun 日 , with its primitive form ⊙ . This represents an interesting phenomenon which adds to the confusion of the beginning student but challenges the language sleuth. What were originally quite different pictographs, barrel and sun, evolved over time to become the same. This is another example of convergent evolution that I spoke of earlier in connection with flesh and moon coming to have the same form.

Putting the two halves together, we have the character 香 , depicting the fermentation of grain in a barrel. By association, the character has come to mean "fragrance of wine," and hence, any agreeable odor. Notice that the fermentation barrel here is different from the 酉 of Chapter 2. Fermentation barrels are so important to Chinese culture that they have produced two separate radicals.

We have already encountered in Chapter 2 the triad of 色 香 味 (color, fragrance, and taste) that cooks strive for in Chinese cuisine. Here, then, is the second character in this triad.

While you may not know it, you have actually heard this character 香 pronounced many times. Pronounced "h'urn" in Cantonese (you can come very close to the sound by adding an aspirated *h* sound at the beginning of the English word "urn"), the character is in fact the Hong in Hong Kong. The name "Hong Kong" 香 港 literally means "fragrant harbor." (See the water radical in "harbor"?)

The barrel 曰 has also given rise to the modern character 甘 meaning "sweet." The character for tongue was 舌 and now 舌 , showing the tongue coming out of the mouth. (Interestingly, it is a forked tongue.) Some busybody scribe put tongue and sweet together to form another character 甜 , now also meaning sweet. Happily, this sort of linguistic redundancy allows the language to make fine distinctions. Over the years, 甜 has come to mean a more syrupy kind of sweetness, as in some desserts, while 甘 suggests the natural sweetness of sugar cane, for example.

Now, the only character left is the first— 魚 , which we immediately recognize as the character for fish. Thus, this menu entry, which is usually translated as Eggplant with Fish Flavor or Sichuan-style Eggplant, literally means "fish-fragrant eggplant," that is, eggplants cooked to suggest the fragrance of fish. Whaat? What is the connection between Sichuan-style and fish flavor? The dish doesn't taste anything like fish.

The taste of fresh ocean fish was unknown in Sichuan, an inland province almost a thousand miles from the sea and surrounded by mountains. Despite its name 四 川 , which you might remember means "four rivers," Sichuan was not known for its fish. (People from coastal provinces have always dismissed the river fish in Sichuan as scrawny and pathetic.) Apparently, one day some Sichuanese cook concocted a novel flavor and with an infinite longing for the plump ocean fish he had heard about but never tasted, he named the new flavor "the fragrance of fish." And thus in

Sichuan cuisine there is a group of dishes all named such-and-such with the fragrance (or flavor) of fish.

The character for fragrance appears in a number of other dishes. As a child, one of my favorite dishes was　五 香 熏 魚　, anise-flavored smoked fish, or literally "five-fragrance smoked fish." (The Chinese call star anise "five-fragrance" perhaps out of exasperation over how to define its unusual flavor.) The fish, cut up in square pieces and fried in oil until it is crisp and dry, is then dipped in a heated marinade of soy sauce, sugar, scallions, and anise until it acquires a dark brown color and an almost rubbery, chewy texture. As a fragrance, star anise has almost that Proustian magic for me. When I go to New York, I still make a point of going to a Shanghainese restaurant that makes five-fragrance smoked fish.

奶 油 菜 心

6. VEGETABLES IN CREAM SAUCE

The giveaway here is　女　, the woman radical in the first character. The character has something to do with woman: it means "milk." The second character has the water radical and is our old friend "oil" from Chapter 2. Thus,　奶 油　, literally "milk oil" and suggestively the fatty part of milk, means "cream." The character 　心　 means "heart," thus indicating that only the tenderest parts of vegetables should be used in this dish. If your restaurant does not, complain.

The character 　心　 looks rather like a heart to me, thus 　♡　 with the aorta and all. Certainly, it is no worse than 　♡　.

There are many characters containing 　心　 as a radical. Anything to do with feelings, emotions, love, and so forth are described by characters containing the heart radical.

A particularly cute example is 忐忑 . Remember from the last chapter that 上 means "up" and 下 means "down"? You got it! This combination means "anxiety." Other examples of heart-based characters include

愛 = love, 感 = to feel, 情 = mood.

(The heart radical is often compressed into 忄 or 忄 , which by the way even looks sort of like the symbol for the American Heart Association.) We also have the combinations 愛情 = romantic love, 感情 = emotional feelings.

Actually, you have already seen the character for "to feel." Do you remember the word for "sexy"? And if you now go back to Kao-tze's saying in Chapter 6 about food and sex, you may notice that the character for human nature 性 consists of the heart radical together with the character for alive. Besides the character for color, this character is also now used as a euphemism for sex.

It is curious to see that the ancient Chinese thought with their hearts. Several characters connected with thinking, such as 思 and 想 , all contain the heart radical. Remember from Chapter 2 the character 意 meaning "intentions" that the gentlemen-gourmet regarded as the true essence of cuisine? It also contains the heart.

Another interesting example is 愁 , meaning "worried" or "depressed." The etymology shows an inspired construction, combining phonetics and meaning. First, we recognize the heart radical on the bottom. Okay, so this character has something to do with emotion. On top, we see side by side the character for crops 禾 and the character for fire 火 . Together we have a character 秋 , meaning "autumn." I suppose the reason for this is because crops are harvested in autumn under the fiery sun. Here, this character for autumn is the phonetic element: the character for "worry" is pronounced roughly the same as the character for autumn.

Fine, that's the phonetic construction in action. However, you may have also noticed that the choice of autumn as the phonetic element is wonderfully apt: summer is over, the weather is turning, and one may very well feel depressed. Indeed, Chinese poetry, perhaps in resonance with Shelley, is full of lines on how depressing the winds and rains of autumn are. Some ancient scribe chose his phonetic elements with feeling.

Next time you are in a Chinese restaurant, if you can remember the grass radical 艹 (picture the plants growing 艹), then you are all set to pick out characters having to do with vegetables.

CHAPTER 10

HOW TO
AVOID BEING
VULGAR

THE PANDA WAS God's gift to zookeepers and manufacturers of stuffed animals.* Its biggest problem is that it eats bamboo leaves. Pandas are now confined to the giant bamboo forests of western China. The People's Republic, in collaboration with international conservation agencies, has been trying to save the pandas from extinction. The situation is exacerbated by a peculiarity of the bamboo. It flowers once every hundred years or so, at which time the entire bamboo forest dies.

---

* The word panda is actually Nepalese. The Chinese term is 大熊貓 , literally "big bear cat," a term also used by biologists.

Just as pandas are found nowhere else in the world but China, eating bamboo shoots is unique to the Chinese. On some prehistoric occasion, perhaps the same fellow who invented the character for fire saw a panda eating bamboo leaves. A lot smarter than the panda, he probably soon figured out that the shoots tasted much better than the leaves. The eating of bamboo shoots was quite likely a prehistoric habit. It was mentioned in some of the most ancient texts known. By the Tang dynasty (618–907) there was even a minister specifically in charge of planting bamboo.

Incidentally, the English word "bamboo" did not derive from Chinese but from Malay. The character for bamboo is 竹 and came from the pictograph 个个 . It also appears as a radical ⺮ in characters that have something to do with bamboo. Such characters are more numerous than you think, since so many everyday objects were made of bamboo before the age of plastic. The radical appears in words we would normally associate with bamboo, such as flute, as well as in words describing objects no longer commonly associated with it, such as pen, pipe, hairpin, chest, and so forth. It also appears in words with no apparent connection with bamboo, such as 算 , to calculate.

The character for "calculate" is etymologically quite interesting. You as a sharp-eyed linguist may have already noticed the character for eye 目 . (Remember the rotated ⟨◉⟩ ?) Underneath, we have 廾 , originally 𠂇𠂉 two hands. You calculate by watching how your hands manipulate the bamboo sticks. I find this example particularly interesting because the derivation of such English words as calculate, calculus, and calcium, for instance, comes from the Latin word for pebble. In the West men counted with pebbles; in the East, with bamboo sticks and beads.

I won't go any further into the group of bamboo-based characters. As

In Chinese art, the calligraphy in the inscription is often admired just as much as the painting; writing and painting are regarded as closely related arts. In particular, the strokes of the character for bamboo, when written with a brush, remind the connoisseur of the leaves and stalks of the bamboo. On the left, we have, in order, the leaves of the bamboo, the character for bamboo, the character for bamboo written in a more flowing hand, and the bamboo radical as rendered by brush. (Mrs. S. L. Zee)

long as you can remember the radical 竹 , which when written with a brush looks rather like Chinese paintings of bamboo, you are all set to pick out the bamboo-dominated dishes. The character for bamboo shoot is 筍 , and it appears often in the combination 筍 尖 (bamboo-shoot tips) and 冬 筍 (winter bamboo shoot). Remember how we had discussed in Chapter 8 the character 尖 for "tip" or a "sharp point"? It has small 小 on top of big 大 .

Winter bamboo shoot is so called to distinguish it from spring bamboo shoot. Bamboo shoots sprout up from thick underground stems that branch out in clusters. They poke out of the earth in the spring, but already in winter they have been growing underground. With experience, the digger can locate the shoots by noticing tiny cracks in the soil, but he may miss those shoots growing deeper down. It is said that a real expert can locate these deeper shoots by looking at how the bamboo branches have been growing. For this reason, winter bamboo shoots are more costly than spring bamboo shoots. *

A celebrated bamboo dish is 蝦 子 燒 冬 筍 . Recognize the insect radical in the first character of the dish? (No, the dish doesn't contain any bugs.) Remember from Chapter 8 that shellfish were given the insect radical? The dish is "shrimp eggs cooked with winter bamboo shoots." (The character 子 indicates the shrimp's "children"

---

* Now you can go back to the water-lily leaves, bamboo-shoot, cherry soup 荷 葉 筍 尖 櫻 桃 湯 we talked about in Chapter 2. See the grass radical 艹 in the first two characters; the bamboo radical 竹 in the third; the wood radical 木 in the fifth and sixth; and the water radical 氵 in the last?

in this case and is not a diminutive for a change.) Another tasty dish is 火 腿 煨 冬 筍 . You may be puzzled at seeing fire twice, once as the first character and once as a radical in the third character. Indeed, the third character indicates the mode of cooking and means "to simmer" or "to braise."

But what about fire as the first character? First, we see that the second character contains the flesh radical 月 . (Remember from Chapter 7 that this is the compressed form of flesh 肉 .) The character means "leg." (The right half is a phonetic element.) Combining the first and second characters we get "fire leg," a leg that has been put to the fire. Guess what? A ham.

The second dish is thus "ham braised with winter bamboo." By the way, it is generally agreed that of American hams, Virginia Smithfield comes closest in flavor to traditional Chinese ham.

You are now ready for a taste of advanced postgraduate menu reading. It is fairly common for Chinese restaurants to carry in the vegetable section of their menu the entry 炒 雙 冬 . Perhaps you recognize the character 冬 for "winter" as that was just mentioned. You certainly recognize the fire radical in the first character. Good. That indicates the mode of cooking, stir-fry in this case. The second character means "double," "two," or "a pair." Perhaps you remember from our discussion of birds that the character 隹 means short-tailed bird. Thus, 雙 shows two short-tailed birds caught in a hand 又 , originally written 又 . (Remember the ancient form for hand?) On menus, the character 雙 is often simplified to 双 . Curiously, the two birds have disappeared, replaced by two hands clutching at thin air!

All right, so 炒 雙 冬 can be literally translated as "stir-fry two winters." What could that possibly mean?

If you remember from our discussion of vegetables that mushrooms are often called winter mushrooms, you can probably guess the answer. The dish indicates winter mushrooms stir-fried with winter bamboo shoots, a dish highly rated by gourmets who prize its clean, delicate flavor.

If you ever order this dish or some other bamboo-shoot dish that mentions 冬 , make sure that you get winter bamboo shoots and not spring bamboo shoots. How would you know? From experience, that is the only way. Well, what do you think? In your average neighborhood Chinese restaurant, will you get winter shoots or spring shoots? Unless you live in one of the major cities, you will probably get canned shoots.

All this is not to give the impression that one should disdain spring bamboo shoots. While winter bamboo shoots are considered a delicacy, spring bamboo shoots are merely regarded as wonderful. One leading Chinese gourmet wrote that with spring bamboo shoots, no matter how you cook them and no matter what you cook them with, they are just absolutely delicious. With the coming of the spring rain, the shoots literally shoot up. A wonderful use of language, this use of "shoot" to describe new growths! The French term *pousses de bambou* is perhaps more forceful but less dramatic. In Chinese the expression "spring bamboo shoots after the rain" is used to describe anything that grows rapidly. About the thickness of a finger, these shoots are delicate white in color, fragrant and crisp. Incidentally, poets have traditionally compared a beautiful woman's fingers to spring bamboo shoots. Try that, if you will, on the next lady you see. "Your fingers are lovely as the bamboo shoots of spring." A lady panda might blush.

Bamboo also figures in Chinese cooking as the material in various utensils, such as steamers. A more delicate use of the bamboo described in some ancient cookbooks has long disappeared, unfortunately. In a time long passed into wistful memory, a cook about to steam some crab meat, say, might wander into the garden and cut off a segment of green bamboo. The crabmeat, together with a touch of ginger and egg white, was then stuffed into the hollow bamboo cylinder. With the two ends plugged up, the bamboo cylinder was then steamed. (This particular recipe was described in a Qing dynasty [1644–1911] cookbook entitled *The Many Secrets of Fine Cooking.*) The subtle interplay of the flavor of crab with the clean aroma of fresh bamboo sounds heavenly.

For obvious reasons, this mode of cooking fell out of favor with urban restaurants and is now practically unknown in China. Since some species of bamboo are native to southeastern United States, I see no reason why some enterprising Chinese restaurants there can't revive this whole way of cooking. Let me know if you have access to a bamboo grove.

If you go out shopping for bamboo shoots, watch out for bitter bamboo 苦 筍 . (In the character for "bitter," the grass radical is self-explanatory, while 古 is a phonetic element. On its own, it means "ancient." Notice that it is formed out of 十 meaning "ten" and the mouth radical. A story that has been told over "ten mouths," or figuratively ten generations, is ancient.)

The bitter bamboo is very much an acquired taste. The people who hate it, really hate it; while the people who like it, love it. The Song dynasty poet and gourmet Su Tung-po, whom we met in connection with his pork dish and his eating the "death fish," grew so attached to bitter bamboo that a friend teased him, saying that if he liked the stuff so much, he should resign his official post and move to the region known for its bitter bamboo.

Somehow I never acquired the taste for it even though I rather like the flavor of 苦 瓜 , bitter melon. (Here we have another pictographic character, with its original form 瓜 showing the melon hanging from its tendrils.) Bamboo shoots of all kinds often have a slightly bitter taste. The bitterness can be eliminated by soaking them in boiling water for a few minutes.

In most parts of this country you will probably be reduced to buying canned bamboo. A large variety of Chinese food has been canned, as anyone who has ever visited a Chinese grocery store knows, and many overseas Chinese communities are forced to rely on them. The quality of canned Chinese food ranges from dreadful to surprisingly good. Of course, fresh products are preferred for fine cuisine, but for many preserved, marinated, and pickled items, canning does little harm. Some items, in fact, benefit from long marinating. I feel that canned 油 炆 筍 , particularly those of the better brands, is actually remarkably tasty. You probably remember 油 for "oil," and you probably recognize the fire radical. Oil and fire: we are talking about bamboo shoots braised in oil. (I should make myself completely clear: the so-called precooked Chinese food made for Americans, canned and otherwise, manufactured and advertised in this country, is universally abominable. Ditto for the frozen Oriental entrées.)

Incidentally, canned food represents one of the few benign by-products of military technology I know of. In his Russian campaign, Napoleon was the first commander ever to provision his army with canned food, a technology invented in response to a prize offered by the French government in 1809. That was, of course, what made the Grande Armée grand and unprecedented in size; previously, armies had to live either by pillaging or dragging along a ragtag column of steers, goats, and chickens.

When you buy canned bamboo shoots, look at the label. Sometimes you will see the character 筍 and sometimes 笋 . The latter is a simplified character used in the People's Republic. (In this case, it doesn't seem like much of a simplification.) Thus, by looking at the name printed in big letters, you can immediately determine the political persuasion of the bamboo shoots you are buying.

The love the Chinese have for bamboo extends far beyond the gustatory. I am not thinking only of its practical uses, but of the symbolic significance it has in Chinese thought. The bamboo is clean and cool to the touch, its color a delicate, almost translucent green; it stays upright but sways with the wind. With its elegantly refined proportions, the bamboo is a recurrent theme in Chinese paintings.

In the paeans in praise of the bamboo written by poets and literati, the bamboo was more often than not an allusion to the writers themselves as being upright and refined. Scholar-officials wrote of their longing for the bamboo grove, far from the corruption and intrigues of the court. Tired of politics, they thought of themselves reading poetry in a cool, green bamboo grove, with perhaps a slight breeze rustling the leaves. With this intellectual perspective that the Chinese bring to the bamboo, it is perhaps little wonder that I have never met a Chinese who dislikes bamboo shoots. Regardless, bamboo shoots are just plain delicious, with or without the intellectual perspective.

A famous saying of Su Tung-po's has it that without pork you will merely become skinny, but without bamboo shoots you will become crude and vulgar:

無 肉 使 人 瘦
無 竹 使 人 俗

Su added that to avoid becoming skinny and crude you should have pork braised with bamboo shoots every day.

The etymology of the character for "without" 無 is so delightfully idiotic that I just have to go into it. The character 十 means ten, as we have seen. If you string two together you get 廾 for "twenty"; three together 卅 for "thirty"; and four together 卌 for "forty." (This last one is now rarely used.) Superimpose "forty" on 大 , a pictograph showing a man with outstretched arms and which, as you may recall, gave rise to the character for "big," and you get a multitude of strong men 奰 .

This multitude then came to a forest 林 (Remember the two trees?) The result is an awkward mess 橆 that eventually got compressed to 無 , our character for "without." Get it? After the forty strong men got done chopping, the land was without forest!

Did you ever hear the joke about the little guy who asked for a job at a lumber camp, saying that he could do the work of forty men? You haven't? Here goes then. "Sure, sure, you expect me to believe that," said the doubting foreman. "You got any references? Where you worked before?"

"Of course, I used to work in the Sahara forest," replied the little guy.

"What? You take me for an idiot?" the foreman growled. "There ain't nothing but sand in them Araby countries."

"So there," said the little guy. "After I was through, the Sahara was 無 林 , without a forest."

Let us go back to the two lines of Su Tung-po's saying now that you know the character for "without." You already know the characters for pork 肉 , bamboo 竹 , and person or man 人 . The third character in both lines 使 means "to cause." (Thus, a literal translation would be

"Without pork causes a person to be skinny" and so on.) Now how would you, many generations after the caveman who drew a picture of fire, represent such an abstract concept as "to cause"? The right half is formed by adding the stroke ⼀ to 史 , a character that came from the picture 史 . Do you see it? There is 中 , the bamboo fountain pen I mentioned in connection with the ignorance of scribes, grasped by ⼈ , a hand. The fingers of the hand disappeared with time. Thus, 史 means "a person writing," "a scholar," "an official," "an historian," and by extension, its modern meaning of "history." The addition of a stroke to form 吏 may mean a "first-grade" official, or a "high-ranking" official. Now add the left half 亻 , the familiar person radical, and we have the idea of a government official 吏 causing the man 亻 to do something. The tyranny of bad government administrators had already started when the character was invented.

The character 俗 for "common," "crude," and "vulgar" is etymologically the antithesis of 仙 (meaning "immortal" or "godlike"). The right half 谷 is a character that means "valley." Thus, the people who live in the lowlands are common compared to those who live in the hills 山 . Check that out with a California real-estate agent!

Of Su Tung-po's poetry, much of which I really like, one particular line is perhaps appropriate in the present context:

好 竹 連 山 覺 筍 香

Look, the characters you have learned are hardly restricted to menus! You actually know five of the seven characters here! Incredible, soon you will be reading Song dynasty poetry!

The only characters you don't know are the third, meaning "spread all over" and the fifth, meaning "to perceive." (In that horribly complicated fifth character, you might have noticed in the bottom half the eye radical 目 on top of the man 人 ; thus, "a man perceiving.")

The third character 連 contains the "movement" radical 辶 we met in our discussion of dumplings. The rest of the character comes from a frontal view of a carriage 車 . See the two wheels and the central axis? It looks like a low-slung, Indy-500 race car to me. The picture was rotated 90 degrees (remember how the character for eye was rotated?) to form the character 車 , meaning "carriage" or "car." The character 連 was well-chosen by the poet because it not only means "spreading over" but also carries the connotation of "connecting" the hills.

We can now translate the line character by character: Good, bamboo, spread all over, hills, perceive, bamboo shoots, fragrance. Let me now try a literal translation. "In the hills covered with bamboos, I smell the new shoots." Or how about: "Hills wild with fine bamboo, the aroma of new growth!"

Su had just been banished from the court to the south and, arriving at his new post, had broken into poetry on taking in the scenery. I can see it myself. The hills are green with bamboo. It is a spring day, resplendent after a rain, and the delicate fragrance of the new shoots suffuses the air.

All right, all right, everyone knows that it is impossible to translate poetry, least of all between languages as disparate as Chinese and English. A literal translation merely conveys the meaning. We lose the cadence and the ease with which the line rolls off the tongue in Chinese. (How would you capture in Chinese the cadence of "When the stars threw down their spears,/And water'd heaven with their tears"?) We miss the pleasure of hearing a great poet evoke the scene with a most judicious arrangement of characters. A lesser poet writing about the same scene could botch things up by using the wrong characters or by arranging the same characters in an awkward order.

Good poetry, in any language, resonates and reverberates. In this one simple line, we can feel the breeze of freedom. The poet, liberated from the stuffiness of the court, is roaming the hills. There is the celebration of nature, of course, but also of growth and renewal. The last character, while referring to the airy fragrance of the bamboo forest, looks forward to the aroma of the cooked bamboo. The poet is touched with anticipation, as he thinks forward to his favorite bamboo dish. *

Chinese has been rightly regarded as a language uniquely suited for lyric poetry. To some extent, reading pictographic characters allows us to see the scene more directly. Consider the shape of the bamboo leaves in 竹 and of the hills in 山 . We see that evocative character for fragrance, with the crop in the fermentation jar 香 . (Admittedly, too much can be made of this point. Most people do not hold the pictographic origins of characters firmly in mind as they read.) More important, Chinese as a language has dispensed with bit words, such as "the," "of," and "with," the words that clutter my feeble attempt at a translation. Cleansed of this clutter, Chinese poetry has a more elegant and smoother feel.

I am catholic enough in my taste to know that great poetry exists in

---

* In my opinion, the crucial character in Su Tung-po's line is the first. A lesser poet might have used the character for "green," say. The character 好 is an inspired choice: it implies a value judgment. The bamboo spreading over the hills is fine; it pleases the poet. This leads into the poet's anticipated pleasure in sampling the shoots.

many languages, but having read my share, I am prepared to say that Chinese lyric poetry evokes for me a more vivid picture. Of their literary forms, Chinese consider poetry to be supreme. And in poetry, the lyric succeeds more than the epic. The canonical Chinese lyric poem consists of four lines, either of seven characters each, or of five characters each. It is in essence a word picture, achieving in a minimalist fashion something of the effect conveyed by Chinese landscape paintings.

Good poetry is hard to come by. Here we have a culture that revered poetry. Consider that the Chinese call the Tang dynasty the golden age of poetry, rating the Song dynasty a distant second, with only a few poets, such as Su Tung-po, comparable to the Tang dynasty greats. Consider that a literatus in classical times might pen thousands of poems. Think of how many poems that adds up to. Out of this flood emerged an anthology known as *The Three Hundred Greatest Poems of the Tang Dynasty* that used to be part of the education of any reasonably literate person. In my childhood I memorized many of these poems and so great is their poetic power they still fill me with emotion. The point I am making, however, is that even among these three hundred, representing the crème de la crème of Chinese poetry, I like perhaps only fifty. Throw in some Song works. Thus in the millennia of Chinese poetry, I find perhaps seventy or so lyric poems worth reading. The great poems are like gifts from heaven—perfect for all time.

Over the centuries, the great poems have of course been gone over word for word, as a kind of literary pastime, to see if they could be improved on. (Again, what about "When the stars cast down their spears,/And water'd heaven with their tears"?) In the annals of Chinese poetry, one raging battle was fought over a simple poem describing the return of a monk to his monastery. Some literary critic thought that the line "Under the moonlight a monk pushes on the door" in the poem should be changed to "Under the moonlight a monk knocks on the door." This seemingly innocuous suggestion sparked such a heated controversy among poets and literati that it gave rise to the expression "to push or to knock," still commonly used to describe problems that demand careful thinking.

Let us now go from the sublime to the ridiculous! Remember the dish 炒 雙 冬 , "stir-fry a pair of winters," with the second character showing a pair of short-tailed birds in the hand? Another interesting character in this connection is 集 , meaning "a collection," as in a short-story collection. If you recognize the wood radical 木 , you can see this character depicts a short-tailed bird on a tree. How is that a collection? Well, the character was once written as 雧 , three birds in a tree. Clearly too cumbersome to write, it was simplified to its present form and hence even one bird counts as a collection.

We are now going to let the language lead us to the truly ridiculous. The character 集 is closely related to 雜 , meaning "a miscellaneous collection of things that do not belong together." You can still see the bird and the tree. (Never mind that extra something on the tree.) The left half of this character appears in yet another character 碎 . Okay. Now this character contains the radical 石 , which also happens to be a character in its own right, meaning "stone" or "small rock." The original picture 石 shows a rock lying at the foot of a cliff. (There, you have just learned the cliff radical as well as the stone radical.) Thus, the character 碎 means "a pile of broken rocks," and hence more generally "a pile of broken odds and ends."

Confused? Let me summarize. The character 雜 means a miscellaneous collection of things that do not go together, and 碎 , a pile of broken odds and ends.

Why am I going into all this? Well, 雜 is pronounced in Cantonese more or less as "chop," and 碎 , as "suey." That famous American contribution to Chinese cuisine is literally a miscellany of cut-up odds and ends!

The story goes that a group of hungry Americans descended upon a Chinese restaurant, or a railroad camp in another version, and demanded dinner. The cook explained that there was nothing but some odds and ends. To oblige his customers, he chopped up everything lying around the kitchen and stir-fried them. The Americans liked the dish enormously. When they asked the cook what the dish was called, he answered in Cantonese that it was merely a mix of odds and ends. Thus was born one of the best-known food items in this country! Indeed, the early rise of Chinese restaurants was due in no small part to the inexplicable popularity of chop suey.

While the dish arguably incorporates some of the principles of Chinese cuisine, it is not part of the traditional repertoire at all. The term would not appear on a Chinese menu, any more than "a miscellaneous collection of chopped-up odds and ends" would appear on an American menu. In fact, in one Chinese book I have read, chop suey was mentioned in a chapter on the curious eating habits of Americans!

CHAPTER 11

THE POCKMARKED WOMAN AND THE PEARLY EMPRESS

A LITTLE KNOWLEDGE can be a dangerous thing. Now that you've learned the character for meat 肉 , you may notice that menus invariably contain a couple of dishes described by the combination 豆 腐 . Look at the bottom of the second character. Aha, as a budding linguist, you'd surely think these dishes contained some kind of meat. But no. In fact, the character 腐 means "decay" or "rot." Clearly, the appearance of 肉 indicates that the character was once associated with rotten meat.

No need to be alarmed! Your restaurant is not selling spoiled meat. Rather, the combination means "bean curd"! Indeed, with the rising popularity of bean curd among health-conscious Americans, you probably already know how to pronounce 腐 . That's right, it is pronounced "fu" as in tofu. And you have probably realized already that 豆 means "bean" and is pronounced "to". (More accurately, the sound is that of the English word "dough." This is another example of the *d* to *t* shift I mentioned in Chapter 5.)

Nowadays, the character 腐 is often used in the combination 腐 化 to describe a corrupt and decaying government. Remember the character 化 that depicts the transformation of a live man into a dead man? (We met it in connection with beggar's chicken.) Thus, a 腐 化 government has transformed itself from its original form to become rotten.

The idea of fermentation was naturally associated with decay, and from there it was a hop, skip, and jump to the idea of curdling. The precise origin of bean curd, however, has been a matter of controversy among food scholars. A Ming dynasty writer states that a local king or baron named Liu An invented bean curd during the Han dynasty (206 B.C.–A.D. 220). Ordinarily, we may be skeptical when an innovation is credited to a king or an emperor. In this case, however, Liu was actively interested in alchemy and could well have stumbled onto bean curd in his attempts to concoct an elixir of immortality.

Well, an elixir bean curd is not, but it is pretty good for you. Because bean curd is easy to chew and digest and because too much meat is generally believed to tax the body, even Chinese who can afford a diet heavy with meat tend to consume more and more bean curd as they grow older. Bean curd—and more generally, a modest and bland diet—came to be associated with longevity.

While it is possible to make bean curd at home, it is traditionally left to specialty shops. The life of the bean-curd maker and vendor is a harsh one as it involves nightwork, with the product ready for sale by four or five o'clock in the morning. There is a folk saying in the rural region around Shanghai that the hardships most difficult to endure include wearing tight shoes, rowing a ferryboat, having a jealous wife, and being a bean-curd maker (I suppose in that order).

The bean-curd maker also produces a number of related products, among them soy milk. You can make soy milk at home by soaking dried soybeans overnight in several changes of water. After the final draining, mix the soybeans with fresh water in a blender until they are well mashed. You then pour this mixture through a cloth bag to get bean milk. One advantage of this homemade version is being able to use the leftover mashed beans much as you would use leftover rice for fried rice. Gretchen likes it so much that it sometimes becomes an end in itself.

An enormous amount has been written by the Chinese about bean curd. Agronomists extol its exceptional nutritional value; nationalists marvel at the inventiveness of a people who could invent it; and gourmets wax poetic about its subtlety and its ability to absorb other flavors while asserting its independence.

Bean curd by itself has almost no taste. In Chinese, reading a dull book is sometimes likened to "eating boiled bean curd." In one classic novel, one character threatened to lock another character in a room for a month and feed him nothing but boiled bean curd! These sort of remarks have naturally provoked some indignant gourmet to counter that he who cannot taste boiled bean curd cannot claim to have a refined palate. The debate goes on.

With the health-food movement and its associated interest in vegetarianism, Americans who care about such things, even peripherally, are well aware by now of the high protein content of bean curd. East Asians are able to get along with a low meat diet largely because of the nutritional value of the inexpensive bean curd. Incidentally, the image of widespread malnutrition in China is somewhat misleading. Historically, it resulted directly from wars and natural disasters, which occurred with depressing regularity, and was aggravated by gross inequities in the distribution of wealth, rather than from any inadequacies in the diet.

I like to theorize that the invention of the bean curd may have been one of numerous factors contributing to the decline of China. With the bean curd providing a ready source of protein, land was freed to support more and more people rather than meat animals. With a large pool of human labor available, there was little incentive to develop labor-saving devices. By contrast, in Europe the dependence on milk, cheese, and to a lesser extent meat, necessarily kept the density of human population down.

Chinese restaurants in the United States tend to present only two or three cliché bean-curd dishes such as 家 常 豆 腐 Recognize the first character? See the pig under the roof? You learned that in Chapter 5. Home is where the pig is. That's right, home-style bean curd, but more often than not, just a sorry excuse for the cook to throw whatever he has on hand in with some pieces of bean curd. Once in a long while, I might order the dish, hoping to rekindle some childhood memory but I am almost always disappointed.

Another common dish is 麻 婆 豆 腐 or Ma Po Bean Curd, a dish that was invented only a scant hundred or so years ago. Of course, if by Ma Po Bean Curd one means the dish that the average Chinese restaurant offers—some shredded pork or beef pushed around in a wok with a few pieces of bean curd together with some dollops of hot sauce—then it would indeed be astonishing that nobody thought of doing the same as soon as bean curd was invented.

Let's play linguist for a while. By now you recognize the last two characters in 麻婆豆腐 as meaning "bean curd." Therefore, the first two characters say "ma po." Examine the second character. See the radical 女 on the bottom? See the pregnant shape of a woman? Remember, it is the character for woman, and po 波女, actually pronounced more accurately in the name "Paul", refers to an older woman. (Life is not easy for the budding linguist. Some of you may have noticed the water radical 氵 and wondered what that character has to do with water. Well, 波 means "wave" and is pronounced "po"; it works here only as a phonetic element.)

The character 麻 has an interesting diversity of meaning. Here, it means "pock-marked."

And thus, Ma Po Bean Curd means "the pock-marked, old woman's bean curd." Surely then, there is a story.

The pock-marked old lady was once an exceptionally beautiful woman, but fate was unkind to her and left its mark upon her face. (It is now rare to see someone marked by smallpox but it was once a dreaded affliction around the world.) Despite this, she married well. In fact, she and her husband were so madly in love with each other that she incurred the wrath and envy of her husband's brothers' wives. At that time, extended family members customarily lived under one roof. Feeling the tension at home, the two left their native Chengdu and moved to Chongqing, where the man found employment as a manager at an oil press on the outskirts of town. (Chengdu and Chongqing are both cities in Sichuan.)* The two lived in great happiness, marred only by their inability to have children. At one point, her husband's younger sister, having had a fight with some family members, also left Chengdu and came to live with them.

The pock-marked woman's husband was a good man and always treated the coolies who carried oil from the press to the market fair and square. They, in turn, never cheated him with such tricks as taking out oil on the way to a client and replacing it with water. The family lived on the road leading into town, between a lamb shop and a bean curd shop. The coolies would reach their place around noon and would take a rest. In gratitude for their fair treatment, the coolies sometimes pressed gifts upon the pock-marked woman, a bunch of fresh-grown vegetables or perhaps even a home-fed chicken. In return, the pock-marked woman would ask them to lunch, and since she lived between a lamb shop and a bean curd shop, she would often whip up some bean curd with a bit of minced lamb.

---

* You may be interested to know that many place names in the Far East are related linguistically. For instance, the "du" in Chengdu means "metropolis" and appears as "to" in Kyoto. Beijing and Nanjing mean northern and southern capital respectively. The character meaning "capital," pronounced as *jing* in Mandarin and Shanghainese, is pronounced more like *king* in Cantonese (actually *ging* with a hard g as in the English word "go"). Hence the older transliterations Peking and Nanking for Beijing and Nanjing. This "king" appears as "kyo" in Kyoto ("capital metropolis") and in Tokyo ("eastern capital"). Now that we have located the northern, eastern, and southern capitals, where is the western capital? West is *xi* in Chinese. After the nomadic tribes of Central Asia were pacified, the western capital was renamed Xian, "western peace" (remember the "an" in Tian An Men, Gate of Heavenly Peace, means peace?). Now that you know the Chinese words for the four directions, you can understand Vietnam ("beyond the south") and Canton ("broad plain east"). The character for east, "to" in Tokyo and "ton" in Canton, is usually transliterated as *tung* (or *dong* in pinyin). Our friend Su Tung-po called himself "of the eastern slope" because of where he lived.

Fate was to deal the pock-marked woman yet another blow: her husband drowned when a ferryboat capsized. Friends and relatives urged her to remarry, but she refused, determined to remain devoted to the memory of her husband.

No opprobrium was attached to widows remarrying in Old China; widows who chose not to remarry, however, were honored for their virtuousness. Indeed, a famous love story dating from the Han dynasty, and much celebrated in popular folk opera, involves a widow. Needless to say, social customs such as whether or not widows are discouraged from remarrying vary according to the historical period, region, and social class.

Social restrictions on women became more severe starting with the eleventh century or so, in a period spanning the Song and Ming dynasties. There was a surge of moralistic puritanism not unlike Victorian attitudes. The Confucian gentlemen elite interpreted the code of proper behavior as it applied to women more harshly than ever before. (Incidentally, in Chinese literature, moralists are often portrayed as pompous hypocrites, much as in nineteenth-century European novels.)

To eke out a living, the pock-marked woman and her sister-in-law worked together as seamstresses. The coolies continued to stop off at the women's place. They would buy some bean curd and bits of lamb next door and ask the women to cook lunch. By agreement among themselves, they would always buy a little too much so as to help the two poor women out.

The tastiness of the dish spread by word of mouth and soon, the pock-marked woman's place became a famous restaurant specializing in Ma Po Bean Curd. Little did she know that after her death, her improvised dish for friendly coolies would become a classic dish of Sichuan. At her death, there was even some talk of a memorial arch of the type often found in Old China and inscribed with words like "To the memory of a virtuous and faithful woman devoted to love."

To the jaded and cynical, this story might seem touchingly ho-hum, but stories like this are told in Chinese as romantic tearjerkers, in a tone just ever so slightly foreign to our contemporary ears. As they savor the dish some people even talk of seeing in Ma Po Bean Curd the endless tears and wasted youths of the two women, sighing over the devotion of true love.

Again, this story has to be understood in its cultural context. We have to understand why this particular story continues to be told while others are forgotten. In many ways, it is reminiscent of the story of the Woman Song and her fish dishes. Both stories extol the independent-minded woman who supports a younger relative. They are detached, apparently by choice, from their extended family and clan, and have to make it on their own. The message is poor people helping other poor people: the coolies in this case, and the people in Woman Song's own milieu familiar enough to call her "my older brother's wife." What makes these people proud is that these poor women succeeded on their own without favors from the rich. The very popularity of these stories, of course, also suggests that in reality it was exceedingly difficult for these independent women to survive.

Also noteworthy is that these dishes—Woman Song's Fish Broth and Ma Po Bean Curd—were not invented by the social elite but by the common folk. Of course, there are also dishes named after governors, generals, poets, and the like, but it appears that in the West named dishes (such as Beef Wellington and Peach Melba) are mostly in honor of the elite. *

---

* When I made this claim to a friend, she immediately set to scribbling furiously. On one napkin, she wrote Oysters Rockefeller, Noodles Romanoff, Caesar salad, and Napoleon.

The day after I wrote all this I went to a Chinese restaurant, and seeing that Ma Po Bean Curd was one of the lunch specials, I ordered it. To begin with, it wasn't lamb, which any gourmet worth his bean curd would have expected. I mused that I hadn't done a stitch of physical labor all morning. How would the dish taste to a coolie who had just carried over a dirt road into town two large barrels of cooking oil hitched to a pole? Very different from how the dish tasted to me, I thought. In our land of plenty, I was served a large plate of Ma Po Bean Curd with a tiny amount of rice. As the bean curd was excessively hot (a common sin of Chinese restaurants these days), there was no way I could have finished it without asking for more rice. I pictured the coolies wolfing down bowl after huge bowl of rice with only a tiny amount of Ma Po Bean Curd.

Talking about coolies, did you know that the word comes from two Chinese characters 苦力 , pronounced "coo" and "lee?" Remember 苦 from our discussion of bitter bamboo? It means "bitter." Thus, the next time you taste bitter bamboo, you can exclaim "coo" and impress any Chinese-speaking friends you may have. This is easy to remember since coolie literally means "bitter force," that is, a person who leads a bitter existence by selling his strength.

The character 力 for "force" used as a radical gives rise to a whole series of interesting characters. Combined with the character 田 , mean-

---

After some thought, she put down on another napkin Sloppy Joe. I suggested Spaghetti alla puttanesca, but then there is also Spaghetti Caruso. With our combined efforts, the list on the first napkin gradually grew to include Veal Oskar, Charlotte Russe, Crêpe Suzette, Lady Curzon Soup, and Jefferson Davis Pie. We weren't sure about Chicken à la King (and as I discovered later it should in fact go on the other list.) This probably only proves that my friend had a selective memory. In the West, the relatively obscure seems to do well in drinks: Tom Collins and Rob Roy for example. Who is Margarita?

ing "field for farming" (and obviously pictorial in showing the subdivision of a ploughed field) with the "force" radical and we get 男 , meaning a "man" or "a male person." A man is one who uses his force in the field. Remember the character 小 for small in size. A variant is 少 , meaning "small in quantity." Put it on top of force and we have 劣 , originally meaning "feeble and weak" and now meaning "crummy and shoddy." In folk sayings, scholars are sometimes referred to as persons who "do not have enough 力 to hold down a chicken!"

Here is a puzzling one: 加 . It is obtained by putting force 力 and mouth 口 together and means "to add" or "to increase." What? How do you figure that? Well, when you combine muscle with talk, you add to your power of persuasion. I picture a smooth underworld type dressed in a sharkskin suit backed up by two heavies!

The story of the pock-marked woman also ties in with the visual appearance of the dish. The outer surface of the bean curd consists of a smooth skin with tiny craters in it. When the bean curd is simmered in the dark black bean sauce, the craters fill up and look like pockmarks.

Another interesting linguistic tie-in is that the character 麻 also means "numbingly peppery." Language obviously reflects culture. English is notorious for its ambiguous use of the word "hot" in connection with food. Living in southern California with its strong Mexican influence, I have learned to ask what "hot beef sandwich" exactly is before ordering. It could be dangerous. Even the French, to whom peppery food is not natural, use the distinguishing word *piquant*. (As a word "spicy" is too generic; "peppery" is perfectly okay though.) In Chinese, as I will explain in a minute, the common character for peppery is 辣 . People from Sichuan, known to the other Chinese as pepper maniacs, like to make a distinction: 辣 is the taste that burns, while 麻 numbs. One gourmet once described 麻 to me as a "numbing of the fleshy parts of the mouth just above the upper lip."

As a linguist, you may have also noticed the wood radical 木 in this character. Indeed, the character also means "jute" or "hemp." There, see the connection? Certain types of plants in the hemp family can be smoked and used as a numbing drug. Indeed, the modern word for "anesthetic" is 麻醉 . Remember the fermentation jar and the character for drunk? To be conscious and numb as if drunk! There is a lot that can be told about a dish.

Talking about pepper, did you know that the chili pepper was brought by the Portuguese from Central America to East Asia in the sixteenth century? It spread from the Portuguese port of Macao to Hunan province and was taken then to Sichuan by immigrants from Hunan after the fall of the Ming dynasty in 1644. Habitués of Chinese restaurants know by now that Hunan and Sichuan cooking are notorious for their use of chili pepper. Well, the Portuguese are partly responsible! When Americans think "hot" food, they think Chinese and Mexican. The Mexicans were first.

Let me tell you about the pestle: first written as 丫 , then 屮 , and now 干 . (Looks like a two-pronged spear to me, but who am I to argue with the professional etymologists.) The character takes on the meaning "to grind" or "to destroy," and hence by extension, "to offend" or "to injure." Next, 丫 acquired another stroke to become 丫 and later 半 , the additional stroke indicating a second offense, and hence a repeat offender, a serious criminal. Finally, two strokes were added to form 辛 and later 辛 , showing the criminal being brought before a tribunal. (See the criminal standing in front of a podium?) By extension, it came to mean "the pain and bitterness of punishment."* For fun, let's also mention 宰 . You should be able to figure this one out if you remember the roof radical 宀 . That's right, it's the house where the serious criminal was punished. Nowadays, the character is used to describe what goes on in a slaughterhouse.

Remember how 木 or wood came from the picture of a tree 朱 . Add some thorns 朿 and you end up with 朿 , a thorny tree. Nowadays, this character, used singly, is rare; instead, 棘 , meaning "thorny undergrowth," is used.

Why are you telling me all this, you are asking. Well, put the pain and bitterness of punishment 辛 together with the thorn 朿 and you have the character 辣 meaning "peppery hot." Sometimes when I go to a Chinese restaurant that makes its food overly hot, I feel as though they are punishing me by pricking my tongue with thorns. Perhaps that is what they ought to do with people who don't know how to cook but open Chinese

---

* The character 辛 has completely lost any connotation of criminality and nowadays merely means "bitter," as in "What bitter lives we mortals lead" rather than in a "bitter" taste. It is often used in combination with the other character for bitter 苦 . Thus you may say 辛 苦 啦 lovingly to a spouse coming back from a strenuous job, without any suggestion that your spouse is a criminal. (The last character is an interrogative used in speech and does not concern us here.) This is merely the equivalent of "You must have had a tough day, dear." In asking a friend to perform some task as a favor, you might also add as a polite form 辛 苦 你 , indicating that your asking the favor has made life bitter and hard for him. (你 means "you.")

Incidentally, the combination 辛 酸 is used to describe a tragic and bitter life. The combination of bitter and sour, however, does not normally appear in Chinese cuisine.

restaurants in the United States anyway. Incidentally, 辣 is pronounced *la* as in "tra-la-la."

In recent years, hot peppery food has been much in vogue, and Chinese restaurants have been changing their signs in the middle of the night to read Sichuan (or Szechuan). In many of these places, I don't hear the proprietor and the crew speaking the Sichuan dialect, and the cook evidently knows nothing about Sichuan dishes. The Chinese generally used to regard Sichuan cooking more or less in the same way that Americans used to regard Tex-Mex cooking. Traditionally, as in all cultures, hot peppery food was associated with the poor who had to down bowls of rice or stacks of tortillas with very little "garnish." At fine banquets it was unheard of to include peppery dishes. Of course, when properly used, hot peppers can do wonders in bringing out the flavor of various foods. For example, in Hot and Sour soup the pepperiness complements the sourness wonderfully. However, many Chinese restaurants have been overdoing it, in my opinion. I am particularly annoyed with dining companions who boast, "Oh this is nothing, this is mild." There is a certain macho one-upsmanship involved, or perhaps merely an excuse for quaffing beer. They are like rock stars for whom nothing is loud enough.

The humble bean curd is not just a staple for coolies. It also has a supporting role in a number of fancy dishes, such as Crabmeat with Bean Curd or Shrimp Eggs with Bean Curd. Certainly one of the most extravagant and bizarre dishes I know has to be Pearl-Studded Bean Curd, a dish consumed daily by the last empress dowager of the Qing dynasty.

The very name of this empress dowager is anathema to the Chinese who curse her for her corruptness and incompetence and for preventing China from being modernized. This is the woman who had her adopted son, a reform-minded emperor, poisoned. This is also the woman who used the money earmarked for a modern navy to build a summer palace. As a gesture of mockery, she had the place decorated with a stone ship, now a favorite spot with tourists in Beijing. Anyhow, the empress dowager was an eager seeker of eternal youth, which she believed she could achieve by having a pearl every day.

Supposedly, a pearl will dissolve completely if embedded in a piece of bean curd and simmered in broth for forty-nine days. Accordingly, the imperial kitchen had forty-nine pots simmering away in an assembly line. Each day, the pots were moved one burner farther down the line. A new pearl was introduced each time the empress dowager finished her bean curd. A pearl a day keeps the wrinkles away!

I have no idea whether this particular elixir worked or not. In the pictures I have seen, the empress dowager looked ugly as sin. And if you have seen the movie *The Last Emperor,* she appears as a weird old witch near the beginning. But who knows, perhaps it worked for a while to retard aging as she did live to some absurd old age before her judgment at the pearly gate.

Between bean curd as food for coolies and as food for emperors and empresses lies an enormous repertoire of dishes for everyday living. As I mentioned earlier, bean curd is valued for its texture and for its ability to absorb and blend together the flavors of the food it is cooked with. Gretchen likes hot pots or casseroles, and a good hot pot or casserole should contain lots of bean curd. True gourmets go for the bean curds.

In hot summer months, when appetites are down, a favorite dish of the Chinese is a plate of cold bean curd, doused lightly with sesame oil or light soy sauce and sprinkled with bits of scallion or dried shrimp, or bits of whatever one fancies. It's a nutritious and tasty dish that takes only minutes to prepare. Another of my complaints about Chinese restaurants in the United States is that collectively they tend to give an unbalanced impression of Chinese cuisine as often greasy or heavy. Such casual dishes as the one just described are underrepresented, if at all.

Like cheese, there is an enormous variety of bean curd, ranging from "tender" to "old" or "tough." Old bean curd, 老豆腐 , as the name suggests, has been aged. Ma Po Bean Curd, for instance, requires the tender kind. Gretchen chimes in and educates me on this point, "Even the refrigerator age of bean curd dictates how it is to be cooked; after several days, you can only make bean-curd dishes that involve frying in oil."

The construction of the character for "old" started with an ancient pictograph showing hair or plumage 毛 (which gave rise to the character now used for hair 毛). Hair was then shown to be growing on a man 人 , thus 耂 . To this was added the idea of change or transformation, as represented by the character 化 . There was not enough room, however, so only the right half 匕 of the character was used, and we got 耂匕 . With some simplifying and distorting, this became the character 老 for old. Thus, "old" is associated with hair changing color and turning white.

Of the many bean curd products, Gretchen particularly likes bean-curd sheets 百葉 used as an outer wrapping in cooking. (Literally, 百 means "hundred" and 葉 means "leaves." Notice the grass radical 艹 and the wood radical 木 in the character for leaves.) For example, one dish that Gretchen enjoys making is 三鮮百葉捲 , literally "three flavors rolled in a hundred leaves." (Perhaps you recognize the second character, that crazy combination of fish and lamb that means "flavor." You may also recognize the hand radical 扌 from the last character. This character, meaning "to roll," also appears on menus as in "spring roll." Look for it on your menu. The hand radical is often omitted, however.) Shelled shrimp and pork are finely chopped and mixed to make a filling. The bean-curd sheets are wrapped tightly to form rolls that are then steamed and served with a garnish of black mushrooms and shredded bamboo.

Of the many variants of bean curd, there is also dried bean curd (called *dofu gan*). Dried bean curd is made by pressing bean curd to squeeze out its water content. It is usually flavored with some sort of sauce and used in stir-fried dishes.

The consistency of dried bean curd is such that it can be cut into shreds. The result, called "dried silk" or "dried shreds," is a delightful alternative to noodles. Personally, I much prefer it to noodles. If you have never had dried bean curd or dried bean shreds, try asking for it in your Chinese restaurant. The run-of-the-mill restaurant won't have it, however.

And they certainly won't have fermented bean curd either, 腐 乳 although it is sold in jars in nearly every Chinese grocery store in major American cities. The stuff comes in small, soft cubes that practically melt in your mouth. I must warn you, though, that it has a terribly strong flavor that some may even find offensive. It is definitely an acquired taste. Gretchen, who most assuredly did not grow up with it, likes it a lot. It is not unlike the taste for cheese. There are some people who like goat cheese and others who like Cheese Whiz. Those who love Brie may not like Danish blue cheese at all.

The key is to know how fermented bean curd is actually eaten. Those naive enough to gulp down a piece may actually gag. Connoisseurs like

Gretchen take a dab of it with the tip of their chopstick and have it with a mouthful of rice porridge. If you are an adventurous eater, try it. In some particularly earthy Cantonese restaurants, fermented bean curd is sometimes used in vegetable dishes as a substitute for salt and other seasonings.

While you are not going to find the characters for fermented bean curd on a neighborhood restaurant menu, the character 乳 is quite interesting. It is used interchangeably to mean either "breast" or "milk." (Thus, fermented bean curd 腐 乳 is "spoiled milk" or "curdled milk": the comparison to cheese is even suggested by the language.) The pictographic content is evident if you remember 子 , the character for son or child. You can now see, quite graphically, on the lefthand side of the character, a son suckling at the nipples of a breast: 孚 or in a more ancient form 孚 . (The three nipples suggest an animal origin to me.) Incidentally, 乚 , the stroke on the righthand side of the character, was added later for no good reason. The character can be, but is almost never, written as 孚 .

I can go on and write a tome about bean curd, but I'd better stop. I close by mentioning that of all the things scholars think of doing, one has been to go through Chinese novels looking for mentions of bean curd. The conclusion? In novels with macho themes—historical novels with lots of battles such as *War between the Three Kingdoms,* heroic bandit novels such as *By the Water Margin* or *All Men Are Brothers,* and hedonistic novels such as *Jing Pei Mei*—the only food invariably mentioned was wine and meat, while in romantic novels and love stories, such as *The Romance of the Mirror and the Flower* and *The Dream of the Red Chamber,* there are references to bean curd. To novelists at least, bean curd is associated with romance and love. What do you think of that?

WORDS
ARE LIKE OUR
CHILDREN

THE ZHOU DYNASTY (11th century–221 B.C.) was destroyed by a man who crowned himself the first emperor of Qin. He turned out to be quite a tyrant. He started the construction of the Great Wall with forced labor, which certainly did not endear him to the people. Among his many detestable deeds, he also burned books. He was so hated that his Qin dynasty lasted only fourteen years, from 221 to 207 B.C. Ironically, it is the name of his dynasty, also written as Ch'in, that is remembered in the West as "China."

The first emperor of Qin did one good thing, however. During his reign, his prime minister Li Si produced a dictionary. The situation with the strange characters I mentioned in Interlude 3 had become so intolerable that Li tried to impose some order. Unfortunately, Li Si kept a lot of the strange characters, perhaps by mistake or because some of these characters were too well established by then.

The situation continued to worsen. Under the expansionist Han dynasty (206 B.C.–A.D. 220), the empire grew enormously. New words, needed to describe new imports, new inventions, and new concepts, were freely invented. Finally, around A.D. 200, a scholar named Xu Shen decided to systematize things. In his dictionary, called 説 文 解 字 or *Talking about the Written Language and Analyzing the Words*, he set down the characters as we now know them.

Much of what we know about the etymology of Chinese characters comes from this work. The book set the standard for later dictionaries. Indeed, all the dictionaries compiled during the next seventeen centuries referred to it as their source.

But by the time Xu wrote *Talking*, a lot of "strange characters" whose etymology was completely obscure had already been admitted into usage and have been with us ever since, to bedevil the students of the language. *Talking* is hardly a sacred text, and in many cases, your theory may be just as good as Xu's, if not better. I am not a language scholar; in this book I have often eschewed a more accurate etymology in favor of a more vivid one, relegating the more scholarly one to an endnote. Professional etymologists can probably argue about the origin of practically every character.

Talking about this classic text of etymology, it may be fun to look at the etymology of the characters in its title. The first character contains the

radical 言 ; as drawn by some ancient cartoonist it shows words, indicated by the four short strokes 言 , issuing from a mouth 口 .

The next character 文 was originally written as 乂 and meant
a crisscrossing of lines. By association, it has come to mean "the written
language" for the obvious reason that writing resembled nothing so much as
lines crisscrossing each other. For instance, a man of letters is a 文
人 . In a typical development, the character has lost its original meaning. To describe "fine lines," a new character 紋 was invented by
combining 文 with the "silk" or "thread" radical 糸 . This radical
came from the picture of a spool of thread 糸 and gives rise to a whole
group of characters connected with threads, textiles, weaving, clothing, and
more metaphorically, connecting and linking together. (For example, one
is used in the Chinese expression for the United Nations to express the tying
together of countries with threads.) In particular, 絲 means "silk."
(Usually, it is written in a simplified form with four dots beneath it.) We
now also see that the character for "red" 紅 , which we have seen a
number of times in connection with red-cooking, was originally a piece of
red silk.

The left half 角 of the third character is a character in its own
right, meaning "horn." Some etymologists think that a fish 魚 with its
tail chopped off resembles a horn. Sounds fishy to me. It makes more sense
to me that the character was derived from a picture of a horn with some
patterns carved into it or some natural pattern like 角 . The fact that it
resembles the character for fish is just another case of convergent evolution.
In the right half 牜 , you recognize "bull." What about 刀 ? It is an
independent character meaning "knife" and appears to have been derived

from a picture of a cleaver, of the kind you probably have if you cook Chinese food ⼑ → ⼑ → ⼑ .* Thus, we have a character containing horn, bull, and knife; if we combine the three elements, we have the character "to analyze" (it's like one of those children's picture puzzles). I invite you now to play amateur etymologist. Knowing that the word "ana-lyze" comes from the Greek to mean "separate into parts," we can interpret the Chinese character as one who uses a primitive knife made with a bull's horn to cut through knots. Or how about using a knife to cut the horns off a bull? The character also means "to explain." We have actually encoun-tered it as a phonetic element in the character for "crab" 蟹 . Thus, etymologically speaking, the crab contains within it a horn, knife, bull, and insect!

The final character 字 gives etymologists fits and makes them wish they had become entomologists instead. You recognize the child under the roof of course. In antiquity, the character did mean "to shelter" and "to nourish," but already by that time, it had come to mean "word." The best the professionals have come up with is that symbolically "words" are like the children of our race: we beget them and we play with them. Do you buy that? Maybe you have a better idea.

---

* The scary-looking character 忍 pictures a knife 刀 placed on the heart 心 . A drop of blood (the dot) is added for good measure. The character means "to endure," to remain unruffled even while somebody is putting a knife to your heart. In Japanese, this character is pronounced *nin*, as in *Teenage Mutant Ninja Turtles*. A *ninja* 忍 者 is "one who endures," a warrior who would suffer indignities in silence and explode only when he couldn't take it anymore.

CHAPTER 12

BUDDHA
JUMPING OVER
WALLS

TOGETHER WITH BUDDHISM, vegetarianism came into China from India in the sixth century. Like Buddhism, vegetarianism was foreign to the Chinese. As an agrarian people, the Chinese had always eaten whatever was available, seeing no good reason to do otherwise. Unlike some other ancient people, the Chinese are remarkably free of arbitrary food taboos. Buddhism came along and declared that the taking of animal life was immoral.

There had always been some skepticism about that moral precept. After all, the peasants were well-aware that in nature the strong ate the weak for food. The response of Buddhism to this is expressed in a famous parable. A sparrow flew to Buddha for refuge from a hawk. The hawk pleaded with Buddha, saying that he must feed his children. Having listened to the hawk, Buddha then cut off a piece of his thigh to give to the hawk so that the sparrow could be spared.

It is all well and fine for the Buddha to do this, but it is hardly practical for your average neighborhood Buddhist. When seeing other people eat meat, Buddhists generally limit themselves to muttering a short prayer under their breath.

Vegetarianism was never practiced extensively in China. This is reflected in the language: there is no commonly used word for vegetarianism or for vegetarian. Vegetarianism was required only of monks but not of Buddhists in general. Buddhism in China was never as structured or organized as Christianity in the West, and the vast majority of those who professed to be Buddhists probably did no more than mumble a prayer or two now and then and visit the temple on festival days to light a joss stick. In historical China, the only class of people other than monks who practiced vegetarianism were old ladies in wealthy families. After all, they could afford to. Besides, people generally did not believe that all monks kept their vows. The expression 酒 肉 和 尚 is sometimes used to describe a hypocrite. If I tell you that the last two characters mean "monk," then you may be able to read this expression. That's right, it literally means "wine-and-meat monk."

Incidentally, the founder of the Ming dynasty, which succeeded the much hated Mongol Yuan dynasty, started out in life as a poor itinerant monk. During the twilight period of the Mongol dynasty, insurrections broke out all over the empire. Eventually, this monk emerged as the supreme revolutionary leader. Once he had established the new order, his Buddhist principles apparently meant nothing to him: he was exceptionally ruthless in having his former comrades executed. Beware of revolutions led by religious figures!

An entire group of dishes that require exceedingly slow simmering is sometimes attributed to cheating monks. The story goes that a monk tried to cook some pork after the other monks had gone to sleep. Using a candle from the altar, he simmered the pork all night, and to avoid detection, he kept the pot tightly closed so the aroma would not escape. The result was a flavorful and tender meat dish. Nowadays, with the invention of the electric slow cookers, the preparation of such dishes is no longer the tedious chore it once was.

A famous dish of this type is called 佛 跳 墻 meaning "Buddha jumping over the wall," which I have never seen in a Chinese restaurant in this country.* Sounds delicious though, doesn't it? The name suggests a meat dish so fabulous that even Buddha himself would have secretly jumped over the monastery wall to taste it. Pork, sea cucumbers, fish, dates, mushrooms, and some ten or so other ingredients are slowly simmered for about two weeks until the flavors all melt into one. One crotchety gourmet, however, dismisses the whole thing as a high-class stew.

Vegetarianism, like all isms, can be carried by some to its logical extreme. Followers of Jainism in India must make sure that any fruits and

---

* The character for Buddha 佛 was invented by combining the human radical 亻 (from 人) with the phonetic element 弗 . The choice of the phonetic element is intriguing. The character comes from the picture 弗 indicating two diverging sticks that one is trying to tie together. The character originally meant "acting against an obstacle" but has gradually acquired the meaning of "opposition," and hence "a negation." Thus, the character for Buddha can also be interpreted as "not a human."

vegetables they eat are free of even the tiniest bugs. Those who want to ridicule vegetarianism find it an easy target, as a passage from a great contemporary novel *Eight Parts of the Celestial Dragon* shows.

Several "good fellows of the green woods," that is, wandering swordsman-bandit heroes of the Robin Hood school, were resting at a roadside pavilion when a young monk came in. "Charitable masters," he said with great politeness, "a little monk is thirsty from walking and would like to come in for a drink of water." The men replied, "The holy teacher is too polite. We are all travelers and this pavilion is hardly ours to use alone. Come in for your water." Before the monk drank, he held the bowl of water in both hands, lowered his eyes, and respectfully recited, "Buddha looks at a bowl of water / Eighty-four thousand bugs / Without this prayer / Would be like eating meat." Then he intoned a string of meaningless syllables. (Many Buddhist prayers were taught to the Chinese in the original Sanskrit.)

The monk was about to drink when one of the men, curious about what he had just heard, asked, "Little holy teacher, what is all this mumble jumble?" The monk replied, "The little monk was saying the prayer for drinking water. Buddha said that in every bowl of water there are eighty-four thousand tiny bugs. We Buddhists are forbidden to take lives, and so we must say a prayer before drinking." The man burst out laughing, saying, "This water is perfectly clean, without a single bug in it. The little holy teacher must be joking." The monk said, "Charitable sir, in the eyes of us ordinary mortals, the water does not contain any bugs, to be sure, but Buddha, with his Celestial Eye, sees thousands upon thousands of bugs." The man asked, "If after you say your prayer, you drink these eighty-four thousand bugs into your stomach, all these bugs won't die, just because you said your prayer?" The monk hesitated, "This . . . this . . . this point, my holy teacher the reverend head monk never did go over this point. Well, most likely, with the prayer the bugs won't die."

Another man dressed in brown chimed in, "Most definitely not true! Most definitely not true! The little bugs still have to die in your stomach. However, with your prayer, the eighty-four thousand bugs will depart, after their deaths, for the World of Extreme Happiness in the Western Heaven. Little holy teacher, by drinking this bowl of water, you will save eighty-four thousand souls. What immeasureable amount of merit!" (Buddhists believe that the Celestial Paradise lies in the West; they also earn some brownie points for saving souls.)

The monk, wondering whether to believe this, stared vacantly at the bowl of water and muttered, "Saving eighty-four thousand souls in one act? How can I possibly possess such holy power!"

Suddenly, the man in brown took the bowl from the monk and, examining the water intently, counted, "One, two, three, four, five, six . . . one thousand, two thousand, ten thousand, twenty thousand . . . . Most definitely not true! Most definitely not true! Little holy teacher, this bowl contains a total of only eighty-three thousand nine hundred and ninety-nine little bugs. Your count is off by one!"

"By the Buddha most holy," the monk said, "the charitable master is joking. The charitable master is also an ordinary mortal. How then can he have the penetrating sight of the Celestial Eye?" In response, the man asked, "Do you have the penetrating sight of the Celestial Eye?"

"Of course not," the monk replied.

"Most definitely not true! Most definitely not true!" the man exclaimed. "I think that you certainly must have the penetrating sight of the Celestial

Eye. Otherwise, how can you, after merely looking at me, know that I am merely an ordinary mortal and not Buddha reincarnated?" The monk looked at him, totally perplexed.

Such stories aside, Buddhist monks contributed greatly to Chinese cuisine by inventing an outstanding repertoire of vegetarian dishes. Much like their counterparts in the West during medieval times, monasteries often functioned as hostels for passing travelers. In principle, Buddhist monasteries were supposed to provide meals to visitors, regardless of the guests' ability to pay. Also, on important religious holidays, the men from wealthy families that patronized local temples and monasteries were expected to spend a day or two with the monks, much as in the Catholic practice of a retreat. Novelists, of course, had fun satirizing the practice by depicting the debauched wealthy going through the elaborate religious ritual of purification once a year just to keep up appearances. Anyhow, the vegetarian cuisine developed by the monks spread rapidly throughout society.

Buddhist monasteries were often built in isolated places, far from the madding crowd. To protect themselves from marauding bandits, the monks had to train themselves in the martial arts. Indeed, the Chinese often speak of their martial arts as having originated in part from the "secret fighting methods" of India that came with the Indian holy men. One famous school of Chinese martial arts was associated with the Shaolin monastery, as addicts of kung-fu movies can tell you. A pervasive folk belief grew up of the wandering monk as a martial arts hero and protector of the weak. In some quarters in the West, it was thought for a long time that a vegetarian diet was not adequate for good health. In China, because of the popular image of the monk as a martial arts expert, and since monks were known to be vegetarians, people never associated vegetarianism with poor health. The bean curd provided protein.

Throughout history, a number of emperors have professed to be devout Buddhists. The tradition persisted even in the reign of emperors who were not Buddhists, and the imperial kitchen often kept a separate vegetarian section.

The Buddhist legacy includes a variety of mock dishes such as Mock Chicken, Mock Roast Pork, Mock Fish. Gretchen is particularly fond of Mock Chicken 素 鷄 . Made of tiger lily, mushrooms, and wood ears, all rolled up tightly in a sheet of bean-curd skin, the dish is a favorite of the whole family.

As may be expected, things can be "mock" in many different ways. For example, Mock Chicken is often simply made of bean-curd lumps. Recently, Gretchen and I visited a Chinese restaurant purportedly offering a vegetarian menu. The waitress, however, appeared quite perplexed when Gretchen asked her whether the Mock Chicken was of the lump or the roll type. After the waitress left, I advised Gretchen not to get her expectations up too high. As it turned out, it was wise advice.

The flavors of these mock dishes do not particularly remind me of the meat dishes they are supposed to be mocking, and they certainly should not be judged by how closely they mock whatever they are mocking. Rather, they tend to have intriguing flavors all their own. I do not like the use of the word "mock" (as in Mock Turtle Soup) with its derisive connotation. The Chinese term for Mock Chicken 素 鷄 is simply "vegetarian chicken."

As I mentioned earlier, there is not a specific character associated with vegetarianism. The character 素 has been drafted to serve. Perhaps you recognize that it has the silk radical 糸 . The character comes from the picture 𡙇 for a particularly high grade of white silk that has not been dyed. White silk to describe vegetarian dishes?

At Chinese funerals, mourners wear white silk, or as is more often the case, just white cotton. The choice of white is diametrically opposite to the Western choice of black to signify mourning, but the underlying idea is the same East and West: that of distancing oneself from a colorful world. The character 素 , with its connotation of "not colorful," and hence "not gaudy" is thus used, for instance, to describe a demurely dressed woman. (Remember that 色 or "color" is used as a euphemism for sex.) From there, it is easily associated with plain eating and vegetarianism.

While Buddhists regarded vegetarianism as a path to holiness, another group in ancient China, the hermit recluses also extolled and developed vegetarianism. During the Southern Song dynasty, around the twelfth century, the literati and the cultured gave the practice added cachet by explicitly speaking of how the "cool and clean feel" of vegetarianism was conducive to introspection and the appreciation of nature. The Southern Song came into being when the decaying Song dynasty fell prey to invasion by nomadic Khitan and Jurchen tribes from the north. The imperial court moved south (A.D. 1127), ceding the north of China to Jurchen warrior horsemen. With the court mired in intrigue and corruption, many mandarins and scholars resigned or were banished, and they went to live in seclusion in the hills and mountains.

There was a renewed sense of communion with nature, and much in the spirit of Voltaire's "Il faut cultiver notre jardin," the refugees from politics puttered around in their gardens and glorified vegetarianism. It was at this time that the first cookbooks devoted to vegetarianism were published. The recipes tend to have a romantic pastoral flavor Jean-Jacques Rousseau would have appreciated. Typical was an entry called 雪 霞 羹 from a cookbook written by a hermit-scholar during the mid-thirteenth century, as the Song dynasty stumbled towards its cataclysmic end. In this recipe, we are instructed to pick lotus flowers, remove the stamens and pistils, pour boiling hot water over them, and then simmer with bean curd. A touch of ginger or pepper was also suggested.

The entry went on, waxing poetic over the elegant contrast between the red of the lotus and the white of the bean curd—just like the shimmering reflection of the setting sun on the newly fallen snow, gushed the cookbook writer. I picture the scholar spending a lazy afternoon floating on a pond, writing poetry and picking lotus flowers, and then puttering around the kitchen a bit as the evening cooled. Well, maybe when I retire . . .

The scholar's poetic imagination was reflected in the name of the dish. As a maturing linguist, you may have noticed already that the first and second characters share the same radical 雨 . Remember from the chapter on swallowing clouds how with some pictorial imagination you can see the raindrops coming down from the canopy of heaven 雨 ? This character gives rise to a group of characters, mostly having to do with meteorology: thus 雲 is the "cloud" we sometimes swallow; 雪 is "snow"; and 霞 "the red glow" of the setting sun as reflected on clouds.

Finally the third character, meaning "broth," is an old friend from our discussion of fish, remember? It is the crazy character composed of a beautiful baby lamb.

Putting it all together, we have 雪 霞 羹 , "the broth of the red glow of the setting sun reflected on the snow," a dish I have never tasted though it sounds easy enough to make. Incidentally, the earliest known Chinese cookbook appeared around A.D. 600 and was followed by an almost countless number of cookbooks published over the centuries. Just as most of the animals who ever lived have become extinct, many if not most of the dishes contained in these cookbooks now appear as historical oddities. Also, many of the recipes are extremely brief, and scholars have to puzzle over how these dishes are actually made.

When I was growing up, hardly any of my parents' friends were vegetarians. Occasionally, I might hear someone mention some ancient lady or other becoming a vegetarian. From their tone of voice, I could tell that my parents and their friends thought this was mildly eccentric but perfectly fine for old ladies silly enough to be Buddhists. Now in the United States, among my friends and acquaintances, it seems that more and more have become vegetarians, Buddhist or not. Most are motivated by a belief in the health benefits of vegetarianism. In recent years, my parents have been urging me to eat less meat, citing cholesterol and all the usual health hazards.

With the nationwide trend towards healthier eating, I have also noticed, just within the last few years, the increasing availability of vegetarian dishes in Chinese restaurants. If nothing else, they serve to broaden the boring sameness of Chinese restaurant menus. Specialized vegetarian Chinese restaurants can only survive in such hotbeds of Chinese food as the Berkeley–San Francisco area. The trend, though, is toward restaurants here and there offering a separate vegetarian menu on request. Still, as our experience with rolled versus lumped Mock Chicken shows, there is still a long way to go. All too often, a vegetarian dish just means a few lumps of bean curd thrown in with some vegetables. The better vegetarian dishes call for expensive ingredients and their preparation involves much more work than the standard stir-fry fare. Some culinary skill is actually required to make them tasty.

When vegetarianism was embraced in China for religious reasons rather than for health reasons, the health benefits must have seemed quite obvious. I believe there was a selection effect: those so inclined toward Buddhism to become vegetarians tended to be of a more even and contemplative temperament. Furthermore, the aforementioned old ladies of well-to-do families typically adopted vegetarianism when they were already quite old and as a group were predisposed to longevity.

In this connection, the choice of the character 素 , with its connotation of purity, to describe vegetarianism is particularly apt. Chinese writings on vegetarianism have always suggested that animal flesh has a "polluting" influence on the body. In contrast, vegetarian foods are said to cleanse and harmonize.

Vegetarians in this country quite naturally have turned to cuisines with a strong vegetarian tradition, such as Chinese and Indian food. Over the centuries, much ingenuity and skill have gone in to making Chinese vegetarian dishes taste good. In Hong Kong and Taiwan, sophisticates often go out for vegetarian food, not for any health or religious reasons, but "just for the taste of it." Buddhist temples in these places often have canteens, where you can order vegetarian food, as something of a holdover of the tradition of feeding travelers. Vegetarianism does not have to mean tasteless food.

CHAPTER 13

ACT WITHOUT ACTING, TASTE WITHOUT TASTING

To ILLUSTRATE THE difference between the three major philosophical-religious-ethical systems practiced in China, let me tell you a story from the Song dynasty (960–1279); it is perhaps particularly appropriate in a book devoted to taste and food.

Buddha, Confucius, and Lao-tze were each given a sip of vinegar and asked about its taste. Buddha sighed, "Ah, bitter, so bitter, all is bitter in the sea of bitterness as we seek passage toward Nirvana." The rather matter-of-fact Confucius replied, "Why, vinegar tastes sour, of course." Finally, Lao-tze grinned and said with a wink, "How sweet!"

This wonderful story sums up in a nutshell, if it can be done at all, the fundamental differences of Buddhism, Confucianism, and Taoism. A Buddhist sees life as suffering and strives to break out of the reincarnation cycle by living each life more virtuously than the previous one. A Confucian is positive about life and seeks to live it as an upright, benevolent person. The ever pragmatic Confucius (he was a police commissioner early in life) would indeed be puzzled if anybody ever asked him about the taste of vinegar. Lao-tze, on the other hand, gives the impression that he is saying everything with a twinkle in his eyes. Much more than Buddha, and certainly more than Confucius, he is attracted by the unknowable.

Of all the people on earth, the Chinese are the only ones who did not invent a religion. While on balance I consider religion to have had a positive influence on civilization, I nevertheless felt a distinct tinge of ethnic pride when I first read this statement.

We can debate the truth of this statement till we are blue in the face. We can split hairs over the definition of religion. One can also hold that it is not so much that religions were not invented in China, but that Chinese religions remain undeveloped and perhaps more important, unorganized and uninstitutionalized. But when all has been said, I still think that much of Chinese culture and history can be understood by realizing that religion was much less a factor in China than in the West and in the Islamic world.

That the Chinese did not develop an organized religion does not mean that the need for a religion was not deeply felt. What is true is that the Chinese lacked organized and dogmatic religions, unless one were to consider, not entirely without justification, Marxism as an organized and dogmatic religion. But even that is a foreign import.

While not ruling out the idea of an afterlife, and indeed most probably believing in it, the educated class in China has always tended to profess ignorance. The tone was set by Confucius. When asked about the afterlife, he dismissed the question by proclaiming, "Barely do I understand life, how can I possibly know death?" On another occasion, he specified the four topics he would never talk about: oddities, forces, chaos, and gods. The Confucian ruling class has always looked down on the beliefs and practices of the common folk and regarded discussions about the afterlife as something not in completely good taste.

Confucianism is really a code of ethics rather than a religion as such. Among its pantheon of virtues, probably the most characteristically Confucian is that described as 仁 . Etymology can tell us a great deal here. The character literally pictures the relation between two (the character 二) people (the radical 亻 from the character 人). The concept of 仁 , sometimes translated as "benevolence," has no precise Western equivalent, but essentially it expresses the notion that the ideal relationship between two humans is based on honor, trust, kindness, and consideration. It may be said that Christianity and Islam are concerned with man's relationship with the supernatural, Hinduism with man's relationship with the natural, and Confucianism with man's relationship with other men. In recent years, Western businessmen going to the Orient have learned that 仁 is of crucial importance.

Confucianism is exceedingly idealistic. While Confucius stated that you should devote your life to attain benevolence, he specifically emphasized that you cannot expect any rewards, neither in this life nor in the afterlife, if there is such a thing. The attainment of benevolence should be a reward in itself. In this respect, Confucianism is much more demanding than Buddhism, not to mention Christianity and Islam. Incidentally, Confucius claimed neither to be a benevolent man himself nor to have ever even seen such a man.

Lao-tze, who lived in the sixth century B.C., wrote *The Book of the Tao*. Tao, 道 , literally means "Way" and is often thus translated into English. The very first line of his book 道 可 道 非 常 道 states that "The Tao that can be spoken of is not the everlasting Tao." The literal character by character translation is "Tao can say not everlasting Tao." (He was playing on words here since the character 道 also means "to say" or "to express.")

If the Tao is interpreted as a pervasive divine spirit, as some people are inclined to, then Taoism may be said to be a religion. But in *The Book of the Tao*, Lao-tze makes no mention of an afterlife. Rather he advocates a personal way of life to achieve inner spirituality. If Confucianism is concerned with man's relationship with other men, then Taoism is concerned with man's relationship with his mysterious inner self.

I would be a fool to try to summarize Taoism here; at the risk of oversimplifying let me just say that the Tao is very much the antithesis of that which made the West the West.

In a book devoted partly to food, I cannot resist, however, quoting the opening of Chapter 63 of *The Book of the Tao*: 為 無 為 , 事 無 事 , 味 無 味 , "Act without acting, do without doing, taste without tasting." You see the triple repetition of the character for "without," which we learned in connection with the saying "without bamboo makes you vulgar"? Remember the forty strong men chopping down the forest?

It is sometimes said that 無 為 , pronounced "wu wei" and

meaning "without action," is one of the central tenets of Taoism. Amusingly, the character 為 was derived from a picture of a monkey. You can still see the four legs. The ancient Chinese associated "action" with the constantly active monkey. "No monkey" as the central tenet of Taoism? Lao-tze would have liked that!

Don't let Chapter 63 frighten you. Each chapter of the book only contains about ten enigmatic lines. The entire *Book of the Tao* is much shorter than a novella. However, you may have to chew over each line for a long time. The language is ambiguous enough to invite different interpretations. For example, 味 無 味 can also be translated as "taste the tasteless." I know lots of people who are still trying to taste that which has no taste.

Another relevant passage is the opening line of Chapter 60:

治 大 國 若 烹 小 鮮

Hey, you can almost read this!

Let's try. First you have already seen the second, third, sixth, and seventh characters.

Though I have only mentioned the third in passing in explaining how the Chinese describe the United States as "beautiful country" (see Chapter 5), you may remember the enclosing square as marking the boundaries of an area. The character means "country." The second and sixth characters mean "big" and "small." Remember the figures on page 81? Finally, I hope you remember the last character as the "fish" and "lamb" combination that appears in the word for seafood.

Of the three remaining characters, look at the fifth. From the four dots, it is a good guess that it either represents some living creature or some form of cooking. Cooking fits in with the next two characters, which most likely represent a small fish.

We now have "x big country y cook small fish." Any guesses?

Character x contains the water radical and indeed, it originally had something to do with water. A legendary ruler named Yu the Great was much celebrated for digging canals to control floods and to irrigate the fields. The character 治 was used to describe how he governed the behavior of water. Gradually it has taken on the larger meaning of "to govern" or "to rule." Finally, character y means "like" or "to resemble" and is now rarely used.

So, what did Lao-tze say? Ruling a large country is like cooking a small fish.

The trouble is, I don't know if any of our world leaders know how to cook. As with all of Lao-tze's sayings, this one is tantalizingly ambiguous. Did he think that governing a country was easy, or that cooking a fish well was difficult?

I certainly do not want to mislead you into thinking that you are on the verge of reading ancient Chinese. Fluency in modern Chinese does not imply fluency in ancient Chinese, as generations of students who have struggled through instruction in ancient Chinese know all too well. However, it is rather amazing, don't you think, that even with the limited brush with the language you have had, you can make some head and tail out of a passage written six centuries before Christ?

You may be curious about the etymology of 道 . (Again, it is pronounced like "dao" rather than "tao.") We already know about the radical 辶 associated with movement and derived from a rather distorted picture of the foot walking. The rest is a character 首 meaning "head" and by extension, the notion of "first" or "leader." You can practically see the caricature of the head with hair coming out of it 囟 .* Thus, the character for the Tao shows a head or a leader walking, and thus "Way" or "Path." It was a fairly inspired choice by Lao-tze.

The names of Chinese philosophers are also etymologically amusing. Lao-tze is 老 子 , and so you knew all along how to pronouce the character 子 , particularly now that the sayings of Lao-tze are so much in vogue in certain circles in this country. Chinese philosophers are called Lao-tze, Chuang-tze, Kao-tze, and so on. (Remember Kao-tze, of the saying about food and sex?)

For a long time I couldn't understand why 子 , meaning child or son, was an honorific title for philosophers. Wouldn't you be offended if someone who was not at least fifty years older than you called you "sonny boy"? (Particularly if you are a woman.) I finally tracked down the answer. The emperor would honor the philosophers by addressing them as his sons: since the emperor is the son of heaven, I guess that makes the philosophers the grandsons of heaven.

As you may recall from our discussion of old bean curd, 老 means "old." (Now you know it is pronounced as *lao*.) Since "old" is not a standard family name, it is generally felt that the appellation Lao-tze, something like "old guy" or "old son," was self-given or given by disciples.

---

* Curiously, the hair was dropped and legs added to a bodyless and hairless head to form a radical 頁 associated with the head. An interesting character containing this radical is 煩 , depicting a fire in the head and meaning "worry" and "mental stress," as you might have guessed.

What about Confucius? The Chinese called him 孔 夫 子 , pronounced as "Kong-fu-tze." This was transliterated into Latin as Confucius. (The philosopher Mencius, he of the fish-and-bear's-paw debate, was given the same honor by the Europeans; he is known to the Chinese as Meng-tze.) The character 孔 , "kong" in pinyin, was Confucius's family name and happens to mean "opening" or "hole." Its etymology is not at all obvious. You recognize the child 子 on the left half; the right half し represents the graceful flight of the swallow. Since the swallows し raise their young 子 and nest in the holes under the eaves of houses, by a strange process of association the character was taken to mean hole. You can say that Confucius is the "holey" one. The other character, 夫 , which comes from a picture of a big man carrying a burden or a plank of wood, nowadays merely means husband but used to be an honorific title. The Chinese often omit this character and simply refer to Confucius as Kong-tze.

In contrast to Lao-tze who spoke easily of cooking fish, Confucius once said that a scholar-gentleman should get out of the kitchen. The guy probably wasn't much of a gourmet anyway. In his travels he was once accosted by an old lady who offered him a bowl of porridge. Later, one of his disciples asked him why he thanked the old lady so profusely since the porridge wasn't at all tasty. The sage replied that it was not the taste but the thought that counted. He sounded just like the elderly gentleman-scholar who spoke to me in Chapter 2 about the meaning or intention behind a meal of fine food.

Confucius, who came after Lao-tze, held the Tao in high esteem. He once said, "If you heard of the Tao in the morning, and then if you should happen to drop dead in the evening, your life would not have been in vain."

But he also differed considerably from Lao-tze. For instance, in the same passage in which Lao-tze talked about "tasting the tasteless," he went on to say that you should repay him who has done you injury with a good deed. Later, a disciple of Confucius asked him, "I've heard said that one should repay an injury with a good deed." Confucius replied, "Repay an injury with straightness, repay a good deed with a good deed." None of this turn-the-other-cheek stuff for Confucians! Straightness presumably implies a firm, clear response, but not outrage.

The thought of Confucius has come down to us in a book compiled by his disciples, *The Analects*. It consists of twenty books, each divided into a number of sections. Most sections consist of just one line, of the form " 子 曰 , such and such." The character 曰 , which looks exactly like the character for the sun, is an archaic character showing a word, represented by the dash, coming out of the mouth. The character 子 refers to Confucius. Because of the peculiar tradition of using the character for child in referring to the sages, you could have translated these sayings as "The child said such and such" rather than "the Master said such and such."

I can convey to you the pragmatic tone of Confucianism by telling you the very first line of the whole book. "The Master said: Is it not a pleasure, having learned something, to be able to apply it from time to time? Is it not a joy to have friends who have come from far away? Is it not gentlemanly not to be upset when others fail to appreciate your abilities?" Contrast this with Lao-tze's opening line, something like, "Whatever I am going to tell you is not the Tao!"

Of the three rhetorical questions in *The Analects* the most remembered is the middle one; it is what an excessively literate person might say to you as he orders up a banquet upon your arrival. In its way, the opening line summarizes well three of the main themes of Confucianism: learning, friendship, and modesty.

The emphasis on learning and scholarship in East Asian cultures is of course almost legendary. One of Confucius's best remembered lines talks about three persons walking together 三 人 行 . (See, you can read *The Analects* too. The third character derives from a picture 彳亍 showing two legs in motion.) The saying goes: Whenever you are walking with two others, you should decide which of them is the better, and then learn from him. The idea is that you should always be learning.

About friendship: In book XVII, section 26, we read, "The Master said: If by the age of forty a man is not well liked by lots of friends, then there is no hope for him." Here Confucius really caused me a lot of anxiety. If *The Analects* sounds like a collection of advice for proper living, to some extent it is. We learn that "At thirty, one is established; at forty, one no longer has doubts; at fifty, one knows one's destiny; at sixty, one's ears are in tune; at seventy, one can do as one's heart desires, without trespassing the rules." Even the greatest Confucian scholar alive professes not to understand what happens at sixty. This passage is often misquoted, even by the highly educated, as saying that at sixty one can do as one's heart desires. The part about not trespassing the rules is considered too much of a mouthful and is usually omitted. Also, since the Chinese traditionally count age in cycles of sixty years (you know, sixty seconds in a minute, and so on), at age sixty you are considered a newborn again.

Finally, the part about not getting upset at people who don't appreciate you is part of a broad Confucian dictum on modesty. The ideal, described as "Hide your talent deeply, not showing it," is somewhat reminiscent of the

Western proverb "Silence is golden." This may account for the excessive reticence and self-effacement ("I beg to offer you my humble worthless opinion . . .") often affected by East Asian people, a trait that works tremendously to their handicap if they live in Western societies.

One of the most serious misperceptions uninformed Westerners can have about East Asian societies is to think of them as Buddhist. While Buddhism is neither uncommon nor without influence, the political, business, cultural, intellectual, and social lives of countries like Japan, Korea, China, Taiwan, Hong Kong, Singapore and perhaps even Thailand are almost totally driven by Confucianism. Whether they are capitalists or communists, the ruling elite are all deep in their hearts Confucians.

When I travel in Asia, going from west to east say, I am always struck by how abruptly the Islamic influence stops, and Hinduism with all its exuberance takes over, and in turn stops abruptly, with Confucianism then setting the order of the day. This shift occurs somewhere before you get to Bangkok.

The Confucian ideals of friendship, honor, trust, kindness, firmness, benevolence, scholarship, dedication, and proper behavior are of course all held highly in the West as well. It is a matter of degree as to how these qualities are stressed, sometimes to tragic extremes in East Asian societies.

As with any system, Confucianism has negative aspects that have surely contributed to China's backwardness. A favorite topic of debate among Chinese intellectuals is the extent to which Confucianism has retarded the development of China. Just as was the case with Christianity and Islam in historical times, Confucianism was often distorted and twisted to suit the purposes of the powerful. Honor, for instance, was often invoked by the venal to persecute women. The Confucian ideal of learning and scholarship shaped the system of imperial examination where in principle each man could rise according to his ability. In practice, of course, the poor hardly had a chance. The examination was distorted to emphasize memorization of the classics. Filial piety and reverence for the aged were exaggerated into a blind devotion to authority and a backward-looking admiration for all things ancient. Ironically, Confucius actually said, "I am in awe of the young. How do you know that the coming generation will not be as good as this one?" Another distortion originates in Confucius's constant distinction between the good man and the small man (小 人), namely the small-minded man. A typical saying is, "The Master said: The good man is at ease without being arrogant, the small-minded man is arrogant without being at ease." (Boy, do I see this in academia every day!) Eventually, the mass of common people were all defined as 小 人 by birth. The underclass was deemed incapable of honor and trust much as how the common people in Europe were regarded by the upper class. Again, the irony is that Confucius himself was born poor.

In politics, the Confucian ideal of a benevolent dictatorship has been a disaster. Confucius likens the ruler to parents and the people to children. The deeply ingrained mentality of Chinese rulers through the millennia to the present has always been that the people are an ignorant mass to be handled and controlled. A court minister propounded a classic policy known as "the policy of keeping the people dumb." The paradox is that even with the Confucian emphasis on learning in China, the ruler has always been afraid to have too educated a populace.

Buddhism is a religion as Confucianism and Taoism are not. It speaks of reincarnation and of a better or worse next-life according to one's behavior in this life. There is also a hell where the wicked are punished. These ideas clearly appealed to the common people. They just weren't willing to accept the austere and agnostic Confucian denial that virtue would necessarily be rewarded, either in this life or in some other life.

Reincarnation also allowed the poor to justify their miserable existence by believing that they were merely being punished for misdeeds of a previous life. This fostered among the masses an attitude of resignation that retarded the development of China. Furthermore, the well-off were able to look at the less fortunate and suppose that they deserved to be poor.

People were also attracted by Buddhism's emphasis on mercy and its strict prohibition against any kind of violence that served to make the society kinder and gentler than it would have been otherwise. Buddhism did much to promote almsgiving and charitable institutions. Of the world's major religions, Buddhism is by far the softest and the most passive. Its hell is reserved strictly for the truly vicious, and not for infidels. Incidentally, the term Buddha was not reserved exclusively for the Indian prince Gautama who founded the movement known as Buddhism; in principle anyone can become a Buddha.

The Chinese, with their need for religion satisfied by neither Confucianism nor Taoism, embraced Buddhism with enthusiasm.

The common folk warmly welcomed the Indian bodhisattvas into their pantheon of gods and spirits. (Roughly speaking, bodhisattvas are various holy men revered in Buddhism or alternatively they are presented as earlier incarnations of Gautama.) The bodhisattvas became Chinese, so to speak. In particular, the bodhisattva Avalokitesvara was given the Chinese name Guan-yin; she was depicted as a benevolent lady and widely worshiped as the Goddess of Mercy.

Around the sixth century in China, one Buddhist sect was heavily influenced by Taoism and developed into a remarkable religion known as Zen Buddhism, after the Chinese word 禪 , pronounced in Chinese roughly as "chan" and in Japanese as "zen." In many ways, Zen Buddhism is as much Taoism as Buddhism, if not more. In the twelfth century, a Chinese monk introduced Zen to Japan, and there it reached its greatest development. In Zen, the individual tries to attain sudden enlightenment through meditation. This sudden enlightenment or awakening is known as *satori* in Japanese and 悟 in Chinese. (Notice the heart radical.) I was foolish enough to try to say in one sentence or less what the Tao was; I will certainly not try again with Zen.

Naturally, any religion can be practiced on many different levels. Among the common folk in China, Buddhism often degenerated into a mass of superstitious mumbo-jumbo. And Buddhist prayers in Chinese often do sound like mumbo-jumbo as they were transliterated directly from the Sanskrit. (Incidentally, this historical fact provides one way for scholars to ascertain how Chinese was pronounced during the Tang dynasty, when many Buddhist scriptures were first translated. The point is that Sanskrit has not been a commonly spoken language for a long time and thus has not suffered any shifts in pronunciation. Another interesting clue is that many Tang dynasty poems would rhyme in Cantonese but not in Mandarin. This type of evidence suggests that the Cantonese were descendants of ancient people who fled south due to political upheavals.)

Just as Buddhism often degenerated into local superstitions, Taoism also suffered debasement as Taoists came to be associated with sorcery and the search for elixirs. With their magic spells and strange sexual practices, Taoists were often looked down upon with distaste by the Confucian elite.

In thinking about the religious life of Old China, we should be careful not to use the frame of reference provided by the religious history of the Western world. Confucianism, Taoism, and Buddhism were never institutionalized in the way Christianity was in Europe. There was not a supreme leader stationed in a permanent setting and powerful enough to dictate to the entire society. There was not an Inquisition to keep the creed pure and to root out heretics. Much was freely invented and belief systems were not mutually exclusive. There was no such thing as declaring oneself to be a Buddhist short of becoming a monk, and a Buddhist could without a moment's second thought embrace Taoist practices.

Of course, the Chinese, like all people, have possessed since time immemorial a mythology with a rich pantheon of gods, spirits, elves, and goblins. The common folk believed in a mélange of these native gods, Buddhist bodhisattvas in their new Chinese forms, together with various Taoist immortals.

This total mélange is illustrated by a folktale about a bridge built over the Lo River by the governor of Fujian province during the Song dynasty. Thirty thousand years ago (many Chinese stories contain jarringly precise details), the Pole-Star Deity, upon achieving immortality, decided to throw his entrails into the Lo River, presumably because he had no further need for them. These metamorphosed into a snake spirit and a turtle spirit. In due time, having absorbed the essences of nature, these spirits were able to assume human forms: posing as ferry boatmen, they would drown unsuspecting travelers seeking to cross the river.

One day, as they were about to capsize the ferry, a voice from the sky cried out, "Stop, for in this boatload of passengers is a lady pregnant with the future governor of Fujian!" Saved by this miracle, the lady vowed to heaven that her son would one day build a bridge so people would no longer have to risk drowning.

Years passed, and the lady's son did grow up to be governor. To fulfill his mother's vow, he set out to build the bridge. The project was troubled by lack of funds and the tide, which would periodically sweep everything away.

Guan-yin, the Goddess of Mercy, whose job it was after all to show mercy on people, floated in on a cloud from the South Sea and assumed the guise of a beautiful maiden. Standing in a boat on the river, she promised to marry anyone who could hit her with a piece of gold from the bank (the banks of the river, not a commercial bank!). The water's edge teemed with the local gallants all throwing gold pieces at her. Boy, sounds like a version of dunk the girl with a baseball at American fairs! Nobody managed to hit the target, but the boat, in the meantime, was filled with gold.

The Immortal Lu Dong-bin, who was known for his pranks, arrived on the scene in the form of a human, and with one throw of a gold piece, hit the Goddess of Mercy. (Lu, a historical figure, was a Taoist who reputedly achieved immortality. This particular Immortal is one of the all-time favorites of the people because of his pranks.) The goddess was furious at this impertinence and rushed off to complain to the Jade Emperor, ruler of the Taoist heaven. The Jade Emperor dispatched the God of Thunder to demolish Lu. The prankster turned himself into a fly and hid inside the hair of a scholar's brush. The God of Thunder, not wanting to harm the scholar, was thus unable to get at Lu.

An angry Jade Emperor banished the God of Thunder. In his rage, he even punished the scholar. (Hey, what was the charge? Aiding and sheltering a fugitive?) Instead of passing the imperial examination at the age of twenty-two as he had been destined to, he would now pass it only at the age of eighty-two! (The poor guy didn't even know what hit him. He saw this fly zinging into the room, and the next thing he knew he was flunking exams!)

The Jade Emperor somehow instructed the governor of Fujian to compose a letter to the Dragon King, the Neptune of Chinese mythology, asking what would be an auspicious day to resume construction of the bridge. The governor then asked for someone to go down to the Big Sea (下 大 海 , pronounced "Xia Da Hai"; we have met all three characters before) to deliver the letter. Among his subordinates there happened to be a young man whose name was also pronounced "Xia Da Hai", and he mistakenly thought that the governor had called upon him. Trembling with fear at the prospect of going to the Dragon King's palace in the depths of the ocean, he begged to be excused, but the governor shoved the letter into his hands and went off to dinner. (Here we have perhaps that most Chinese of religions, the worship of good food!)

Judging death by drowning to be preferable to disobedience (very Confucian here!), the young man went off to do his duty, but not before getting as drunk as "a lizard pickled in alcohol" (this Confucius would not have approved of). He staggered to the beach but fell asleep. When he woke up at dawn, he was amazed to find a different letter in his pocket. It was a reply from the Dragon King! On a sheet of paper was written a single character 醋 , meaning "vinegar" as you may recall. The governor, after looking at the letter, declared that they should resume building the bridge at dusk on the twenty-first day of the next month. (He came to this conclusion by taking the right half of the character apart into 卄 一 日 , literally "twenty-one-day." The left half, the fermentation radical, happens to be the ancient name of the hour of dusk in the Chinese clock. Incidentally, in traditional China, picking a character at random and taking it apart to look for hidden meanings was a popular method for telling fortunes.) Lo and behold, at the appointed hour the sea receded to low tide and the work went like a charm. Thus was constructed what the locals call "the most beautiful bridge under heaven."

What a mix! An American sinologist once remarked that it is as if a Western raconteur had brought together Zeus, the Virgin Mary, Thor, Satan, and Krishna in one story. In addition, real historical figures, such as the governor, appear. (E.L. Doctorow, take note!) We have the divination of secret messages (or of tide tables). Note also the fatalistic notion that there are reasons why events happen. How else could you explain flunking exams over a period of sixty years?

Clearly, as in all folk literature, such stories grew with time, absorbing earlier folktales and incorporating historical events as they happened.

I have already explained that in Chinese mythology gods and immortals are divided into those with responsibilities 神 and those without 仙 . The hapless God of Thunder 雷 神 (see the rain radical?) is definitely one of the former, while Lu is certainly a 仙 .

Incidentally, the etymology of the character 神 reveals the concept of nature worship in primitive Chinese religious thought. The left half is derived from an ancient sign 示 , meaning "sign from heaven." The two horizontal lines are said to represent heaven, while the three vertical lines represent the sun, moon, and stars. Scholars concede that this is mere speculation; the true meaning of these five strokes has probably been lost forever. Compressed as a radical 礻, which we may call the "divine-revelation" radical, this character gives rise to characters such as 祈 "praying"; 祝 "blessing"; and 福 "good fortune"; as well as 神. We also have characters like 祭 "offering to the gods." Notice that Zen 禪 also contains this divine-revelation radical. Meanwhile, the original character 示 has lost its divine aura and now simply means to show.

The right half of 神, 申, is also an ancient picture showing two hands on a rope , later with the rope straightened out to form . It also appears in decorative art as the motif 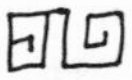. Its meaning is variously "to pull forth" or "to extend." The association with gods is said to come from the notion of the God of Creation drawing forth all things from nothing.

The character 福 for good fortune brings us to an amusing aspect of folk culture that is directly linked to the language. Some connoisseurs of things Chinese have been puzzled by why bats appear so often as a motif in Chinese decorative art. If you haven't noticed, start looking around and you'll be surprised at how many bats you will see. You just didn't recognize them as bats before. Indeed, they often appear in bowls and plates. Waiter! There's a bat in my bowl!

The solution to the puzzle is simply that the character for "bat" 蝠 and the character for "good fortune" or "happiness" 福 share the same phonetic element, and hence are pronounced the same. The difference is that one belongs to the insect radical, the other to the revelation radical.

A Tang dynasty design showing the character for "good fortune" together with four bats. (S. Ng)

Thus, the bat is used to symbolize good fortune.* This class of folk superstitions is made possible by the fact that Chinese is monosyllabic, that is, each character corresponds to one syllable, and inevitably, many different characters are pronounced exactly the same way.

---

* Even more elaborate character-sound plays are possible. I once saw the character 福
written upside down on the door of a Chinese restaurant in Los Angeles. I commented
to my mother on the laughable mistake these people had made. She pointed out to me
that the characters for "arrival" and for "upside down" were pronounced the same.
Hence, the restaurant owner was in fact hoping for good fortune to arrive. By the same
token, bats are often represented upside down in folk art.

As another example, the character for fish is pronounced exactly the same as the character meaning "remainder" or "left-over." Thus, on festive occasions, an entire fish is served in the hope of a prosperous future in which there is something left over after the daily necessities have been taken care of. It is customary to leave a bit of fish uneaten on the plate. For the same reason, people buy folk art depicting fish to hang on their doors on New Year's Day.

The fish, because its character happens to be pronounced exactly as the character for "remainder" or "excess," is extremely popular in folk art.

As yet another example, the characters for "book" and for "loss" or "to lose" sound the same. As a child in Hong Kong, I learned that I'd better not be holding a book while wandering into the room where my mother played mah-jongg with her friends. That would be sure to incur the displeasure of one of her friends!

In reading a book partly about food, you may be expecting a god in charge of the kitchen. More precisely, the god 灶 神 is in charge of the stove or hearth 灶 . You see the character for "stove" combines the fire radical 火 with the earth radical 土 . I would have thought that the stove god's job is to make sure that the food is well cooked or at least that the stove works properly, but no, his primary responsibility is actually to report to the Celestial Emperor once a year the good and bad deeds committed in the household. It is not clear how this particular god, presumably starting out in primitive times as a god of fire, ended up being a sort of secret police for the Celestial Empire.

Traditionally, such household gods are represented in wood carvings, or more simply, in a picture pasted on an appropriate wall of the house. Every year on the twenty-third day of the twelfth month in the lunar calendar, the God of the Stove leaves for heaven to file his report. To bid him bon voyage on his trip to heaven, people offer up a variety of food, a paper horse, and even some bits of hay for the horse. The horse and the hay are burned in the ceremony, while the food, of course, is eaten by the celebrants. In some regions, among the food offered is a kind of candy that sticks to your teeth and gums. The idea is to "glue" the Stove God's mouth shut so that he can't tell the Celestial Emperor about all your bad deeds.

On New Year's Day, people welcome the Stove God back to his post. The ritual consists simply of buying a new poster and pasting it up on the wall. I have always wondered if during his absence people could carry on as they pleased.

The birthday of the Stove God, which somehow has been determined

戲婢女灶
神記賬

While a scholar flirts with a maidservant, the Stove God and his assistant are keeping account of his bad behavior (based on an illustration in a Ming dynasty chronicle). You should be able to pick out at least some of the radicals in the inscription. The "woman" character appears as a radical in the second character and, as a character in its own right, in the third. The "fire" radical appears in the fourth character and the "divine revelation" radical in the fifth. (S. Zee)

to fall on the third day of the eighth month of the lunar calendar, is also celebrated. The Stove God is usually portrayed with a wife. People believe that the good lady is much more understanding of their peccadillos and will intercede for them. As you can imagine, there are conflicting accounts of the Stove God's life. According to one tale, the Stove God was once a human named Chen who lived happily with his wife until he decided to take in a concubine. He fell into a life of extravagant debauchery with the concubine and divorced his wife. Eventually, he frittered away his fortune;

the concubine left him and he ended up a beggar. One day, he collapsed, nearly dead from starvation. A maid from a nearby house found him, and bringing him into the kitchen, fed him. When he asked the maid who the owner of the house was, he was told that it was a virtuous lady who had been divorced by her no-good husband. Chen realized that the lady of the house was in fact his ex-wife. Contrite and ashamed, he climbed into the stove and burned himself to death. The Celestial Emperor, touched by Chen's contrition, appointed him the Stove God.

Perhaps this is why the Stove God is particularly alert to sexual improprieties. In a story recorded in a Ming dynasty chronicle, a scholar tried to seduce the maid while his wife was asleep. The wife dreamed that the Stove God, witnessing the attempted seduction, asked his assistant whether they should shorten the scholar's life or make him not have any sons. The wife woke up and told her husband about the dream. The very next day, he arranged a marriage for the maid and lived virtuously ever after. Psychologists could of course have a field day with the wife's dream. It is interesting to note that punishments are meted out in this lifetime, and not in some afterlife.

On the other hand, perhaps because of the Stove God's own dalliance with the concubine, people in some regions say that he really enjoys looking at nude women. You will understand this curious belief if you think about it. In simple households in Old China as elsewhere in the world, the hot water was of course in the kitchen and that was where people took baths. And so the Stove God became a voyeur perhaps in spite of himself!

LIKE EATING
POTATO CHIPS

LEARNING CHINESE CHARACTERS is like eating potato chips: you can't just learn one. For example, when you learned the character 使 "to cause" (as in "the lack of bamboo causes you to be vulgar"), you also learned the character for "history" 史 and for "official" 吏 , and breaking things down even further, the character for "hand" 手 , not to mention the character for "man" 人 . Every time you learn a new character, its component parts may appear as characters in their own right. I think of a multitude of characters all linked together by either the phonetic principle or the pictorial principle. To be sure, learning any language is an accelerating process, but the acceleration is even more pronounced with Chinese. Once you have learned your first hundred characters, the second hundred is going to come more easily because many of the first hundred (and their component parts) are going to reappear in the second as radicals or phonetic elements.

My method of teaching you some Chinese through food is fun, but I also can't really show you how one character can lead us to many others without straying a little. Let's have some fun here and just wander from one character to another. You will see what I mean by not being able to learn just one character at a time.

Let's pick an example, say 木 "wood" or "tree." Add a mouth 口 and you have 呆 , an idiot, a person whose mouth is attached to a log. A man resting by a tree gives us 休 , "to rest." A sun 日 rising out of the trees 木 indicates "east" 東 .

And talking about the sun, we have 旦 "dawn," showing the sun rising above the horizon, and 早 "early" or "morning," showing the sun rising above a stick.* The sun setting amidst the grass 茻 , with its modern form 莫 , gives us "evening." Eventually, this character came to mean "disappearance," and by extension, "no more" or "not." From the sun rising amongst the trees and setting amidst the grass, we can even picture where the guy who made up these characters lived! Some busybody scribe later added the sun as a radical to 莫 to form 暮 , now used to mean evening. One sun is setting on another sun! When the sun sets

---

* The 十 in the character 早 was originally a soldier with a helmet, indicating the height to which the sun had risen. Perhaps he was standing at attention at early morning reveille. The helmet has since disappeared.

over the earth or soil 土 , we have "tomb" 墓 . Early man naturally associated sunset with death.

Put sun 日 and moon 月 together and you obtain the character 明 meaning "bright." Pronounced as "ming," it is in fact the "ming" of the Ming dynasty (1368–1644). Thus, when you show your friends your treasured Ming vase, you are showing them a vase from the Bright dynasty. Incidentally, the dynasty was so named because the leaders of the revolt that toppled the preceding Mongol Yuan dynasty (1271–1368) belonged to certain quasi-secret religious sects with origins in the Zoroastrian sect of Persia and the Zoroastrians worshiped light. If you want to lead a revolution against the oppressive Mongols it would be useful to belong to a secret religious sect with its tight organization and fanatical membership. The unpopular Yuan dynasty was exceptionally brief because the warrior-horsemen from the north lacked political and administrative abilities and also because they quickly discovered the pleasures of civilization and lost the martial spirit that once took them knocking at even Europe's door.

Put mouth to wood and we get an idiot, as we just saw. Put mouth to some good-tasting grain 禾 and we have "a good thing." The character 和 means "harmony." The conjunction of mouth with grain is so natural that this character also means "and." Incidentally, a republic is a 共 和 country. The character 共 shows twenty (remember ten 十 plus ten 十 equals 廿) 𦥑 hands working together, thus 廿𦥑 . Thus, the Chinese word for republic or republican means "together harmony," but etymologically it means "twenty pairs of hands putting grain into mouths!"

We have seen that words coming out of a mouth gives us "speech" 言 . A word just being uttered in the mouth gives us 言 , meaning "sound," now distorted to 音 . The extra dot is the word still in the mouth. In the character 計 we see a mouth counting to ten, thus a character meaning "to count" or "to calculate," and by extension, "a scheme" or "a smart move."

I am reminded of one of my favorite examples of etymology. The character for dog is 犬 (see endnote to Chapter 11, page 351). This character, when used as a radical, is compressed to form 犭 . The dog radical appears in such characters as the ones for wolf and fox. Curiously, some scribe, having forgotten the original 犬 , later invented another word for dog 狗 by adding a phonetic element to the dog radical. Anyway, one of my favorite characters is 獄 . See the two dogs speaking to each other? The character means "jail": when two nasty doglike persons argued with each other, they ended up in jail.

Add "sound" 音 to the character 樂 , which comes from a picture of an old musical instrument 樂 (a wooden frame with bells), and we have the word for "music" 音 樂 . Music is associated with joy, and so the character 樂 now also means "happy."

This brings me to a famous American drink that I would like to talk about now that I've mentioned potato chips. The drink is 可 口 可 樂 . You know all the characters! The first and third character 可 appeared in 道 可 道 , the first phrase of *The Book of the Tao*, remember? It means "could" or "should" and also originated in a command 丁 issuing from the mouth 口 . ("The Tao that could be spoken is not the Tao.") Okay, get the drift of what the name of this famous American drink means? "Could mouth could happy." Aha, could taste good in your mouth and could make you happy!

Three guesses as to what the famous American drink is! I have to tell you how the characters are pronounced: 可 sounds very roughly like the *co* in "covet"; 口 like the *co* in "coal"; and 樂 like *lo* in "lost." Say *co-co-co-lo* aloud a few times and see if you get it.

When an American product is introduced to the Chinese, the manufacturer is faced with the problem of transliterating the name of it into Chinese. The manufacturer has to find a string of characters that when pronounced sound like the name of the product in English. It would be neat if at the same time the chosen characters, when read as Chinese, would also convey some message about the product. This particular example is a classic in the field. What a felicitous choice, finding four characters pronounced like *co-co-co-lo* and meaning "could mouth could happy." Not to be outdone, the archrival of this famous drink got their product transliterated as 百 事 , pronounced *bai-shi-co-lo* and meaning "hundred affairs could happy," in other words, "may all your affairs work out happily!" (We have met the character 百 in Chapter 11 in connection with "hundred leaves roll.") That's pretty good, too.

An interesting group of characters to talk about are those containing the "woman" radical 女 . Their etymology would surely arouse the ire of feminists. I once read in a feminist book that the Chinese is one of the worst male chauvinist societies.

Consider 婦 , meaning "married woman." Well, does the right half look like a broom or what? Interestingly, the notion of a woman with a broom is universal. Consider the picture of a witch in the West. As another example, an American reading text for primary school children from about 1810 has a passage called "Mama and Miss Ann," in which

Mama tells Ann to go and buy a toy. After being told various toys are only fit for boys, Ann asks, "May I buy a top?" Mama replies, "No, but you may buy a mop."

It gets a lot worse than woman as janitor. For example, 奸 means "traitor" or evil person." You may remember the right half as the primitive character for criminal. Even though it contains the woman radical, it is used without regard to gender and since most traitors in history have been male, the character usually describes men in historical texts. The worst example may be 姦 . The man who invented the character, and surely it was a man, must have been convinced that three women together are certainly up to no good. The character is associated with such badness that it has come to mean "rape," and the male character doesn't even appear!

Of course, there are also numerous woman-related characters with positive connotations. We have already seen a woman with child is good and a woman in the house spells contentment. A charming example is 媚 . You may recognize the eye character 目 rotated from ◁▷ . The 尸 on top of the eye indicates the hair above the eye. Thus, the character 眉 means "eyebrow." The Chinese regard the eyebrows as a particularly expressive feature of the face. Put the eyebrow and the woman radical together and we have a character 媚 meaning "flirtatious." To verify this piece of etymology, I asked Gretchen to show me how a woman can move her eyebrows. I think the Chinese were right.

If you remember that 生 means "alive," you can probably read the character 姓 , literally "born of woman," which includes everybody except Adam, whom the ancient Chinese presumably did not know about. This character has evolved through a number of metaphorical meanings to arrive at its present-day meaning of "family name."

Westerners are often curious about Chinese names. The Chinese practice of putting their family name 姓 first and the given name last has caused endless confusion. Supposedly, an ancient document set the number of possible family names at one hundred. Thus, the combination 百 姓 , literally "the hundred family names," means "the populace" or "the people." That there are only a hundred family names spells disaster for the modern-day telephone directory. Trying to find a MacKenzie in Scotland is nothing compared to trying to find a Chen in Hong Kong through the telephone book.

The paucity of family names in Chinese is just the reverse of the relative paucity of given names in the West. In Chinese, the given name generally consists of two characters which may be arbitrarily chosen from the universe of existing characters. Of course, in practice, only characters with laudatory connotations are chosen; still that allows for an almost astronomical number of possibilities.

Literate or upper class families often have what is called a family poem, which may simply consist of a list of the cardinal virtues. Each character in the poem corresponds to a generation. Every person in the family has one character from the poem in his or her given name. That character appears in the given names of everybody else in the same generation. In other words, the same character recurs in the given names of all the members of one generation. The next character in the poem then recurs in the given names of all the members of the next generation. Thus, if you know the family poem, you can immediately determine which generation any individual in the family belongs to. The second character in a given name then serves to distinguish members of the same generation.

Of my family poem my father knows only two lines of four characters each. My generation corresponds to the second character of the second line, which happens to be the simplest of all characters, namely ⼀ , meaning "one," or in the context of the poem, "unity." As a child, I had a tremendous advantage over other children in learning how to write my name! My brothers and sister all had the same advantage; all their names contain the same character.

Since my generation corresponds to the second character of the second line and each line has only four characters, I know how to name my children and my grandchildren according to the system, but not my great-grandchildren. I can either write some new lines or I can regard the poem as representing an eight-generation cycle and go back to the first character of the first line.

Amusingly, that very simple character in my name can drive calligraphers crazy. On several occasions, I was presented with scrolls by calligraphers. The tradition calls for calligraphers not only to write their names on their works of art but the recipient's name as well, along the lines of "for the idle amusement of so-and-so," for instance. Paradoxically, the simplest possible character ⼀ is also considered the most difficult to write. How do you make it look lively when it contains only one stroke? How do you make it squarish so as to harmonize with all the other characters? How do you give it structure so that it doesn't look boring? One calligrapher who wanted to favor me with his work ended up spending a whole morning practicing how to write ⼀ !

I started out by telling you how in learning one Chinese character you learn many others and ended up by talking about family poems and calligraphy. In learning characters, you also learn about Chinese culture. That's the fun part of learning a language, isn't it?

CHAPTER 14

THE
SUBLIME FAITH
IN ILLUSIONS

WHEN YOU DRINK tea in a Chinese restaurant, do you ever think of the Boston Tea Party? These days it is hard to imagine how tea was once considered such an essential of life that an added import tax on it would incite the colonists to violent protests and vandalism leading eventually to a revolution. In fact, the British Empire was not the first to use tea to control its people. Several Chinese imperial administrations enforced a stated policy of "using tea to control western China." The selling of tea to the people of western China was strictly controlled and monopolized by the state. The horses the Empire needed for its military came from the West and tea was used to insure a steady supply of horses.

While tea has been drunk in China for a long time, it didn't become the drink of the common people until the Song dynasty (960–1279) when it was first listed as one of the "daily necessities of life." The imperial administration was quick to understand the enormous amount of revenue a tea monopoly would bring in. Indeed, from dynasty to dynasty, the Chinese empire derived a great deal of its revenues from state monopolies on tea and salt.

In Europe, the Italians were the first to hear of tea. The traveler Haji Muhammad told them about it in 1550. (For some reason, Marco Polo never mentioned tea in his otherwise often rather detailed chronicle.) A century later, in 1658, the first advertisement for tea appeared in a London newspaper, introducing to the public "That Excellent, and by all Physitians approved, China drink, called by the Chineans, Tcha, by other Nations Tay alias Tee."

At first, tea prices were so high that they were suitable as "regalia for high treatments and entertainments, presents being made thereof to princes and grandees." Nevertheless, tea drinking spread rapidly throughout England. Samuel Johnson referred to himself as a "hardened and shameless tea-drinker, who . . . with tea amused the evening, with tea solaced the midnight, and with tea welcomed the morning."*

Prices soon came down but apparently were still not low enough. In the 1790s, an Act of Parliament condemned the widespread practice of adulterating and counterfeiting tea. Police went around catching the unscrupulous who would dry thorn leaves, color them green with poisonous verdigris, and sell them as tea. Even more simply, some merchants would buy used tea

---

* Even today, the English still consume twice as much tea per capita as the Japanese.

leaves from tea houses and from the servants of the rich, stiffen them with gum, and color them with a solution of black lead.

Given the sometimes greasy cooking in some Chinese restaurants, a pot of hot tea is indispensable to help the digestion, "to cut the grease." To their credit, most Chinese restaurants in this country supply a bottomless pot of steaming hot tea without additional charge. In contrast, the Chinese restaurants in France charge for tea, and often even by the cup, a practice I find quite annoying. The tea served up in Chinese restaurants is certainly not of high quality, but it is reasonable for its purpose. After all, you wouldn't want to mask the subtle flavor of truly fine tea with food. My only requirement of restaurants in this regard is that the tea be steaming hot. There is nothing worse, in my mind, than to have Chinese food with lukewarm tea.

Some Chinese are known to deride people who put cream and sugar in tea. Little do they know that the ancient Chinese put all sorts of stuff into *their* tea. One fifth-century book advocated boiling tea with rice, ginger, salt, lemon slices, orange peel, spices, milk, and scallions!

Various gourmets denounced this practice as vulgar and foolish. I think this attitude came about when more subtly flavored tea became available as a result of improvements in production techniques. Finally, around 760 A.D., during the Tang dynasty, a man named Lu Yu published a definitive treatise, 茶 經 or The Book of Tea, in three volumes and ten chapters. He specified the twenty-four pieces of utensils necessary for the proper preparation of tea and defined the best tea leaves as those that "have creases like the leather boot of Tartar horsemen, curl like the dewlap of a mighty bullock, unfold like a mist rising out of a ravine, gleam like a lake touched by a zephyr, and are wet and soft like fine earth newly swept by rain." My, oh my. More important, he declared that people should stop adding whatever they could think of to tea. Strangely enough, however, he did recommend adding salt.

Surely, in the title of the classic on tea, you can figure out which character stands for tea. See the grass radical *and* the wood radical. Indeed, it is pronounced something like "tcha"—the London newspaper got it right.

Remember that the newspaper went on to say that while the Chinese called it "cha," other nations called it "Tay alias Tee." In fact, in some of the coastal dialects of southeastern China, tea was called something like "tay." Interestingly then, by playing linguistic sleuths, we can even determine whether a country first obtained its tea from China through land routes or through coastal ports. Thus, in Russia, India, and Central Asia tea is called "cha," while in most European countries, tea is "tea," "thé," or something similar.

The other character in the title of this tea classic is interesting. You may have recognized the silk radical 糸 . (Remember the picture 糸 ?) Originally, 經 described the warp on a loom. (For those of you who haven't done much weaving lately, the warp describes the "vertical" threads through which the shuttle passes.) The crisscrossing of the warp threads with the woof threads sets up a system of coordinates, and thus the character also means "longitude." Since the warp threads regulate the movement of the shuttle, the character acquired the symbolic meaning of "to regulate." Its most common modern usage is "to manage a business." Etymologically speaking, a Chinese manager is "one who keeps the warp threads in order." In the present context, it means a canonical treatise, a scripture, a definitive book, a meaning derived from the idea of regulation—a book in which rules and regulations are set down. Not the most obvious etymology! Upon seeing the silk radical, a pop etymologist might plausibly theorize that important books were written on silk. *

Despite the injunction of *The Book of Tea*, the practice of adding all sorts of spices and miscellaneous ingredients persisted for centuries, and various cookbook writers felt compelled to advise their readers against the practice. A Song poet lamented that the three most deplorable lapses in the world were "the spoiling of fine youths through false education, the degradation of fine paintings through vulgar admiration, and the utter waste of fine tea through incompetent manipulation." Hear, hear! I hate all these too, but with particular passion the spoiling of youths through false education.

Serious connoisseurs of tea designate the three great periods of tea as the Classic, the Romantic, and the Naturalistic, corresponding to the Tang (618–907), the Song (960–1279), and the Ming (1368–1644) dynasties. In the Classic period, tea was boiled; in the Romantic, whipped; and in the Naturalistic, steeped, as is still done at present.

After the Ming dynasty, it was all over, according to one connoisseur. Nobody understands tea drinking anymore. The northern horsemen-warriors who ended the Ming dynasty and founded the Qing dynasty (1644–1911) knew nothing about tea, just like their predecessors, the Mongol horsemen, who conquered the Song dynasty and brought an end to the Romantic period of tea. People continued to drink tea, but they no longer understood that the act of drinking it was tantamount to a "worship of the

---

* Perhaps you have heard of the transliterated names of some Chinese classics, such as *I Ching* (or *Yi Jing* in pinyin), that is *The Book of Changes*; or *Tao-te Ching* (or *Dao-deh Jing*), that is *The Book of the Tao*; or *Shih Ching* (or *Shi Jing*), that is *The Book of Songs*. If so, then you know that the character 經 is pronounced *jing*.

Imperfect." The latter-day tea drinker "has lost that sublime faith in illusions which constitutes the eternal youth and vigor of the poets and ancients." Tsk, tsk.

Tea scholars attribute the execrable tea-drinking habits of Westerners to the fact that they started learning about tea during the Qing dynasty (1644–1911) when the ancient knowledge and wisdom on the subject was already in decline. In Japan, where its emperor first tasted tea in A.D. 729, however, the ancient way of tea drinking is preserved to some extent in the tea ceremony 茶道 , known in Japanese as *chado*. The first character is the one for tea. Recognize the second character? Yes, it is the character for the Tao. Thus, the tea ceremony is literally the Tao of tea. Some historians believe that the Koreans have preserved the ancient Chinese ways more faithfully than the Japanese, who may be accused of imposing too rigid and too tedious a ritual on one of life's simpler pleasures.

In Qiuzhou, in southeastern China, tea drinkers still like to go through some relatively elaborate motions in preparing their tea, known as 工夫茶 , "kung fu tea." The term "kung fu" has become almost a household word these days in connection with the martial arts. Actually, the character 工 simply means "work" or "skill." (It represents a builder's square used by the ancients to draw right angles.) The character "fu" 夫 is the same as the "fu" in Confucius. Together, "kung fu" merely means "a difficult skill that takes years of work to master." Such is the skill said to be required to brew a good tea.

Observers of Asian cultures have sometimes remarked that these different approaches to tea reflect national characters. While the Japanese go through the tea ceremony largely as a form of mental discipline or even as a quasi-religious experience, the motions the Chinese go through in their "kung fu tea" have all been carefully thought out in order to brew the best cup of tea possible.

In the twelve centuries since Lu Yu laid down his canon, literati with plenty of time on their hands have argued endlessly about every conceivable aspect of tea drinking, as you can imagine; the comparative virtues of different varieties, the best kind of water, the proper way of boiling the water, the best kind of cups, and so on. For instance, the bubbles appearing in boiling water are described as "crab eyes" and "fish eyes" according to their sizes. One issue of debate is whether the fire should be turned off as soon as crab eyes appear or only when fish eyes appear. Then there are those who advocate bringing the water to a rolling boil. And so on and so forth. The Chinese are probably the only people with a dozen or so technical culinary terms describing the various stages of boiling water!

As for the water, it is generally agreed that mountain spring water is best. If spring water is not available, then rainwater is the next best thing. And here the acrimonious debate really starts. Is the water from a drizzle or from a thunderstorm better? The consensus appears to favor a steady autumn rain, while summer rain is said to be utterly unacceptable. All this is before anybody knew about acid rain of course.

The technical terms used to describe the relative merits of the different varieties of tea are also endless, as you can imagine. One important term is the liveliness of the tea. The flowery parlance of this genre is no less excessive than that parodied by Thurber in his classic line "It's a naive domestic burgundy, without any breeding, but I think you'll be amused by its presumption."

I will thus not presume to even begin citing the many varieties of tea, names such as Iron Goddess of Mercy, Dragon's Well, Old Man's Eyebrows, and Water Nymph. Earlier in Chapter 8 I had mentioned "black dragon" or oolong tea. I will only caution you that for each variety many grades exist, depending on such crucial factors as how close the leaves are to the tip of the branch. Some grades even specify the precise time of day when the leaves were picked. By the way, you now know enough characters to recognize the names of two of the varieties I just listed: 龍井 and 水 仙 . (The "tic-tac-toe" character 井 is clearly pictorial: it indicates the mouth of the well.)

One tea aficionado wrote that you should never serve your guest your finest tea right away. Rather, you should serve him a fine tea and wait for his comments. If he knows what he is talking about, then you bring out your finest tea.

This kind of one-up-connoisseurship was described with almost wicked glee in a scene from the classic romantic novel *The Dream of the Red Chamber*. At one point, several characters in the novel went to visit a high-born relative who chose to retire from the world as a nun. The nun served tea in a pumpkin-shaped, jade cup inscribed with a beautiful miniature calligraphy, whereupon our protagonist remarked that the cup was rather inferior. In response, the nun brought out a cup in the shape of a coiled dragon with antler horns and carved from an ancient clump of gnarled bamboo root. Our young aesthete nodded approvingly and taking a sip, inquired whether the tea was brewed with rainwater. Now the nun really got her this time. "How could you be so poorly brought up," she chided. "I had gathered the snow from the branches of a plum tree, sealed, and buried it in a demon-green glaze jar for five years. Oh, how very disappointing that you cannot tell the difference!"

This scene can be read as a satiric portrayal of the excessive refinement of a dying culture, but it also gives you a sense of the aesthetic ne plus ultra that the Chinese have always striven for.

In the Song dynasty, wealthy connoisseurs would hold tea contests to see who owned the most elegant tea set and brewed the best tea. (Remember the rise of the nouveau riche in the Song dynasty due to the growth in maritime trade?) One tea called "Small Rounds" went for one-tenth its weight in gold. The relative merits of different firewoods were also hotly debated. In a gesture of extravagance, one rich, young dandy was said to have impetuously chopped up a priceless antique desk to brew the ultimate cup of tea.

Apparently entire fortunes could be squandered away on tea. One chronicle tells of a wealthy connoisseur reduced to begging. Stripped of all his worldly possessions, the man managed to hang on to his treasured teapot. One day, the beggar heard that a wealthy merchant had gotten hold of an exceptional tea. He showed up at the merchant's home and asked for a taste. The merchant, no doubt by giving him a quiz first, ascertained that this ragged beggar was in fact a connoisseur. Upon taking a sip, the beggar approved of the tea but remarked that the merchant's teapot, though of excellent make, was too new to allow the tea to breathe. The merchant was a bit annoyed, no doubt thinking how much dough he had blown on that pot, whereupon the beggar produced out of his sack his own teapot, mellowed with centuries of use. The merchant, recognizing a treasure, offered the beggar a thousand pieces of gold for it. The beggar declined but suggested that they could use his pot if the merchant would invite him whenever he came into some good tea.

When it comes to teacups, connoisseurs now agree that only those produced during two periods in the Ming dynasty and one period in the

Qing dynasty at a monastery in the town of 宜興 (pronounced "Yee Shing") in Jiangsu province are worth talking about. The master of the first period was a boy servant named 供春 . While his master, a literatus, spent some time in the monastery, the boy would observe the monks making teacups. The boy was later to found an entire school devoted to the art of making teacups. Even today, fine teacups are produced with the marking 仿供春 . The character 仿 means "in imitation of," so don't even think that you've gotten the real thing for a song if you see the last two characters.

Such is the esteem for such masters that hundreds of years would pass before another master would emerge. The master during this revival period in the Qing dynasty, Yang Peng-nien, was celebrated for his free-form creations. He is known as an expressionist.

Connoisseurs of teacups distinguish between a hundred or so varieties from the Ming dynasty, with names like Monk's Hat, a Beautiful Lady's Shoulder, and Dragon Pearl. Me, I just buy my mug at the nearest dimestore. Such is the passing of civilization.

CHAPTER 15

PIECES OF
HER HEART

Janis Joplin sang about giving away pieces of her heart. If you can't afford to do that, you may consider treating your loved ones to a dim-sum lunch instead. The word "dim sum" 點 心 means literally "pieces of heart."

Perhaps you remember the heart character 心 , which I thought was no less pictorial than ♡ . The other character 點 means "a black spot," "a dot," or "a small piece." It contains the character for "black" 黑 that I discussed in Chapter 9. You may remember that it depicts two fires burning under a chimney and draws its meaning from the soot produced.

The other component 占 is phonetic. (Amusingly, the character 點 is often simplified to 点、, so that the chimney and half of the soot-producing fire are removed, leaving what remains of the fire burning under the phonetic element.)

Since the character 點、 can also be used as a verb to mean "to draw a dot" or "to touch lightly," the evident interpretation of this curious word "dim sum" is that the bite-size morsels "touch the heart lightly." The other interpretation of the morsels as "pieces of one's heart" is more whimsical. The title of the much acclaimed movie *Dim Sum* uses this latter sense as a play on words: the daughter in the movie is seen to offer metaphorically pieces of her heart to her widowed mother.

The proper method for serving dim sum is to have a constant procession of carts on which the goodies are displayed. You simply ask for those plates that catch your fancy. Part of the fun is gone when you have to order from a menu. Traditionally, the bill is computed by counting the dishes on the table at the close of the meal.

The dim-sum lunch as known in this country originates largely from the south of China, particularly the region around Canton. Actually, the Cantonese do not speak of going to dim sum; instead, they say they are going to drink some tea 飲 茶 . Do you recognize the eating radical 食 ? It is used here as the radical for all characters having to do with food and drink. Perhaps you also recognize the character for tea, or at least the grass radical.

Traditionally, teahouses were patronized by men who gathered there to chat. The emphasis is on a leisurely pace, a notion anathema to many modern restaurateurs. A good rule is to avoid the temptation of taking too many plates at the very start. At some restaurants these days one tends to be besieged by carts as soon as one sits down and it takes some willpower not to overload immediately. A traditional Cantonese formula counsels two plates of dim sum for each pot of tea. This pace is certainly too leisurely for our times. Incidentally, the waiter is supposed to ask you what kind of tea you want. Many people prefer chrysanthemum tea 菊花茶 to go with dim sum. Remember the character for flower?

An interesting sociological change is that the dim-sum lunch was once a dim-sum breakfast. In places like Hong Kong, people today do not have time to linger over breakfast. On the other hand, the dim-sum lunch offers an opportunity to chat over business at a relaxed pace.

By the way, the idiomatic Cantonese expression for "to chat" originally meant something like "to talk Zen." You may have heard that Zen practitioners meditate on paradoxes such as the sound of one hand clapping. Over time, folk usage came to associate "talking Zen" with talking nonsense, a connotation conveyed wonderfully by that excellent American idiomatic expression "shooting the breeze."

Having told you the etymological origin of dim sum, I should mention that dim sum is actually a generic word meaning "snack." Given the multitude of regions in China, it is hardly surprising that the variety of snacks is staggering and constitutes a substantial portion of the Chinese culinary imagination. Unfortunately, most of these snacks are unknown in this country. The average restaurant-goer may have had almond cookies, or perhaps almond float, and not much else. (And the almond float he had was in all likelihood an abomination with gelatin substituting for soft bean curd.)

Interestingly, but quite naturally, many of the popular snacks of China have American equivalents. For example, a common and simple snack in North China consists of a bunch of haw apples—the fruits of the hawthorn bush—strung together on a bamboo spit and dipped and glazed in syrup. (The haw apple is the size of a large grape but looks like an apple. It grows wild in the hills and is thus known as 山楂 or 山裡 紅 ["red in the hills"]. You may recognize the characters for "hill" or "mountain" 山 and for "red" 紅 as in red-cooked.) I am reminded of the glazed apple on a stick sold in county fairs. A gourmet I consulted feels that the haw-apple version is superior because the tartness of the haw apple balances the sugary syrup and because the smaller size of the haw apple allows for more glazing. Incidentally, a candy sold as haw flakes is widely available in Chinatowns.

At the other end of the spectrum, far from simple snacks peddled in the streets, are sophisticated concoctions savored by the well-to-do. The region around Suzhou and Shanghai is recognized as excelling in this culinary genre. For example, the rose candy of Suzhou is made from rose petals. Delicately pink outside, it contains white cotton candy inside. *The Dream of the Red Chamber,* being a romantic novel about a declining family of fabulous wealth, is noted for its loving description of the elegant snacks the protagonists were always having.

Many Chinese snacks are seasonal and associated with a variety of festivals; for example, the moon cakes of the mid-autumn's night festival, held on the fifteenth day of the eighth month in the lunar calendar. On that night the moon is regarded to be at its roundest and most alluring. The roundness of the moon is reflected in the roundness of the moon cake and, in traditional thinking, also in the roundness of the family circle. Family members make it a point to get home for a reunion during this festival. The mid-autumn's night festival thus corresponds to the American Thanksgiving in more ways than one. Occurring at roughly the same time of year, they both have their origins as harvest festivals. In earlier days, villagers would dance around a bonfire worshiping the moon. In some regions, women would worship the moon on this night since the moon is regarded as rich in the female essence. The moon cake also figures in history. The plotting of the revolution to overthrow the Mongol Yuan dynasty involved the passing of secret messages hidden in moon cakes.

Incidentally, the Chinese word for reunion is 團 圓 , which means "forming a circle" or "making roundness." We met the second character, meaning "roundness," in the saying that tells us which month to eat female crabs in. Notice that both characters have the enclosure or encircling radical 囗 associated with the character for "country" that we discussed in connection with the word for the United States. It is amusing that roundness is described by a character with a square shape; the square is easier to write with a brush.

One snack that brings back the nostalgia for my childhood is 湯 圓 , literally "soup round." They are round balls made of glutinous rice flour and filled with different sweet pastes. I have not found it often in the United States. Once Gretchen and I wandered New York going from restaurant, vowing that we would find it or else.

From this discussion of snacks we move naturally on to desserts. While certain desserts, such as apple pie for example, can be considered a snack, many common snacks are not suitable desserts. Few hostesses would consider serving potato chips as a dessert, for instance.

American patrons of Chinese restaurants sometimes complain of not being able to cap their meals with a good dessert. I feel that there are at least three reasons why desserts are hard to find in Chinese restaurants.

First, many traditional desserts require a great deal of work to make, at least when compared to stir-frying some shreds of this and that together. Most restaurateurs are simply unwilling to go to the trouble, particularly since the profit margin on desserts is generally smaller than that on the main dishes. The same phenomenon occurs in other ethnic restaurants. In the old country, desserts and snack foods are made in specialized shops where the volume keeps labor costs down.

Another and perhaps more fundamental reason is that the Chinese are almost excessively concerned about good digestion as part of their preoccupation with food and health, a topic which I will discuss later. The eating habits of my family as I was growing up were probably typical of those of the people from the Shanghai region. At the end of a full meal, soup was served, followed by fruit.* The soup, and even more so the fruit, were thought to promote good digestion. My parents just would not feel right if they didn't have some fresh fruit at the end of a meal. It's a good thing they live in Brazil, with its wonderful variety and abundance of delicious fruit. Gretchen was astounded by the enormous piles of fruit to be found in my parents' house.

Third, while there are plenty of sweet snacks suitable for desserts, the Chinese generally prefer to consume them throughout the day rather than at the end of meals.

However, it is customary to serve a sweet dessert at the end of a proper banquet. For instance at birthday banquets, it is almost obligatory to serve a

---

* While it is fairly well known that a number of the fruits we now enjoy in the West, such as the tangerine and apricot, originated in China, there are two fruit facts that you may or may not know. The Sunkist orange was named after a Chinese village called Sun Kee. The marketing man who changed "kee" to "kist" must be a genius. Incidentally, orange was originally a Hindi word: it was cultivated in India, China, and Southeast Asia. The kiwi fruit, made famous by nouvelle cuisine, was taken to New Zealand from China. I believe that in New Zealand it is called Chinese gooseberry.

The character for "longevity" has many stylized representations. Here are a few. If you own any Chinese objects, be they teacups or chairs, chances are that you will be able to find a representation of longevity on one of them.

bun filled with a sweet paste made from dates; it is often decorated with green leaves and colored slightly pink so as to resemble a peach. Often, the handiwork is perhaps more appreciated than the taste. I and many a celebrant at birthday banquets have often found it a trial to down this so-called longevity peach 壽 桃 after a full banquet.

That incredibly complicated character for longevity is popular as a decorative motif.* If you visit one of those Chinatown gift shops catering to tourists, you are bound to find something—a plate, a bowl, an ashtray, or

---

* The character for longevity evolved partly from a picture 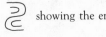 showing the endless pattern made while ploughing the field.

perhaps a robe—emblazoned with this character, often in a stylized form. In the second character for peach, you can easily recognize the wood radical 木 . The rest is just a phonetic element.

The peach is associated with longevity and hence birthday parties because, in Chinese heaven, there is an orchard where magical peaches of immortality grow. The God of Longevity is conventionally portrayed as an old man with an extraordinarily high forehead who is holding a peach.

Stephen Schwartz, the composer of several noted Broadway musicals, has written a children's book called *The Perfect Peach.* The book, one of my children's all-time favorites, uses in its illustrations a mélange of elements from Chinese and Japanese cultures. (If you are at all familiar with the art of China and Japan, you will have fun distinguishing the two in the illustrations.) Incidentally, the God of Longevity appears in the book as an architect.

In *The Monkey King,* a humorous adventure novel from the sixteenth century, the Monkey King went to heaven and, among the many mischiefs he caused, stole and ate the peaches of immortality just before the Celestial Queen Mother was going to give a birthday party featuring them. Angry that he wasn't invited to the party, he then also stole and drank the wine. This whole episode is the subject of a popular folk opera.

Talking about snacks, I enter an area of Chinese food that is essentially unknown to Americans. When I prowl around the kitchen looking for a midnight snack, I think of a steaming bowl of porridge. In places like Hong Kong, the night city is crowded with night owls filling the porridge shops. Incidentally, the late night snack, literally known as "consuming the night," is very much a part of the Chinese culture. There is an entire repertoire of which porridge is but a component.

The notion of boiling a staple grain is so obvious that almost every civilization has had some form of porridge or gruel. For example, the Roman Empire was fed in part by a millet porridge, coming down to us in Italian cuisine as polenta; and Mexicans from the Aztecs on have had a maize porridge spiced with red pepper or sweetened with honey. And then of course, there was Goldilocks and the three bears. But somehow, porridge has fallen out of favor in the United States. The last holdout, the breakfast bowl of oatmeal, has now been largely displaced by cold cereal. Most of us are in such a rush in the morning.

The variety of porridge is essentially limitless. All sorts of flavorings can be added. Those with refined tastes, the Song dynasty poets for example, like to add a piece of lotus leaf. Here is a much touted, and rather simple, way of making chicken porridge. The chicken is boiled and simmered together with the rice. It is then taken out and boned. The meat is cut into shreds and put back into the porridge, which is then served with scallion shavings and ginger shreds.

While porridge is served traditionally as a staple of the poor (just as in the West), a lifestyle, perhaps even a mystique, has developed around it among the literati and the leisure class. Poets sang the praises of porridge and wrote about its subtle flavors. The premier Song poet, literatus, and gourmet, Su Tung-po, practically our old friend by now, wrote:

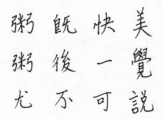

We have already met a number of characters in this passage: 粥 = porridge (the first and fifth character, remember the steam rising on both sides of the rice?); 美 = beautiful (the fourth character, remember the big fat lamb?); 一 = one or a (the seventh character); and 説 = speak (the twelfth character, remember the stream of words coming out of the mouth?). To be able to read this passage, you have to know in addition that 不 means "no"; 可 means "could" or "should" (as in "The Tao that could be spoken of is not the everlasting Tao"); and 覺 means "sleep" or "nap." You get the general drift? Well, here is a rough translation: "The porridge is already delicious, but then to have a nap after the porridge, ahh, such pleasure could hardly be expressed in words!"

An interesting ambiguity of language occurs here. The character 可 can mean either "could" or "should." Perhaps Su had meant to say that the pleasure should not be described in words.

Porridge is thought to promote longevity. An ancient tract offering medical advice prescribed laughter and porridge as the two keys to longevity. In a poem to longevity, another famous Song dynasty poet wrote that while others searched high and low for the secrets to longevity, he already felt like a god 神 仙 by simply having porridge regularly. This guy exaggerates some, but it is true that a steaming bowl of porridge promotes relaxation. It is easy to digest, so one can fall asleep without feeling a lump in one's stomach. (That's why porridge is thought to be particularly suitable as a midnight snack.) Boy, as I write these words, I feel like having some porridge with chicken shreds, lightly touched with some scallion shavings, and then, a nap!

In ancient China, indigent scholars often stayed at Buddhist monasteries where they got free food and lodging. At mealtimes, the monastery cook would sound a drum to call all the monks together for porridge, a staple in monasteries since purity and cleanliness were also associated with it. Thus, a number of scholars have left us with poems describing how they were awakened from their nap by the "porridge drum," and hastened to join the assembled monks for porridge. Boy, some of these people seem to nap before and after porridge! One scholar must have overstayed his welcome. He complained of uncharitable monks who beat the drum after they had already finished off the porridge.

Taste in porridge varies, of course. There are regional and personal preferences. Some like it soft, others like it hard, and some don't like porridge at all. At one extreme, people who like it hard simply pour boiling water over cooked rice. This version, known as 稀 飯 and meaning "thinned-out, cooked rice," is prevalent in the Shanghai region and in the north. However, all porridge fanciers agree on one basic principle, summarized in the expression:

$$\text{寧 可 人 等 粥}$$
$$\text{不 可 粥 等 人}$$

You probably recognize the characters 人 = people, and we had just seen 粥 = porridge; 可 = could or should; and 不 = no or not. The first character means "rather," the fourth and ninth character, "wait." Thus, "Rather than people wait for the porridge, let not the porridge wait for people." In other words, have the porridge while it is hot, before it congeals.

Now I am going to let you in on a little secret that may be of great use to you if yours is a two-career family like mine and also part of a growing demographic phenomenon. When we don't have time to cook, we often have porridge. Over the millennia, an enormous variety of prepared food has been developed to go with porridge. Most of these are available canned or bottled in the sort of Oriental grocery store now found in almost every major American town. Some can be found right on your supermarket shelves, such as salted cocktail peanuts. Here is a totally incomplete list: fluffy shreds of pork, beef, or chicken 肉鬆 ; fried dace 鯪魚 , available either with or without black bean sauce; braised bamboo 油炆筍 ; salted vegetable—particularly recommended is 雪裡紅 , red-in-snow, a type of winter cabbage; chili radish 辣蘿蔔 (if you like hot food); fermented bean curd 腐乳 ; pressed or dried bean curd 豆腐乾 ; spicy fried gluten 辣味麵筋 ; Sichuan pickle, sliced paper-thin 四川榨菜 ; salted duck eggs; thousand-year-old eggs; "babaolajan" or eight-treasure spicy mix 八寶辣醬 (recognize 辣 = peppery and 醬 = sauce?). Boy, there are hundreds more items I can think of.

To this list should be added food items easily obtainable outside the Chinese grocery store. I have already mentioned salted cocktail peanuts, one of the major staples of my household. Also suitable with porridge are other types of salted nuts such as almonds, and hard-boiled eggs (sliced and lightly doused with soy sauce). You may also want to add closely related ethnic food items such as Korean kimchee, a spicy pickled vegetable. The leftovers you brought back from your last foray to a Chinese restaurant may also work.

When Gretchen is in a pinch to cook dinner, she will often boil some rice into porridge, open some cans and bottles, and take out all the porridge food items we had left over from our last porridge meal and kept in little containers in the refrigerator. With a bit more time, she might also slice up some Chinese sausage and boil it in the porridge. For nutritional balance, she may also stir-fry some bok choy for a fresh vegetable, or defrost some peas, a real classic Chinese culinary maneuver. Also, some of the canned items like babaolajan would benefit greatly by being shoved around for a minute or two in a wok.

In adopting porridge as a quick meal, you should follow two key principles: experimentation and variety. You are not going to like everything on the list given above. You should try different items. If you ever visited a Chinatown grocery store, you were probably overwhelmed, as I often am, by the bewildering wealth of dried and canned and bottled foods. Out of all that, you should be able to construct your own list of favorite porridge foods. Variety is also essential. I don't like to have porridge with just one or two items. At a time when Gretchen and I had a more leisurely pace of life before we had children, we would have midnight porridge snacks with twenty or so different accompanying little things to eat. It was fun.

Having porridge with kids is also fun though. Peter likes fluffy shredded pork 肉 鬆 , and those are the first Chinese words he knew how to say. The fried dace was a big hit with both our kids. Its bones are soft and edible. The idea of eating bones and growing strong bones really appealed to both Peter and Andrew.

More trumpeting for Chinese here. If you come upon the word "dace" out of context, would you know whether it is a fish or fowl, high tech gizmo or a carpenter's whatnot, a nautical term or theatrical slang? I also had never seen the character 鲮 before until I looked at a can of fried dace, but with the help of the radical system, I immediately knew what it described. To borrow kids' talk, the radical system is rad. Well, of course, I also saw the character printed next to a picture of a fish blowing bubbles.

CHAPTER 16

ELIXIRS
AND THE FOOD
OF HEALTH

WHEN I PLANNED this book, I envisaged a chapter on dishes rarely seen in Chinese restaurants, but I soon realized that such a chapter would be enormous. Chinese restaurants in this country present such a minuscule segment of the culinary repertoire. So instead, let me talk about the kind of food that you would never see in a Chinese restaurant. How about elixirs of immortality?

Since the beginning of history, men East and West have searched for the elixirs of immortality and the fountains of youth that would make them 長生不老 . You have already met 生 = alive or uncooked (see the luxuriant plant growing out of the ground?); 丆 = no or not; and 老 = old. The first character means "long." Thus, the phrase actually means "long (or eternal) life without getting old." Who wants to be a Methuselah if that means being aged and decrepit?

The character 長 , meaning "long," comes from a picture 𣲥 , depicting hair so long that it has to be tied with a headband or a brooch (the horizontal line). Later, the idea of transformation is included by adding the transformation radical ㇄ to make 𣱾 . (Thus in modern usage, 長 also means "to grow.") With quite a bit of distortion, the character evolved into its modern form.*

Amusingly, to make the character less cumbersome, the ancients added only the right half ㇄ of the character for transformation 化 . But you may recall from the chapter on bean curd that this right half actually depicted a dead man.

The etymological idea behind the character for "long" is exactly the same as that behind 老 the character for "old," which as you may recall, came from a picture showing hair transforming, that is, hair turning white. Imagine, the notion of a dead man and an old man hidden in the stock phrase used for the fountain of youth! Almost guarantees that they won't find it, eh?

The ancient Chinese spoke of magical islands in the so-called Eastern sea. Quite likely, storm-tossed fishermen could have reached Japan and come back with such a tall tale. The chronicles record that the first emperor of Qin, the guy who built the Great Wall and unified China, had sent a

---

* The modern character for hair 髮 contains the character 長 (which itself shows long hair) and three strokes 彡 for hair. It has hair all over the place.

certain Xu Fu, together with a hundred virgin boys and girls, on an expedition to the magical islands in search of elixirs of immortality. It was also recorded that Xu never came back. Some said that he didn't find the right stuff and was afraid to face the emperor's wrath. Others said he did find it, and in that case, what was the point of coming back? The Chinese enjoy speculating that Xu's descendants may be living in Japan today.

Another point of view, particularly well-summarized in a famous Tang dynasty love poem, asserts that it it better to enjoy earthly love than to be a lonely immortal. The poem recalls the myth of the lady in the moon. Where Westerners see an old man, the Chinese see a beautiful lady resplendent in flowing robes. To understand how she got there, we have to go back to a time when the world was scorched by ten suns in the sky. The people were having a hard time working the parched land. Luckily, a great hero emerged and with his mighty bow and arrow shot down nine of the ten suns. The gods rewarded the hero with the elixir of immortality. But while he was out, his wife drank the elixir. She floated up into the sky and became the lady in the moon. Although she achieved immortality, she was doomed to a life of loneliness. (She does have a pet rabbit for company.) The poem describes how the lady was punished for all eternity to long for love in vain night after night. On the night of the mid-autumn's festival, people look up and recall the eternal regret of trading love for immortality.

Throughout history, Taoist sorcerers have claimed to have found the elixir. Some of the claimants were not shy about naming names and giving actual recipes. Me, I am of a modern cast of mind, and I am rather skeptical. But some of you may want to try an actual recipe. Proceeding on the principle that those recipes with the most modest claims were the most likely to work, I have picked out a Yuan dynasty recipe with a relatively small claim. Indeed, immortality was not even promised, only longevity. Amusingly, the degree of longevity was promised according to a formula. If you started taking this so-called jade paste regularly before the age of 27, then you could live to the age of 360; if you took it before 45, then you could live to be 240; and if you took it before 63, then you could live to be 120. But if you took it after the age of 64, then the most you could hope for was a lifespan of 100.

What is intriguing is that the recipe does not appear to be too difficult. The ingredients consist of honey and various Chinese herbs, all readily available even in the United States. The ingredients are mixed together, sealed in a silver or earthen pot, and simmered for three days and three nights over a fire of wood from the mulberry tree. This concoction is then kept at the bottom of a well for a while, "to get rid of the poison from the fire." It is simmered again for a day. Then it's done! You are supposed to light some incense, bow to the paste, and take out three spoonfuls as an offering to heaven and earth and all the spirits contained therein. The prescribed "dosage" is a spoonful washed down with a fine wine three times a day. (I suppose that the efficacy of the potion must depend on how fine the wine is.)

What? You want the recipe? Okay, I will give it in a note to this chapter. Let me know if it works. Just think of the commercial possibilities if it did! Never mind longevity—go for the megabucks!

More seriously, let us move on from recipes that promise immortality and longevity to recipes that merely claim to promote health. Over the last two decades or so, Americans have become increasingly interested in the role food plays in determining one's general health. Notions from the health-food movement have entered the mainstream consciousness. Not surprisingly, the Chinese, with a culture so notably preoccupied with food, have always been extremely concerned about determining the precise effects various foods have on health.

The Chinese view of food is very much based on their general philosophy of harmony and balance between the yin and the yang. As you may know, the Chinese constructed an elaborate worldview according to which the cosmos is an arena where the force of yin 陰 and the force of yang 陽 are continually dominating and yielding to each other. The yin-yang symbol depicts how the two forces renew each other cyclically. Yin is the essence of the female, yang the essence of the male. For example, the moon belongs to the yin (and thus women worship the moon in the mid-autumn's night festival), while the sun belongs to the yang. The dichotomy expressed by the yin-yang idea is probably deeply and universally seated in the human psyche and follows rather obviously from primitive man's perception of nature and change. Your notion of what is yin and what is yang would in all likelihood correspond rather closely to what the ancient Chinese put down. For example, you probably would guess that night is yin and day is yang.

The whole scheme is at once simplistic and universal. While the underlying principle can be grasped by a child, its influence on the cultural outlook of the East (and in turn on its history) is profound. A man of the East is more inclined than his counterpart in the West to see things in terms of balance and harmony, of compromise and accommodation rather than in terms of confrontation.

Let us look at the etymology of the characters for yin and yang. You may have noticed already that they have the same radical 阝 , whose pictographic origin is far from obvious. Originally, 阝 was drawn to depict, clearly enough, a cliff. You may even remember the cliff radical in connection with chop suey! A number of characters associated with cliffs still contain this form as a radical. In time, three strokes were added 厓 , presumably to indicate steps carved into the hillside. In time, this became 㠯 and then 阝 . For ease of writing, one of the protrusions was dropped, giving 阝 , and the modern form 阝 . The ancient meaning of yin was "the north," and hence shady, "side of a hill"; and of yang, "the south," and hence sunny, "side of a hill."

According to *Talking About the Written Language and Analyzing the Words,* the classical etymological compilation, the right sides of the characters for yin and yang are merely phonetic elements. It seems to me that other interpretations are possible. An ancient form of yang is 阝彡 .

It looks to me like a picture of the sun shining its rays onto the hill. You may recall that the character for sun is in fact 日 . Incidentally, another commonly used term for sun is 太 陽 , *tai yang,* literally "the ultimate yang," more or less a definition of the sun. (The character meaning "the ultimate," is formed by adding a dot to the character for "big" 大 . Amusingly, in modern usage, a respectful form of addressing a wife is "tai tai," 太 太 or "the ultimate ultimate.") Similarly, an ancient form for yin is 阝侌 . The lower right half looks to me like the jar used to ferment wine in. The top half may be a thatched roof over the wine that is fermenting or the sketch of a peak of a hill. The shady side of the hill is a good place to brew that moonshine. Moon, one of the ultimate manifestations of the yin; moonshine, shady business, get it?

Intriguing though the world of etymology is, we should return to the world of food. We were talking about the Chinese conception of the effect of food on health. Instead of merely saying that a certain kind of food is good for you, the Chinese tried to classify the effects of a given food under the general rubric of the yin and the yang. Every food item is categorized as either 涼 "cool" or 熱 "hot." As the terminology suggests, cool food is supposed to have a cooling effect on the "internal viscera" of the body, and hot food, a heating effect. Here, the words "cool" or "hot" do not refer to the temperature of the food, but to some intrinsic essence of the food based on whether that essence belongs to the yin or the yang.

While most Chinese are aware to some extent of this notion of cool and hot food, no other regional group is as preoccupied with the subject as the Cantonese. The Cantonese have developed the most detailed location of foods along the cold-hot continuum—a continuum that defines certain foods as extremely cold, moderately cold, slightly cold, and so on. From childhood, the Cantonese learned about where each type of food lies along the continuum. Before a Cantonese takes a bite, he or she is keenly aware of whether that morsel of food is going to be cooling or heating. People outside of the Canton region sometimes laugh good-naturedly at the Cantonese for being such fussbudgets about their food.

I am a bit hazy myself about whether a given food is cooling or heating. But again, the classification scheme is more or less what you might expect: meat and fatty foods are hot, while most vegetables, watercress, are cold. Cooked rice is thought to be balanced between hot and cold, but porridge (though it may be steaming) is cooling because of the effect of the water. This illustrates the further refinement in the system of how the cooking process can make the food colder or hotter.

Crabs are thought to be exceedingly cold, and the Chinese invariably serve crabmeat with a dip made of shredded ginger, sugar, and vinegar. Fish and shrimp are also always cooked or served with ginger. The association of crab with wine is thus not only poetic and romantic, but also motivated by health considerations, as I have already mentioned in Chapter 8. After having crab, some particularly health-conscious Chinese will drink a "tea" made by pouring boiling water over thinly sliced ginger, with sugar added to taste. The same tea is recommended after exposure to inclement weather. As you might have guessed, the Chinese regard ginger as warming. Interestingly, the melted butter traditionally served in the West with crab may have the same warming effect.

Ginger imparts to Chinese cuisine one of its characteristic flavors. Besides its warming effect, ginger is also thought to stimulate the digestive tract, and thus a slice of ginger is included in almost every dish. In fish dishes, it plays the same role as the lemon slice in Western cuisine. Incidentally, the Romans developed a taste for ginger, and the caravans plying the Silk Route supplied them with it and other spices from China. Ginger is mentioned in the Koran. It is a disgrace that our mass-marketed ginger ale is so underflavored.

Ginger is rich in vitamins A and C. As far back as the fifth century, Chinese ships carried fresh ginger grown in pots to ward off the dreaded scurvy and other vitamin-deficiency diseases that plagued the Europeans in the age of long sea voyages. The Dutch were apparently the first to learn from the Chinese of the importance of ginger and citrus fruits. And by the end of the eighteenth century, the British admiralty was issuing to each sailor a daily ration of lemon juice mixed with rum, the infamous grog, named after the admiral who first diluted the rum with water. In the middle of the nineteenth century, lime was substituted for lemon, thus earning British sailors the nickname "limeys." From the drink we now have the wonderfully sounding word "groggy," as in "a groggy limey." A horse with stiff joints is known as a grog. Such is the way of languages. (No, the admiral was not named Grog, but he wore a coat made of grogram cloth.)

While I have not told you explicitly what the purpose of all this talk about cool and hot is, I suppose you can readily guess that the Chinese strive to follow a diet that is perfectly balanced between cold and hot. As a further refinement, a woman should maintain herself slightly on the cool side but at the same time take care not to become too cool. The opposite holds for a man. All of this talk is fairly reminiscent of the medieval European notion of calorics and the humors of the body. They took much more extreme measures to achieve balance though. For instance, a man inflamed with the passion of love was to have his hot blood let out of him.

Superimposed on this cold-hot dichotomy is a dry-wet 乾 — 濕 , dichotomy. Thus, a given food may be hot and dry, or hot and wet, and so forth. Again, the words "dry" and "wet" do not refer to an external physical property but to some elusive intrinsic essence. For example, some soups, but by no means all soups, are said to be "moistening" 滋 . I mentioned earlier that the Cantonese have an enormous variety of soups. They have them completely classified according to this health system.

Notice the water radical in these characters associated with wetness and in the character for cool. You may have also seen the fire radical compressed to four dots in the character for "hot" 熱 .

As with many traditional Chinese concepts, this classification of food cannot be fitted, at least in detail, into the schema of Western medicine. On the other hand, the general notion of eating a balanced diet and of not indulging in any one kind of food to excess is one that we could all agree with. Whether or not the specific description of a given vegetable as moderately cold and slightly wet can be trusted is another story. The believer could point to the classification scheme as the distillation of millennia of experience with food. The skeptic would suspect, however, that once the position of a certain food along the cold-hot continuum was fixed somehow, that position was handed down from generation to generation without any possible challenge to the accumulated authority.

In this connection, I may also mention that some of the ancients also spoke of how one type of food would clash with another. Certain food combinations were thus prohibited. By and large, people pay little attention to these prohibitions, many of which appear to be totally ridiculous to us today. For example, an imperial court doctor of the Yuan dynasty wrote a book warning against eating beef with chestnuts and eating rabbit with ginger. He gave some sixty other such prohibited combinations. Presumably, some prince once got sick eating beef with chestnuts. It is of course quite conceivable that of his sixty or so prohibitions, some may have a medical basis. There is after all a difference between folk belief and what a court doctor believed, particularly if the guy might get his head chopped off.

It is interesting to note that the Chinese have no significant food taboo, certainly none comparable in magnitude to the taboo in Judaic and Islamic cultures, for instance. I feel that the reason is that there simply wasn't any central religious authority capable of enforcing such taboos. People were going to eat beef with chestnuts whatever the court doctor said.

My family was from the Shanghai region and there wasn't much talk by my parents about cold and hot nor dry and wet. We had a Cantonese maid, however, and she was always telling us that we needed to be cooled down or heated up. In my adult life, I have paid little attention to this entire business of balance and harmony. All I know is that if I went to Paris and had, immediately upon arrival, a rich meal swimming in butter and wine sauce so "hot" that it's off the Chinese scale, I would be in big trouble. Thus, I am rather impressed by how the Cantonese have integrated this striving for balance and harmony into their daily lives. When I go to a place like Hong Kong, and sit down with some friends to order in a restaurant, someone might say that I look awfully hot and dry and that we'd better order a cooling and moistening soup.

All of this is lost on patrons of Chinese restaurants in this country. Who knows whether the last meal I had was in the net cooling or heating. It was all probably overwhelmed by the MSG anyway! If you are intrigued by this theory of cold and hot foods, perhaps the next time you go to a Cantonese restaurant you can ask your waiter to suggest a meal that is neither too cold nor too hot, neither too dry nor too wet.

Of course, all of this is of help only if you know where you are on the cold/hot–dry/wet continuum. Are you too hot and in need of a cooling meal, or is it the other way around? To know that you have to consult a Chinese book on nutrition. Such books, of which there are quite a few, tell you not only where each food lies on the cold/hot–dry/wet continuum but also where each illness lies.

In traditional Chinese culture, only a fine line separates food and medicine. An ancient saying asserts that "Food and medicine come from the same source." The thought behind this saying is hardly unique to the Chinese. However, it is probably true that no other culture has developed and elaborated herbal medicine to such a degree as the Chinese. A legendary figure named　神農　, literally "divine farmer," is traditionally revered for having established agriculture by systematically tasting all plants to determine their nutritional and medicinal values. The fellow is often represented with a greenish face as a result of repeated food poisonings.

Historians have sometimes remarked that while the Chinese had extensive knowledge of the world, they failed to systematize their knowledge. As a result, their knowledge remained fractured and disconnected. The study of plants, however, was a notable exception to this sweepingly general remark. There were a number of botanical compilations containing detailed drawings and discussions of just about every known plant. Obviously, a thorough understanding of the properties of plants is of prime importance to an agrarian society.

Many herbs and plants with medicinal properties are also used in everyday cooking, notably in soups. This is one aspect of Chinese culture that I have paid little attention to. It appeared to me much too complicated to have an apothecary of Chinese herbs on hand to make soup with. But as I mentioned earlier in connection with soups, even in this aspect of life we have entered the convenience age! You can now buy packaged soup mixes in Chinatown grocery stores. The relevant herbs and grains are all there in the right proportions in a plastic bag. An example is the 清 補 涼 soup mix, consisting of pearl barley, lily bulbs, lotus seeds, radix dioscoreae, dried longans, fox nuts, and polygonatum. You simply dump the soup mix into a pot of water together with some chicken, beef, pork, lamb, or whatever you want to make the soup with. Bring the soup to a boil and then simmer for at least two hours. That's it. The first time I used this soup mix I had lamb, and because of the barley in the soup mix Gretchen and I thought that we had made a Chinese Scotch broth. It is recommended that you also add some vegetable of your choice. Many Chinese like to add dried or what my children call "petrified" vegetable, 菜乾 , literally "vegetable dried" and generally available in Chinatown grocery stores. Try the many soup mixes available to see which one you like best. The tastes of some of the medicinal herbs are definitely acquired.

Speaking of soups and herbs, I have to mention one of my favorites 川 貝雪梨豬肉湯 . The botanical name of the herb 川貝 is *Fritillaria Roylei Hook*. Now you know what it is, of course. You can buy it in a Chinese pharmacy in the form of a ground-up white powder. You may have noticed the weather radical 雨 in the third character and the wood radical 木 in the fourth character; together, these characters mean "snow pear." Finally, you may remember the last three characters, meaning "pork soup," from Chapters 2 and 5. This is a subtle and understated soup: the soft blending of the flavors of the sliced pears and of the pork into each other is underscored by the slightly medicinal taste of the 川貝 .

Apples, and sometimes dates, are often substituted for pears. I am reminded of pork chops with apple sauce—some of the basic principles of blending flavors are transcultural. On the other hand, according to the canons of food balance and harmony, beef should never be used instead of pork in this soup. Beef is hotter than pork and would overwhelm the mildly cooling effect of the 雪梨 .

Boy, sometimes I really wish that the Chinese restaurants in this country would branch out from Hot and Sour Soup. You don't really believe that the Chinese have developed only the four or five soups you commonly see on menus, do you?

Among Chinese herbs perhaps none is as well known in the West as ginseng 人參 , with its alleged quasi-magical properties. In the past, extreme claims were made for ginseng: with a timely dose, one suppos-edly could even bring the dying back to life. More rationally, many Chinese swear by it as an invigorating tonic, particularly for the elderly and the infirm. As for me, it just makes me feel jumpy. Modern science simply lists ginseng as a stimulant. The Latin name for ginseng is *Panax schinseng.* Does that ring a bell? *Panax* for panacea!

The part of the ginseng plant actually used is its root. Part of the mystery surrounding ginseng is that the root vaguely resembles the human form. Linguistically, you may have noticed the character 人 for "human" in the word for ginseng. Thus, ginseng may be translated rather loosely as "human essence." (The second character means "essence" and appeared in the word for "sea cucumber" 海 參 in Chapter 8. Thus, sea cucum-ber is linguistically "ginseng of the sea.")

I find it intriguing that in the European tradition the same sort of mystery surrounds the root of another plant, the mandrake. The mandrake also resembles the human form; in fact, many see in it a male and a female form intertwined. The ancient Greeks believed that a human, or at least a homunculus, could be bred from the mandrake. (In Europe, the mandrake was used as a narcotic and, in the hands of the Borgias, as a poison.) Similarly, in some Chinese stories, ginseng could take on human forms.

Incidentally, ginseng is pronounced in Mandarin as something like "ren sun," and in Cantonese, as "yun sun." The phonetic transliteration ginseng is a corruption.

Did you know that the United States has become a major producer and exporter of ginseng? (It is also, by the way, the world's largest exporter of chopsticks.) It turns out that conditions in Wisconsin are ideal for the cultivation of ginseng. To distinguish American ginseng from Asian ginseng, some Chinese refer to the American product as 花 旗 參 . Remember that the first character means "flower." See the grass radical 艹 ? The second character means "flag." What? "Flower-flag" ginseng?

Well, a Cantonese nickname for the United States is "flower-flag country" or "florid flag country." Come to think of it, the Betsy Ross, with its stars and stripes, is considerably more florid than the flags of the western European countries that were seen in China.

In Asia, ginseng grows wild in the mountains of northeastern China and Korea. Ginseng was so expensive not only because of its supposed life-restoring properties but also because of the hardships involved in gathering it. In Chinese adventure stories, there are tales of specialized traders traipsing over the wilds of the frigid northeast in search of ginseng.

Even with American cultivation, the price of ginseng remains impressive. The demand is there, judging from the mob scene in Chinatown ginseng shops. I have pretty much stayed away from ginseng partly because I feel that the claims for it are surely exaggerated and partly because of the price. I was advised that were I to buy ginseng I could just as well do with the lowest grade "florid flag" ginseng. I was also told that Asian ginseng is more suitable for the elderly while the "florid flag" kind is more suitable for the young and middle-aged. In recent years, rather shady-looking ads have appeared in the back pages of some American magazines hawking ginseng. If you have any doubts as to whether or not you are going to get the real thing for the prices mentioned in these ads, you should visit a ginseng shop and find out how much the top-grade stuff costs.

Chinese herbal medicine is a vast and venerable subject, but also unfortunately shot through with exaggerated and unsubstantiated claims. In recent years, biochemists in Hong Kong and elsewhere have launched long-term projects to do controlled experiments and to determine the chemical basis of some of these herbs. I feel hopeful that these efforts will lead to a deeper understanding of them and the development of new, herbally based drugs.

Let us go back and look at the three characters 清 補 涼 in the name of the soup mix. You encountered the first character, meaning "clear," in Chapter 2 and the third character, meaning "cool," which we saw in connection with the tossed sea-cucumber salad. The second character means "to mend clothing." (It contains the clothing radical 衤, a compressed form of the character 衣 for clothing. The character is pictographic: you are supposed to recognize a robe with its two sleeves! The clothing radical and the divine-revelation radical look exactly the same and hence are often confused even by highly educated Chinese readers.)

Thus, the soup mix is an example of an enormous complex of food items known as 補 品 that are supposed to "mend" your body. For example, bird's nest is highly regarded as a "mending food." Meat is also generally considered "mending." Traditionally, the Chinese think of consuming lots of mending food in the fall. This is the reason why some restaurants put out signs with the character 補 splashed all over. One has gone through the summer with a lackadaisical appetite and now one has to build up one's vigor for the winter ahead. You may remember that in the north, in old Beijing, on the first day of fall people flocked to have roast lamb in order to put on some fat for the winter.

Meanwhile, other creatures are also getting fat. A favorite southern Chinese saying goes:

秋 風 起 兮 三 蛇 肥

"As the autumn wind blows, the three types of snakes are getting fat." Such is the rallying cry of those who like to eat snakes. (You may recognize the first character as meaning "autumn" (with the fire radical next to the stalk of grain); the fifth character for three; the insect radical 虫 in the sixth character for "snake"; and the compressed flesh radical 月 in the last character meaning "fat.") The Cantonese consider snake to be extremely mending and invigorating, particularly for the male. The most expensive part of the snake is its gallbladder, said to be extremely beneficial to one's eyesight and to be effective against inflammation. In specialized shops, snake gall bladders are kept soaked in strong liquors. The liquor is taken as a tonic.

The taste for snakes is by no means universal in China. Northerners consider it a peculiar habit of the south. When our friend the Song dynasty poet Su Tung-po was banished from the imperial court, his wife accompanied him to southern China. There she was given a snake broth without realizing what it was. When told that she had eaten snake, she threw up and got sick.

In talking about "mending" one's body, the Chinese hold as a basic principle the saying: 以 形 補 形 , literally "with the shape mend the shape" (形 = shape or form; 以 = with). According to this principle, if you feel your liver needs mending, you should eat liver; if you feel your brain needs mending, you should eat brain, and so on. This appears to be a rather natural principle that fairly leaps to mind. When the English first learned of this principle among the Chinese, they derided the whole idea as absurd. But then the English as a people tend to avoid eating internal organs, certainly compared to the French, with their sweetbreads and liver and all. Nowadays, this simple principle appears less absurd. Surely there is an element of truth in it.

This principle, however, can be carried to an extreme. Besides brain (and fish), many Chinese have long believed that walnuts are good for your brain, arguing that its wrinkled shape resembles the folds of the brain. This is clearly stretching it. Nevertheless, generations of Chinese mothers have pushed walnuts on their children.

East and West apparently agree on one thing, that fish is brain-food. Lately, there has been much talk in this country about the benefits of fish, and the consumption of fish has reached an all-time record. If the truth be known, it is considerably easier to prepare fish than brain.

All this talk about the balance and harmony between hot and cold and about mending the body is part of a larger holistic outlook on health. Another important component is exercise, particularly exercise to promote "chi" 氣 or "inner energy." Of these exercises, tai chi chuan 太極拳 is by far the best known to Westerners. Many of you have probably seen the exercise with its slow, dancelike movements performed, movements variously described as shadow boxing or meditative ballet. It is a common sight in China: the parks in the early morning are filled with people going through the motions, and it is becoming an increasingly common sight in this country, at gyms and adult education centers and the like. The exercise stresses calmness of mind, slowness and fluidity of movement, and a flowing smoothness of breath. One of the basic tenets of the exercise is "Be like a child."

Incidentally, the transliteration of the term is rather inaccurate: you can see the "chi" in tai chi chuan, namely the character 極 , and actually pronounced more like "jee," is quite different from the character 氣 for "inner energy." The character 極 means "extreme." You may remember the first character as meaning "the ultimate." The third character—notice the hand radical 手 it contains—means "fist," or in this context, a martial art using fists. Thus, the full name of the exercise is literally "ultimate extreme fist."

Let us now come back to "chi." It is a peculiarly Chinese concept and hence virtually untranslatable. I used "inner energy" tentatively above. It can variously be identified as "breath," "inner essence," or perhaps "inner harmony." One author suggests the rather more elaborate "psychophysiological power associated with blood and breath." Wow!

Let us first look at "chi" as etymologists. The radical 气 , originally 气 , shows vapors rising. Thus, this is the radical associated with gases and vapors. For example, the modern characters for oxygen, nitrogen, and so on, all contain this radical. The character 氣 for "chi" is formed by combining the vapor radical with the character for "rice" 米 . The simplest interpretation would be the steam rising as rice is boiled. Or it may denote the essential vapor contained in rice. In any case, the character is common enough and occurs in a multitude of compound words of two characters describing, for example, air, cooking gas, and the weather.

When applied to humans, "chi" can mean simply "breath." Thus, 氣 功 or "chi kung" may be called "breathing exercise" but it is really a practice based on meditation and breath control whereby one hopes to gain mastery of one's chi. ("Kung" is as in kung fu.) Since the ancient Chinese spoke of how "chi" circulates inside the body, it doesn't quite mean merely "breath." Perhaps the humor talked about in medieval Europe comes close. Here we have two equally vague concepts. In the end, one simply throws up one's hands and says that there is not an exact equivalent in English.

Anyhow, in the traditional Chinese view, the mastery of "chi" and keeping it in balance and harmony should be the goal of all those concerned with health.

We have gone from elixir to the food of health, and in the end it all comes down to harmony and balance. It's just as your mother told you. There is no elixir, and a balanced diet is best, certainly better than any pill you can find. Keep yourself neither hot nor cool, neither dry nor wet!

CHAPTER 17

FROM BANQUETS
TO VOYAGES
OF DISCOVERY

THE CHINESE BANQUET first came into the public consciousness in this
country with Nixon's trip to China. For some months after that historic
trip, friends would ask me from time to time to organize a Chinese banquet.
They had in mind that I should gather up a suitably large group of friends,
herd them all to a local Chinese restaurant, and order a multitude of dishes.
It was, admittedly, lots of fun, but a properly served Chinese banquet is
much more than a large number of dishes piled together and after a while,
all mixed up and indistinguishable from one another.

A proper Chinese banquet has its own internal logic and balance, like a symphonic poem. The pace of the banquet should be as leisurely as a summer's dream. The dishes should arrive in a stately procession, succeeding one another at such a pace as to allow digestion but not to promote impatience. The size of the dishes should be appropriate for the gathering. Each person should get just enough for a satisfying taste but not so much as to leave no room for the twenty-nine other dishes to come.

The order of the procession is the soul of the banquet and must be carefully thought out in advance. The presentation may take the diner's palate in one direction, with each succeeding dish building up in taste, perhaps exploring a few side paths along the way, up to a height not reachable in ordinary dining, and then let it down slowly to a punctuated finish. Or perhaps the presentation may alternate in taste, each heavily flavored dish followed by a dish elegant in its bland subtlety, much as in the finest French dinners I have tasted, where each course is followed by a small serving of a lightly flavored sherbet to refresh the palate. A sizzling hot dish should be followed by a cool dish, a crunchy concoction by some meltingly soft morsels. In any case, banquets should have an identifiable structure: there should be a prelude, a buildup, a climax, and a détente.

At a fine banquet, the excellence of the individual dishes is taken for granted, but the presentation reflects on the gracious thoughtfulness and worldly sophistication of the host. The logic of the banquet should be such that the diner can more or less anticipate the type of dish to be served next, but not so rigid that he or she is not pleasantly surprised from time to time. A fine banquet should have rhythm and melody, interlaced with twists and turns.

The art connoisseur and historian Walter Pater once asserted that all art tends toward the condition of music. I feel that so too does the Chinese banquet. A fine Chinese banquet represents one of the refinements of a civilization much given to worldly pleasures, but much too often, a Chinese banquet as interpreted in this country is simply a pigs' feast.

Incidentally, the word for banquet is　酒 席　. Perhaps you recognize the first character as the one for wine and liquor. Thus, to the Chinese mind, drinking alcohol is an intrinsic part of banqueting. The primary meaning of the second character is simply "a banquet." Interestingly, the character originally meant "mat" and later "large table." Perhaps the notion of a banquet originated with sitting together on a mat. In modern usage, the character for "mat" is often written as　蓆　, with the grass radical　艹　added to distinguish it from the character for "banquet."

Much of what I now think of banquets are remembrances of feasts past. I remember accompanying my parents to Chinese banquets during my adolescence in São Paulo, Brazil. The sort of restaurants my parents would patronize all had private rooms upstairs. A fine banquet should really be held in a private dining room: I was given to understand how vulgar it would be to eat surrounded by strangers. The waiting host and hostess would greet the guests as they arrived. Before the banquet started, the owner of the restaurant would make an unobtrusive appearance, exchanging pleasantries with the diners, perhaps apologizing for the cook's incompetence. The banquets of my adolescence lasted for hours, with animated conversation and drinking games punctuated by the arrival of yet another dish. As the dining party departed when it was all over, the entire staff, from the owner to the cook on down, would line up outside the door to say good night to us and to express hope that we would come again.

On the way home I would often hear my parents discussing the presentation, perhaps saying that the arrival of a certain dish at a particular time was without rhyme or reason. Why would Mrs. So-and-so have that duck before the fish? At such banquets, the presentation was worked out in advance by the owner in consultation with the host. Often, the entire arrangement would be left to the discretion of the owner.

During my years in college and in graduate school, I drifted away from the world of fine banquets. It was only while on occasional visits to my parents that I maintained some contact with that world. And then some years ago, thanks partly to Nixon I suppose, I was once again brought back into that world. On one trip I found myself part of a delegation from the United States visiting the People's Republic of China, and I got to enjoy a seemingly endless stream of banquets given by various government officials.

Surely the most memorable was one given by Deng Xiao-ping. The food was excellent and refined but it was far from extravagant. The banquet contained none of the traditional delicacies held in esteem by gourmets. What was memorable was the occasion, the setting in the Great Hall of the People (cavernous and vast and so far from the private dining rooms I knew in my adolescence), and most of all, the service. It's got to be the best-served meal I have ever had. Two servers were assigned to each diner; one of them was stationed permanently behind the diner while the other came and went. The service stopped just short of spoon-feeding each guest.

While enjoying official banquets in China, I have on more than one occasion wondered about the government leaders who have to attend these functions every day. How did they ever get any work done? After all, Mao Zedong himself once asserted that carrying out a revolution was not the same as attending a dinner party. Thus it came as no surprise that in 1987 the Chinese government announced a drive to cut the time spent at official banquets from an average of three to four hours down to a maximum of ninety minutes. The number of courses was to be limited to four, plus a soup.

Of course, the complaint of having to attend official dinners is an ancient one. A Ming dynasty official wrote that he would attend only those banquets given by family and friends, in spite of the potential ill effects on his career. (In the Ming dynasty, banquets often started at 11 A.M. and would last for six hours or more.) That complaint is also hardly limited to China.

The elaborateness of official banquets reached an absurd height during the Qing dynasty (1644–1911). But first, some historical background. The Qing dynasty, the last imperial dynasty before the republic was established in 1911, was founded by Manchu horsemen invading from the north in 1644. (China contains five major ethnic groups: Mongols, Manchus, Tibetans, Moslem Weis, and Hans. The vast majority of Chinese are ethnically Han.) The Manchu rulers found themselves a tiny minority governing the majority Han and thus felt it necessary to resort to rather repressive measures. Particularly in its early years, the Manchu dynasty was resisted and hated by the Han Chinese. Within a couple of generations, however, the Manchus had been culturally assimilated into the Han.

The Qing dynasty followed the same pattern that had governed the rise and fall of Chinese dynasties for millennia. A dynasty is founded by a military leader of extraordinary ability and vision. Perhaps one or two capable and discerning emperors would emerge during the dynasty's first phase. But then, as power is passed from father to son and as the gene pool gets steadily diluted, an inevitable period of decay sets in, in which emperors barely know the difference between night and day. The cataclysmic collapse is then followed by revolution and chaos. With tragic regularity, this script has been played out in Chinese history. In the movie *The Last Emperor* the almost pathetic decadence of the Qing dynasty in its death throes was beautifully portrayed. In just two hundred or so years, the charging horsemen who were terror incarnate as they swept through the Chinese empire had been reduced to whimpering sybarites.

It is the tragedy of China, among her almost countless other tragedies, that the West came in the nineteenth century during the disintegration of one of her dynasties. Japan, in contrast, had the good fortune of having one of her most capable emperors on the throne at the time.

As the Manchu warriors settled down to the comfort and luxury of their new empire, they promptly developed a taste for Han food, that is, what we would call Chinese food. Official banquets at the imperial court were soon given in both a Manchu version and a Han version. There were six grades of Manchu banquets and five grades of Han banquets. Precise rules governed what grades of banquets were to be served. For instance, foreign envoys, including those from the West, were served the sixth-level Manchu banquet while the top three students in the imperial examination got the fifth-level Han banquet. Presumably, the Chinese government also has a similar grading system. Hmm, I wonder if the less than extravagant banquet in the Great Hall of the People was of the lowest grade!

Less than forty years after the founding of the dynasty, the emperor Kang Xi decided in 1680 that henceforth the imperial court would be served only Han banquets for its New Year's feasts. While the Hans lost on the battlefields, they emerged victorious on the dining table.

After the first major Chinese insurrection, the Manchu emperors announced some relaxation of their oppressive rule. For instance, the prohibition on intermarriage between the Manchus and the Hans was lifted. As a further symbol of the emerging peace between the Manchus and the Hans, it was also proclaimed that the Manchu banquet and the Han banquet were to be merged into what was known as a Manchu-Han Full Banquet 滿 漢 全 席 . The result was a truly humongous feast since both culinary traditions had to be represented fully.* A menu from the reign of the emperor Qian Long (or Ch'ien Lung) has survived and lists seventy entries. The banquet lasted three days. Actually, the menu contains some rather bizarre dishes, one was Steamed Pig, Lamb, Chicken, Duck, and Goose. One food writer found this rather puzzling, citing that Qian Long's favorite concubine was a Moslem and wouldn't possibly allow lamb and pork to be mixed together. He concluded that the entry must mean "steamed pig, steamed lamb, steamed chicken, steamed duck, and steamed goose." I think I have to leave that one to the serious historians. Actually, the favorite concubine might simply have passed over this dish or not attended the banquet.

Incidentally, the emperor Qian Long had an enormous zest for life. A self-proclaimed gourmet, he played a role in the development of several dishes. He liked to travel and upon visiting each place always insisted on trying the famous local dishes. His diet, as recorded in the imperial annals, was chock-full of cholesterol. Nevertheless, he lived to be eighty-eight, an all-time record among Chinese emperors. Historians have calculated that

---

* Manchu food reflects the flavor of the northern steppes. Interestingly, a number of Manchu food items entered the mainstream Chinese food repertoire. For instance, a sweet rice cake commonly sold in Chinatown and known as 薩 其 馬 is of Manchu origin. The three Chinese characters strung together have no meaning but transliterate the Manchu name of the cake. Its name makes it obvious that it is not Han Chinese in origin.

the average lifespan of the 208 emperors that reigned between 202 B.C. and A.D. 1911 was only forty-two. (We see that they don't get to reign for very long, either. On the average each emperor got barely ten years.) The ones that did not die of sexual debauchery were probably poisoned. Only four emperors made it past the age of eighty, and it is the guy who had all those Manchu-Han Full Banquets who beat them all!

In recent years, the Manchu-Han Full Banquet made a comeback in Hong Kong as a sign of extravagance. Actually, a pale shadow of its former self, it merely consists of four separate banquets spread over two days. It is hardly surprising that the world of extravagant banquets is in full flowering in Hong Kong, in that land where anything can be obtained just for the asking.

At fine banquets, the whole complex of behavior associated with social formality and table manners that the Chinese call 客氣 dances over the gathering with the precision and grace of a ballet. The host and hostess anticipate the guests' every wish. Each person is watchful of his neighbors and serves them as soon as he thinks they should be served. Ideally, no one needs to serve himself but is unceasingly busy serving others. While you politely try to stop others from serving you, protesting your unworthiness, you always make sure that in the end you do not deprive them of their pleasure. It all goes on according to an unspoken code based on one's place in the social structure. The pacing is leisurely. The ladies eat with such grace that they are said to be "counting pearls."

The term 客氣 literally means "the *chi* or essence of being a guest." (Remember that we met 客 in discussing the Hakka people, the "gypsy wanderers" of China. The character shows an extra person by the hearth under the roof. The second character 氣 is the mysterious "chi" of the Chinese concept of bodily well-being.) Perhaps not paradoxically, no one at a fine banquet embodies more fully the essence of being a guest than the host and the hostess.

Nowadays, when you order a banquet, many restaurants make it easy by simply offering banquets with fixed lists of dishes. The banquets offered are simply graded by the price. More traditionally, banquets are graded according to whether they contain swallow's nest, shark's fin, or sea cucumber, known respectively as 燕窩席 , 魚翅席 , and 海參席 .

Times are changing, however, and many banquets now don't even contain any of these delicacies. Incidentally, the Manchu-Han Full Banquet contains all three. There are of course also many regional variations.

I have already talked about the sea cucumber, or bêche de mer, in Chapter 8. In the Orient, the shark's fin, prized for its texture, is worth lots more than shark's flesh. The character 翅 actually means "wing of a bird": 羽 is strikingly pictographic, isn't it? (The rest of the character, 支 , is just a phonetic element.) Thus, shark's fin is represented on the menu as "fish's wing."

Shark's fin is tricky to prepare and should not be ordered unless you have a well-founded faith in the restaurant. Depending on how it is prepared, it can be rather chewy and in that form is not recommended for people with loose teeth. The story is told that when a shark's fin banquet was served to Bismarck, his aide-de-camp had a tooth come loose. Not wanting to breach protocol, the general swallowed his tooth together with the shark's fin. When this soldierly act of courage became known, the imperial Qing dynasty court apparently issued a standing order not to serve shark's fin to German diplomats again.

While prized, neither shark's fin nor sea cucumber is considered as fancy as swallow's nest. The three types of banquets are listed above in order of decreasing fanciness: thus, the swallow's nest banquet is the most expensive; the sea cucumber banquet, the least.

The very mention of swallow's nest evokes in the uninitiated a disgusting image of eating a bird's nest whole. Actually, the swallow in question is not any old swallow but a sea swallow that lives along the Malaysian coast, and what is eaten is only the glutinous secretion used by the swallow to cement the nest together. The actual material of the nest, such as twigs and the stray feather or two, all have to be carefully washed away. If you ever discover such foreign material in swallow's nest banquet, you can cry for the restaurant owner's head. The best quality nests are supposed to be those collected before the eggs hatch.

In the annals of culinary literature, perhaps the most laughably ignorant piece I ever came across was that of a Western food writer speculating that the swallow's nest was discovered by some peasant during a famine. Nothing can be further from the truth. While certainly many Chinese food items were discovered during famines, the swallow's nest was first introduced into China during the Ming dynasty (1368–1644) as a luxury import. It's the Ferrari of the Ming table. Only the wealthiest could possibly afford it. In the novel *The Dream of the Red Chamber,* Dai-yu, the rather languid and sickly female protagonist, was advised to have a swallow's nest every morning for her constitution. In the minds of readers in the know, this passage immediately conjures up an image of vast extravagance. (You lady readers may want to take note that the swallow's nest is reputed to have excellent effects on the female constitution.)

Why in the world should a swallow's nest be so expensive? Well, it turns out that the particular swallow whose nest is held in such esteem builds its nests on sheer cliffs along the sea or on cave walls. In ancient times, monkeys were trained to gather the nests. An evolutionary biologist would remark here that even if that swallow did not used to build its nest on cliffs, it would have learned pretty darn fast to do so once the Chinese developed a taste for its salivary secretions.

Why does it have to be the sea swallow? What is wrong with a garden variety bird's nest? One theory is that this sea swallow feeds on a particular kind of seaweed, dissolving the seaweed in its saliva to form its own special secretion. Incidentally, no less a biologist than Charles Darwin had studied this question. I suspect that a number of bird species would produce secretions every bit as good as the vaunted sea swallow. Indeed, with the prices of swallow's nest as they are, the gourmet ordering swallow's nest is always in fear as to whether he or she is going to get the real McCoy. There are apparently fakes made with gelatin. Personally, I wouldn't be surprised if half of the swallow's nest served in New York City comes from a rubber cement factory in Elizabeth, New Jersey.

Now for a quick language lesson even though you probably won't see swallow's nest 燕 窩 on the menu of your neighborhood Chinese restaurant. I will just tell you enough so you can spot it if you see it. See the four telltale dots at the bottom of the first character; you may remember them from the various early chapters as denoting the tail of a bird, the tail of a fish, or the feet of a quadruped. See the two wings, ⟩ and ⟨ , on the two sides of the character? Perhaps the picture is a little bit clearer in the archaic form 燕 . As for the second character, meaning "nest," you need only notice the roof radical ⼧ that appears in characters connected with housing. Remember how a pig under the roof signifies "home," a woman under the roof, "contentment"? Interestingly, swallow's nest is never written in Chinese generically as "bird's nest," as it is translated into English on menus. On the other hand, shark's fin is rendered simply as "fish fin" on Chinese menus: it is only in English that shark is specified.

So how did the sea swallow's nest come to be a luxury import in the Ming dynasty?

Ming court ladies in their ennui, not unlike their latter-day counterparts, had always clamored for imported exotica. According to some historians, the rise of the Ottoman Empire had cut off the normal flow of luxury items from the West to China through the Silk Route. Another motivation was the search for the unicorn, of all things. At that time, Arab traders presented a giraffe to the imperial court. The appearance of an exotic animal was interpreted by court astrologers as an auspicious sign from Heaven indicating the benevolence and wisdom of the emperor's rule. This was further colored by a power struggle between different court factions: an increase in the emperor's prestige would strengthen one faction at the expense of another. Even more important, the Ming emperor at the time was worried that a pretender to the throne was not yet dead but somehow in hiding in the south seas. He wanted to send his trusted eunuch Zheng He to find out.

For all these reasons—the desire for imported luxuries, the need for a unicorn to enhance the emperor's prestige, and the fear that a pretender might be at large—a mighty armada under Zheng's command was organized.

Zheng was an exceedingly capable navigator and from 1405 to 1433 led seven voyages of discovery, reaching as far as East Africa. Incidentally, Zheng was ethnically Wei and a Moslem. The historical-minded tourist can still find temples and statues erected in his honor throughout southern Asia. The Chinese colonization of Southeast Asia also started with these voyages.

Anyway, one of the "exotic treasures" brought back by Zheng was the swallow's nest.

This brings us to an interesting point of culinary history. Did the natives of Southeast Asia already know how to consume the swallow's nests? There appears to be evidence to support this. Or did Zheng merely like the translucence and pretty shape of the nests?

A Chinese writer once remarked with bitter wit that when the Europeans went on their chronologically later voyages of discoveries they gained entire continents, while the Chinese merely discovered the swallow's nest. Quite naturally, the comparison and contrast between European and Chinese history is a favorite topic of discussion among Chinese intellectuals. While the European voyages were driven by the need for spices and commerce, the Chinese voyages were motivated by mere court intrigue. There is, of course, also an accident of geography: the Pacific is much wider than the Atlantic. But most important, once the Ming emperor decided to call an end to these voyages, they were over. Power in China has always been concentrated. By contrast, the Europeans were forced to compete with each other. With the monolithic dominance of East Asia by China, there was a disastrous lack of competition. Instead, a sense of self-sufficiency prevailed. The Celestial Empire felt it lacked for nothing. In truth, there was preciously little Zheng could have brought back besides the swallow's nest.

The unicorn was not found. The pretender was surely dead. The court ladies were thrilled by the new banquet delicacy. No more sea expeditions set forth, and the Empire once again closed upon itself. Everything was as before, and the Chinese civilization inexorably lumbered slowly down the road to stagnation and decay. The tragedy continues.

ALL BANQUETS
MUST
COME TO
AN END

THE CHINESE HAVE a saying that "there is no banquet under heaven that does not end." I have enticed you into learning some Chinese by chatting with you about the food. Through food and language we have had a glimpse of Chinese culture and history. It has been fun, but all good things must come to an end.

Some of you are happy that you can now pick out a character here and there on your Chinese menu. A few of you are more ambitious and will want to go on. You are asking, how difficult is it to learn to read Chinese?

How easy is it? you should have asked.

Americans are fascinated by how many characters there are. Popular articles, in the mode of "Believe it or not," are always quoting some huge numbers. These numbers are exceedingly misleading. For instance, it has been estimated that some fifty thousand characters existed at one time or another, but the vast majority are archaic and obsolete. Basic literacy is defined variously as mastery of one thousand to one thousand five hundred characters. A well-educated Chinese may know three or four thousand characters, while an exceedingly learned scholar may get up to the six-thousand level.

More relevant is how often Chinese words occur in contemporary material such as newspapers, magazines, novels, nonfiction books, and so on. The result of such a word count is shown in a table on page 300. According to this table, if you know ten words, then you can read almost 20 percent of a typical Chinese text. This is, of course, extremely misleading since the first ten words are all words like "I", "you," and "of." But notice that if you can learn a hundred words, you get almost 50 percent of the written text! I think this is enough to know roughly what the writer is talking about. If you can handle a thousand words, then you are probably almost there, with 80 percent comprehension.

In English we have compound words such as "seafood." If you know "sea" and "food," then you can readily guess what "seafood" means. But while compound words are relatively rare in English, they are ubiquitous in Chinese. A survey of contemporary written texts shows that more than 70 percent of Chinese words are compounds, that is, made out of two or more characters. Words consisting of just one character comprise less than 30 percent.

I have already given you several examples as we went along. Perhaps you remember 肉 感 = flesh feel = sexy. Or 點 心 = dot heart = snacks. Granted, it is not entirely obvious to guess that "dot heart" means "snacks." Still, the number of characters you have to learn is far less than what you might have imagined.

To give you a better idea of how words are formed, let me give you a rather miscellaneous collection of compound words. (Notice that you have already met many of the characters involved.) 明 白 = bright white = understand, that is, a word consisting of the character for "bright" followed by the character for "white" means "to understand";

文 明　language bright = civilized

說 明　say bright = explain

結 果　form fruit = result

運 動　carry move = sports

動 物　move thing = animal

學 問　learn ask = knowledge

大 學　big learn = university

化 學　transform learn = chemistry

担 心　burden heart = worried

熱 心　hot heart = enthusiastic

馬 上　horse up = immediately

體 貼　body stick = quality of a spouse who gives tender, loving care

These compound words often give fascinating insights into the culture. For example, an educator may note with satisfaction that the word for "knowledge" or "scholarship" underlines the importance of asking questions. The word for "result" reveals the agrarian roots of the language. You see that when the Chinese want to do something immediately, they jump on their horses. Some words are hilarious, such as "body stick." (The character for "stick" is precisely the same as that in "pot sticker.")

You may also note with satisfaction that in the characters you don't know you can in most cases make out the radical: you can see the fruit on the tree, the mouth in "to ask," the child staggering under the weight of authority in "learning," and the flesh in the spouse's sticky body.

Naturally, concepts that arose in relatively recent times, such as diplomacy, are all represented by compound words. The difference is that in English new concepts were often accommodated by borrowing: a scholar would recognize, for instance, that diplomacy comes from the Greek word for a piece of folded paper, suggesting the document accrediting the official. (In Greek, the word is related to "double"; double, diplomacy, very apt indeed: double-dealing, double-talking diplomats?) In contrast, in Chinese "diplomacy" is represented by two simple characters 外 交 , meaning "outside" and "interact," respectively, which any literate Chinese would recognize.

Chinese also contains a large class of compound words whose individual characters mean more or less the same thing. The characters are simply strung together for emphasis. An example is 朋 友 for "friend": both 朋 and 友 can be used individually to mean "friend." You have already seen the character 友 describing two hands pointing in the same direction. How good are you as a linguist? Try to figure out 朋 .

Remember the flesh radical 月 ? Aha, two pieces of flesh placed side by side. That also makes a friend. Interesting, eh?

Of course, if someone says, "I will do it on a horse 馬 上 ," it is not immediately obvious what he means. Does it mean he will do it sloppily? Usually, one can figure out the meaning of compound words, perhaps with a hint from the context, but in this case, there is admittedly an ambiguity. Nevertheless, once you are told what "on a horse" means, you are probably all set.

Analogously, in English we can say "at once" or "right away" instead of "immediately," and it is a heck of a lot easier to learn "at once" or "right away" than to learn "immediately." The point is that Chinese is a language full of words more like "at once" than "immediately."

This preponderance of compound words is good news for you would-be students of Chinese. Learning a thousand words probably means learning no more than five hundred characters.

So, it is not that bad!

Indeed, we have already encountered about two hundred characters in this book. To be sure, you couldn't possibly remember all two hundred from a casual reading of this book. Besides, many of the characters and words mentioned are culinary and rank low in frequency of occurrence, but it does give you an idea that learning five hundred characters is not that tough!

How is that for encouragement?

CUMULATIVE FREQUENCY OF OCCURRENCE OF CHINESE WORDS

Number of Words	% Cumulative Frequency
10	19.81
50	37.49
100	47.07
500	69.23
1000	79.07
2000	88.38
3000	93.14
4000	96.08
5000	98.09
6000	99.59

The meaning of this table is as follows: If you know the 500 most common Chinese words, for instance, then you can read 69.23% of typical reading materials, say a newspaper. This table is taken from C. Y. Suen.

HOW TO EXERCISE YOUR ARM AND THROAT WHILE DRINKING

As I EXPLAINED in Chapter 3, drinking at Chinese banquets is often accompanied by the "fist-guessing" game, particularly among businessmen. The two "contestants" swing their fists and on the third swing each extends out a certain number of fingers, from zero to five, while at the same time yelling out his guess of the total number of fingers extended. Whoever guesses correctly wins.

In this game, one does not yell out plain numbers, but certain stock phrases expressing good wishes. As I mentioned earlier, these stock phrases are one aspect of folk culture that has gradually disappeared, especially in the overseas Chinese community. I learned these phrases from my father, a businessman and lifelong contestant in the fist-guessing game, and I would like to explain them in detail here.

As you will see, these phrases are rich with folk culture and references to traditional Chinese life. I am also going to have lots of fun with the etymology. Now that you have gotten through "Swallowing Clouds" you are practically an expert, so I am really going to bite into it. At the same time, this will give you an opportunity to learn the numbers in Chinese.

Obviously, the total number of fingers extended in the game can only range from zero to ten. There is a phrase associated with each of these numbers.

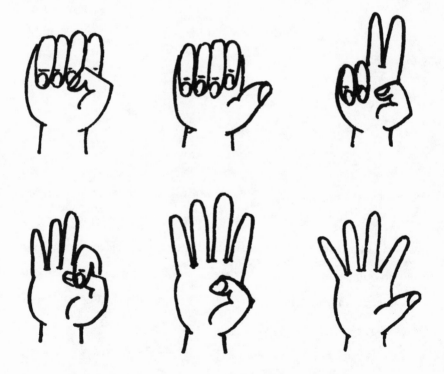

Hand gestures used to represent the numbers zero through five in the "fist-guessing" game.

Zero:　　對 宝 拳　　= Treasured fists facing off.

You can see the hand radical　扌　in the third character, meaning "fist." We have already met this character in connection with tai chi chuan (Chapter 16), as in "treasured fists." It is characteristic of Chinese usage to exaggerate and to describe any fine object as "treasured." Phrases such as "your treasured daughter" are common in polite conversation. The etymology of the character for "treasure"　宝　derives from the character for "jade"　玉　. It shows the jade kept in a safe house. (Remember the roof radical　宀　?) The character for jade was originally　王　, showing three pieces of jade threaded together by a string. How did these jade pieces acquire the dot in the modern form? Herein lies a tale of linguistic confusion between two characters.

The character meaning "king" was also written as　王　, based on the abstraction that the king, represented by the vertical line, was the one who brought together heaven, earth, and men, represented by the three horizontal lines. Imagine this group of ragtag cavemen falling to the ground in front of you. Hail the great leader, the king! To them, you were not only a leader of men, but also one who could shelter them from the powers of nature and commune with the spirits in heaven. Pictographs can teach us about the minds of primitive men.

To resolve the confusion, scribes put a dot on the jade. Amateur etymologists may imagine the dot to be a blemish—it's easy to make up theories. Later, the character for king also acquired a top part and became　皇　. The ancient form　王　, however, is still used.

The importance of jade in Chinese arts and crafts is, of course, well known. The Chinese consider the jade the noblest of all stones and attribute to it five virtues: benevolence, justice, wisdom, bravery, and cleanliness. I think that it is significant that the character is so simple. The simplicity suggests antiquity.

One: 一 定 恭 喜 你 = Definitely congratulating you.

The character for "one" is certainly easy to learn. It is just 一 , as we have already seen in Chapter 8, for example. The etymology of the second character is peculiar. The roof radical 宀 may give you pause. How does the house come in again? We have to begin with 止 , a character representing the foot. With a really vivid pictorial imagination, you may be able to see the heel, the ankle, and the front of the foot. (No, the toes are not shown.) This gives rise to the character 正 showing the foot coming to a line and stopping. This character acquires the abstract meaning of staying within bounds and hence of propriety, and it is so used in modern Chinese. Now get it? With propriety reigning in the house, as depicted in the character 定 , things are settled, ordered, and definite, rather than random and chaotic. Going from 定 to the form 定 is a calligrapher's improvement, making the character look livelier.

The word for "definitely" 一 定 is an example of a compound word (recall the Epilogue). Why is the number one associated with the meaning of definitely? This compound word is actually an abbreviation of a standard phrase literally meaning "With one word this is settled" and is used in sealing business deals and other contractual arrangements. It is the Chinese equivalent of the Western "With a handshake this is settled." In Confucian ethics, breaking a verbal promise is regarded as a terrible breach of honor.

The word for "congratulation" 恭 喜 is also a compound of

two characters. The first character means "to respect." I just want to point out to you that it contains a rather distorted version of the heart radical 心 . See it? It's 小 . You know how certain English words are invariably misspelled. Well, some Chinese characters are also invariably miswritten and the character for respect is one of them. It feels unnatural to write non-symmetrically, with one dot on the left side and two dots on the right. The distorted heart also looks so much like the character for small 小 that even the well-educated would often write 恭 (sic). Thus are characters changed. Future etymologists will be puzzled by why respect should be small.

The other character 喜 in the word for congratulation means "joy." Thus, congratulation amounts to paying respect at a joyous occasion. The top half represents a (barely recognizable) drum complete with stand. The bottom half is a mouth, presumably singing. Joy, joy to the world! Sing to the drumbeat. In some Chinese restaurants you might see screens or wall pieces decorated with this character repeated twice and joined together, thus 囍 . This is the traditional symbol for marriage, two joys joined together. The screens are used for wedding banquets. In fact, the evening after I wrote this, I went to dinner and saw this double-joy character on my chopsticks.

Two: 兩 相 好 = A couple getting on well.

Given that the character for "one" is 一 , you may have guessed that the character for "two" is 二 . You guessed right. However, in Chinese as in English, the word "couple" often replaces "two." The character 兩 means "a couple," and has its origin in two weights balancing as they hang from a simple scale 秝 . Indeed, this same character is also used to indicate a unit of weight, either the Chinese ounce or the English ounce. In modern American usage, the term "a couple" suggests a male-female pair. In the Chinese phrase, there is no such suggestion, and in this context, a couple of friends or business associates is perhaps indicated more often than not.

The character 相 has both a concrete meaning, "to watch" or "to inspect," and an abstract meaning, "mutual." The concrete meaning is easy to understand if you recognize the wood radical 木 and the eye radical 目 . (Remember the rotated eye ⟋⟍ → 目 ?) Somebody is watching you from behind a tree. Obviously, in the phrase 兩 相 好 , the abstract meaning of mutual is being used. You may recognize the third character as the character for "good." See the woman radical 女 on its left? Literally, we have "two mutual good," that is, two persons being good to each other.

How did the abstraction of mutuality come about from putting together wood and eye? A good etymological puzzle here! The best theory is that it represents a witticism: the characters 木 and 目 are both pronounced like "moo." They share something in common but make quite an odd couple. Some ancient scribe thought that he was really funny. See if you can make up a better theory!

Three: 三 星 高 照 = Three stars shining high above.

Surely you could have guessed the meaning of the first character, and the second character, "star," was described in an endnote to Chapter 7. It represents the essence of matter rising up out of the ground and crystallizing into stars. Its lower half is the character for "alive" or "raw," as in raw fish porridge. The third character, meaning "high," is an architectural construction. It comes from a watchtower high above the city wall 高 . Finally, you may also notice the sun radical in the fourth character, meaning "to shine." The four dots at the bottom represent, as we have seen before, a distortion of the character for fire 火 .

Okay, but what are the three stars? They are not quite the stars of the modern astrophysicist, but the stars of 福 "happiness and good fortune," of 祿 "a good income," and of 壽 "longevity." You have seen the character for "good fortune" (it's the one that rhymes with "bat") and the character for "longevity" already.

There is also a variant phrase. Instead of "three stars shining high above," you can also yell out " 三 元 及 第 ," meaning "passing all three exams." No, these are not the SAT, the Achievement Test, and the GRE, but the imperial examinations at the village level, the municipal level, and the court level. If you passed the exam at the village level, you could go to the big city to take the exam at the next level and so on. Incidentally, this phrase is for obvious reasons now archaic and few Chinese, even those who can yell it out while half-drunk, would know its meaning.

Four: 四 季 發 財 = Acquiring wealth during all four seasons.

You met the character for "four" in Sichuan 四 川 , "the province of four streams." The etymology of the characters for four, six, and eight reveals something about how the ancients viewed the numbers. The ancient symbol for four 𝍪 shows an object divided evenly into two halves and thus embodies the general concept of even numbers, rather than the specific concept of four. Four is evidently the most prominent even number after two itself.

Okay, suppose you are a smart cavewoman inventing characters. What would you now write for six? Lots of possibilities of course! The ancient Chinese actually decided just to add a dot on top of the symbol for four, thus ⽥ . Now as you keep writing this, the two downstrokes would often stick out, so that six would look like 𠈓 , and eventually 六 .

The character for "eight" ハ is obtained simply from six by lopping off its head, leaving only its legs.

Thus, the characters for four, six, and eight all derive from the concept of even numbers and pictorially they are all symmetric between left and right. I think that the ancient concept of even numbers being special must be to some extent universal. Witness the use of odd, also meaning strange, to describe the non-even numbers in English. You will see presently that the characters for five, seven, and nine are all not symmetric between left and right.

Evidently, the characters for the three simplest numbers one 一 , two 二 , and three 三 were fixed before this concept of even and odd, and the associated concept of left-right symmetry. Etymologically, it is also obvious that the concept of zero came much later, as is well known to historians of mathematics. (The Romans, for example, did not have a symbol for zero.) The character for "zero" 零 is significantly more complicated. As an accomplished etymologist by now, you must be puzzled by the appearance of the rain radical 雨 . So was I until I discovered that 零 once meant a barely noticeable light drizzle. It was conscripted into service when a character for zero was needed.

So much for the numbers. The etymology of the rest of this phrase also tells us quite a bit about the ancients. The character for "season" 季 , with its combination of the crop radical 禾 (remember from chapter 9 the picture of a stalk of grain?) and the child radical 子 , has an obvious agrarian derivation.

While the character for season tells us about agriculture, the character for "wealth" 財 tells us about the origin of money. The right half in this character was a later phonetic addition. The original character for wealth was simply 貝 , representing a picture 貝 of a marine snail called the cowrie. The cowrie's shell, humped and beautifully colored, was once used as international currency from Southeast Asia to India and East Africa. Indeed, its use in the Pacific Islands persisted into modern times. The word "cowrie" itself comes from ancient Sanskrit. Around the time of the Qin dynasty (221–207 B.C.) the Chinese wised up and no longer accepted shells for payment. (It was the end of the shell game.) Incidentally, the Chinese were also the first to realize the pointlessness of carrying heavy bags of metal coins around. With the burgeoning of commerce and the emergence of large trading houses, letters of credit and then paper money were invented as a prospering merchant class emerged during the Song dynasty (as I discussed in Chapter 7). It is a tragic irony that there are now government officials in China who barely understand what credit and banking mean.

The character 貝 for "wealth" serves as the radical for a whole group of words having to do with money and commerce. Look back at the Ming dynasty illustration in Chapter 13 showing the Stove God and his assistant taking note of the scholar's immoral behavior. You will see in the inscription the character 賬 meaning "a business account." (The right half is a phonetic element.) The scholar's good and bad behavior was recorded into the Stove God's account book as credits and debits.

Finally, on to the third character 發 . Let's break it apart and examine the 弓 hidden inside. See the Chinese bow? 弓 Indeed, 弓 is the modern character for "bow." The top part 癶 is a picture of two feet pointing in opposite directions. By extension it came to mean "separation." The rest 殳 is a totally distorted picture of an arrow. A bow and an arrow separating—we have here a verb describing the shooting of arrows. This militaristic term lingers on in modern usage in connection with the firing of guns and cannons, but it has acquired a more important meaning. The notion of the bow and arrow separating suggested to an ancient scribe two parts of an expanding object separating, and thus the character has acquired the more abstract meaning of "expansion." It is also used in cooking to describe soaking in water of dried bok choy for instance. These dried food items soak up water and expand.

Instead of yelling out "Four!" you yell out "May your wealth expand during all four seasons!"

The character for "expansion" is, for obvious reasons, a favorite of businessmen. In Cantonese, it is pronounced something like "fat." As you wander around Chinatown, if you see a store whose transliterated name contains the word "Fat," you have a good chance of finding the character 發 . In fact, if you live in a big city with a Chinatown, you may have heard the phrase "Gung Hay Fat Choy" as the Chinese greeting for "Happy New Year." "Fat choy" represents the Cantonese pronunciation of 發 財 , "expansion of wealth," while "gung hay" represents the Cantonese pronunciation of 恭 喜 , "congratulations," a word we just met a little earlier. As a new year begins, the Chinese tell each other, "Congratulations on the expansion of your wealth"—a wish couched as an assertion of fact.

Now that you have learned the ancients used cowrie shells 貝 for money, remember the character for treasure 宝 , showing the jade pieces inside the house? Some busybody scribe couldn't leave well enough alone and decided to cram in some shells. By this process, the character for treasure became more complicated so that it is now 寶 . In the simplification campaign promoted in China, a garage sale was held on this character: all that extra junk got thrown out again. The simplified character is once again 宝 . After all, shells are not worth that much anymore.

You can find the character for treasure (usually in its more complicated, more modern form) on restaurant menus quite readily: there are dishes named Eight Treasures Stir-Fried, Eight Treasures Duck, and Eight Treasures Sweet Rice, for example. I mentioned another example in passing in Chapter 15. For some reason, dishes are always named as containing eight, never seven or nine, treasures, even though the actual number may not be eight. The term "eight treasures" is an exaggeration of course. For example, in Eight Treasures Stir-fried the treasures are typically pork, dried shrimp, bamboo shoot, carrot, cucumber, dried pressed bean curd, peas, and peanuts. You may very well have had this dish without realizing it.

Five: 五 金 魁 = Five golden monsters.

The Chinese believe the devil to be pointy-headed, drawn as ⊕ . Add two legs and a tail and we have 鬼 , evolving into the modern form 鬼 , meaning "devil," "ghost," "goblin," and the like. As a radical it gives rise to a group of characters associated with monsters. In particular, 魅 means "monstrous goblin."

Well, the phrase 五 金 魁 actually means "to place in the top five in the imperial examination." What is the connection with five golden monsters?

For some reason, the god of scholarship is portrayed as a monstrously ugly man, pock-marked and crippled in one leg, sometimes with protuberances coming out of his head. How the god of scholarship comes to be so monstrously ugly is a complicated story that scholars have yet to unravel completely. According to one theory, there once lived an uncommonly ugly man who placed first in the imperial exam. Apparently, because of his features, he was compelled to concentrate on his studies and excel.

In Old China, the imperial exam provided essentially the only route to fame and fortune, and thus the god of scholarship was widely venerated. Scholars would make offerings to statues or paintings of their favorite god, portrayed traditionally as standing on one leg since he was crippled. In one hand he holds a writing brush and in the other an inkwell.

Why the association with the number five? You were entitled to high offices only if you placed among the top five. During the proclamation of the exam result, the imperial announcer would call out the names of those who passed starting from number six down. With this strange system, if your name was not called you could either have failed or placed in the top five. Now came the big part of the show. Everyone associated with the exam, from the examiner to the servants and cooks, would hold up candles. In a formal ceremony, the names of the first five scholars were announced in reverse order. These five were known as the "five golden monsters," apparently because the God of Scholarship was monstrous looking.

To be complete, let me also explain that the character for "gold" 金 comes from a pictograph of a gold mine: a shack 亼 on the earth 土 in which gold nuggets 𡉉 are found, thus 𨤾 . If you go back to Chapter 1, you will find that it appears as a metal radical in the character for "pot," as in fire pot.

Six: 六 六 順 利 = Everything is going smoothly.

The literal translation here is "six-six smooth profit." Why six-six? Want to venture a guess? It comes from throwing a pair of dice and having both turn up sixes.

You know the two parts of the character for "smooth": on the left 川 , a stream (as in Sichuan), and on the right, 頁 , the head (remember how the hair was left out and the legs added?). A plausible theory is that it describes the smooth movement of a boat with its head pointed downstream. Perhaps you can think up another theory.

The character for profit is again agrarian: the knife 刂 (it is a distortion of the knife character described in Interlude 4) is applied to the crops 禾 . The harvest naturally came to mean "profit."

Seven: 七 巧 圖 = Loosely, the lovely tableau of the seventh day of the seventh month.

This phrase really requires an explanation. One of the major festivals on the traditional Chinese calendar occurs on the seventh day of the seventh month: it's the lover's festival. On that night, lovers hope to reunite. It's the day that travelers try hard to get home to their spouses.

The festival is based on the tale of eternal love between the Weaver Girl 織 女 and the Cowherd Boy 牛 郎 , perhaps the best known and most enduring of all Chinese folk-tales. (See the silk radical 糸 in the character for "to weave," the character for "woman," and the character for "bull" or "cow"?) *The Book of Songs,* that collection of folk ballads compiled around 600 B.C., already contained a song devoted to it, but the tale's origin must go back to the very beginning of the agrarian economy.

It is revealing about Chinese culture that there are two versions to this tale, a more-or-less official version set down by Confucian scholars and a popular version handed down in the oral tradition and set down in popular writing. First, the version chronicled in more official texts. The daughter of the Celestial Emperor was a virtuous and diligent girl who spent much of her time weaving. Her father arranged a marriage with the boy who worked the celestial herd of cattle. The two were so much in love that they spent their entire time dallying "in the land of warmth and tenderness," to use the Chinese phrase for such things. The field and the loom were left idle. Such sloth so incurred the wrath of her father the Celestial Tyrant (my name for this guy) that he created what Westerners called the Milky Way and what the Chinese called the Silver River, a river separating the Weaver Girl and the Cowherd Boy. They were allowed to come together only once a year, on the seventh day of the seventh month. On that day each year, a flock of magpies would form a bridge across the Silver River. Stepping on the magpies, the Weaver Girl gets to see her husband for that one day.

It's bad news to be married to the daughter of the Celestial Emperor.

The Confucian severity and didactic message come across loud and clear. In an agrarian society the men are to work in the fields and the women to weave at home. You've got to have a work ethic if you want to prosper.

The popular version is more colorful and less didactic. Once upon a time, there was a celestial maiden wonderfully skilled in the art of weaving. Indeed, the ever-changing color and texture of the sky were but reflections of the celestial fabric coming out of her loom. She was the youngest and prettiest of seven sisters. Meanwhile, on earth among the mortals was a young boy. He, too, was the youngest of several brothers. After their parents died, his older brothers and their wives were mean to him. In dividing up the family inheritance, they conspired to give him only a scrawny old bull. Our hero was thus reduced to a life of poverty with only the old bull for companionship.

One day, the old bull opened his mouth and said to our hero in perfectly fluent Chinese: "Hey, listen, some celestial maidens are planning to come down to earth today to take a bath in the river. If you could sneak up and steal their clothes while they are bathing, they will be stuck here on earth and will have no choice but to marry you." Our hero hid among the reeds and sure enough, seven maidens came and bathed in the river. But as he tried to steal their clothes, they took alarm and he managed to get only the clothes of the youngest maiden.

And thus the Weaver Girl and the Cowherd Boy fell in love. They settled down to the bliss of married life and had two lovely children. Alas, their good times did not last forever. The Celestial Emperor got wind of this breach of the rules of the Celestial Kingdom. Celestial beings were strictly forbidden to mingle with mortals! He dispatched celestial soldiers to forcibly drag the Weaver Girl back to heaven.

When the Cowherd Boy came home from the fields to find his beloved wife gone, he was devastated. The old bull spoke again and said, "Master, to go up to heaven and to try to get your wife back, you would have to slaughter me and wrap yourself in my skin. With my skin around you, you will be able to ascend into heaven." Tearfully, our hero insisted that he didn't have the heart to put his devoted companion to death, whereupon the bull rammed his head into a tree and killed himself. With his sorrow now compounded, the Cowherd Boy skinned the bull. He balanced on his shoulder a pole carrying two buckets in the manner of the Chinese peasant and put his two children in the buckets. Wrapping the bull's skin around him, he rushed up to heaven and gave hot pursuit to the celestial soldiers making away with his wife.

Just as he was getting near, the younger sister of the Celestial Emperor, the Dowager of the West (the Wicked Witch of the West?) threw down her silver hairpin between the pursuer and the pursued. The hairpin turned into a Silver River, separating the Weaver Girl and the Cowherd Boy.

Faced with the roiling waters of the Silver River but possessed with an all-powerful love, the Cowherd Boy steeled himself with determination. He said to his children, "Let us bail the river dry with these two buckets." And so they set to taking out the water of the river bucket by bucket.

Such devotion and love moved even the Celestial Emperor. He decreed that once a year, on the seventh day of the seventh month, magpies should form a bridge across the Silver River allowing the lovers and the family to be reunited.

You like this version better? Imagine if you will, under the dark sky of the seventh day and seventh month, in villages all over old China, lovers telling each other this tale, the elders telling the children, the wives telling their husbands. When they get to the part about love moving even the Celestial Emperor, there's not a dry eye in the house. They point to the sky, clear and sparkling with stars at this time of year, and show each other the two groups of stars separated by the Silver River. (Well, if you must know, it's the Aquila and Lyra constellations on the two sides of the Milky Way. One group of three stars, more or less in a line, represents the Cowherd Boy and his two kids. On the other side, with some imagination, you may be able to make out a group of stars resembling the shuttle of the Weaver Girl.)

This beloved tale has generated a variety of folk customs, as diverse as

the regions of China. Typically, there are offerings of food, to wish the
Weaver Girl and the Cowherd Boy well. Since the Weaver Girl is skillful
with threads, there are also contests among the women, typically in thread-
ing needles. Young girls listening carefully may even hear the love murmurs
of the Celestial Couple. In some regions, people believe that as the Weaver
Girl walks over the bridge of magpies, feathers flutter down. In other regions, the feathers somehow become bridge stones. (The Weaver Girl must
be pretty heavy-footed!) Villagers even say that if you ever found such a
stone, it would be made of solid gold.

Love poems throughout the centuries allude to this story. A favorite
saying among literate lovers who cannot be together comes from a Song
dynasty (960–1279) poem based on the story: "If our feelings are truly
everlasting, what does it matter that we cannot see each other day in and
day out?"

Folktales speak to us through their universality and power. I am particularly fascinated by the common themes in the folk-tales of different cultures. This business of sneaking up on bathing maidens is certainly standard
practice in Greek mythology and it must reflect a commonplace in rural life
everywhere. Women, and particularly young maidens, must bathe occasionally in rivers, and stealing their clothes is surely a universally enjoyed diver-
sion among young men. The youngest son who gets cheated out of his
inheritance is of course also a standard character in Grimm's fairy tales, not
to mention talking animals.

A belief in a celestial kingdom whose beings would occasionally mingle
with mortals also recurs in many cultures. In Chinese folktales, it is often
implied that celestial beings want to go down to "the world of many flowers"
to have some fun, that celestial life is not exciting enough. The love be-

tween a celestial maiden and a mortal youth may also reflect the impossible love between a rich man's daughter and a poor villager.

Another reality of village life reflected in the story is the poor man's difficulty in finding a wife, again a universal in agrarian societies, particularly in Old China where the rich could take several wives. Obviously their longing produced the myths of celestial maidens coming to earth. Having one's wife dragged away by soldiers was also not a rarity in a time when despotic barons and landlords terrorized whole villages.

A theme rather characteristic of Chinese culture is that one can accomplish anything with sheer determination. That the Cowherd Boy and his children would attempt to bail the river dry is never derided as foolish. Rather, it is considered moving precisely because it is foolhardy. In another famous Chinese tale, that of "The Foolish Gentleman Who Attempts to Move a Mountain," the protagonist announces to the village that he will keep at it day after day, shovel by shovel, and after his death, his children will carry on, and after their death, their children, and so on, and surely one day the mountain will be moved. The message is conveyed in another tale told to children, that of "Young Mencius Meeting the Woman with the Iron Rod." Young Mencius preferred play to study. One day he ran into a woman rubbing an iron rod against another piece of iron. The boy asked the woman what she was doing, and she replied that she was determined to make a pin. Mencius was inspired to apply the same determination to his studies. All very Confucian!

The story of the Weaver Girl and the Cowherd Boy also reflects the feeling that Chinese villagers have for their plough animals. Chinese tales are full of farmers who didn't have the heart to slaughter their aging bulls. This particular tale certainly plays up the theme of loyalty and devotion.

I can go on and on, but I'd better move on to eight.

Eight: 八 仙 過 海 = Eight Immortals crossing the sea.

You have seen the second character, "the immortals with no responsibility" (remember the men in the mountain?), and the fourth character, "the sea," with its water radical. You may not recall the third character, meaning "to cross," but you may recognize the movement radical 辶 .

We have already met one of the Eight Immortals, Lu Dong-bing. Remember him? He is the prankster who hit the goddess Guan-yin with a gold coin and then, when pursued by the Thunder God, turned himself into a fly and hid inside the brush of a scholar, causing the poor guy to flunk all his exams. He and his cohorts have emerged as the people's favorites. Most Chinese statuettes (you know, the kind made of porcelain that they sell in antique shops), represent one of the Eight Immortals.

A particularly popular Immortal, Quan Zhong-li, is portrayed as a fat, bare-bellied man holding a fan. Sound familiar? If you have ever wandered around in Chinatown gift shops, you have probably seen him, often affectionately called by his given name Zhong-li. There is a story associated with the fan. One day, while out walking, Zhong-li came across a woman dressed in widow's garb who was fanning her husband's grave vigorously. She explained that her late husband had implored her not to remarry until the soil on his grave had dried. The jovial Zhong-li offered the woman his help. Taking the fan, he mumbled a magic spell and fanned the soil dry instantly. The happy woman rushed off, leaving Zhong-li with the fan. When Zhong-li sauntered home, his wife asked him where he got the fan. Upon hearing what happened, Zhong-li's wife became extremely indignant at the faithlessness of the happy widow. The prankish Zhong-li decided to play a trick on his wife. Casting a spell on himself, he suddenly dropped dead. After he was duly buried, he took on another form and turned himself into a dashing young gallant. As a young gallant, he went to court the widow of the late and lamented Zhong-li and soon managed to get her to marry him. He then told her that he wanted to exhume her late husband to make a magic potion out of his brain. She agreed to it. When the coffin was opened, to the woman's horror, the corpse popped back to life. Ha, ha, fooled you!

It's bad news to be married to an Immortal.

The single female Immortal among the eight is a historical person who lived in the seventh century A.D. Daughter of a shopkeeper in a small town in Hunan province, she ate a magic peach and achieved immortality. In another version, she went to great pains to find bamboo shoots for her ailing mother and thus achieved immortality. She is portrayed floating on a lotus petal and holding a whisk used to brush away dust. You may have seen her, too.

There is also a child Immortal, the nephew of the famous scholar Han Yu, who lived in the ninth century. Somehow the Immortal Lu Dong-bing (the prankster who caused that luckless scholar to flunk all his exams) was taking care of this kid and took him up to the Celestial Kingdom to play high up in a peach tree. (Remember the Peaches of Immortality the Monkey King ate and the longevity peaches served at the end of birthday banquets?) You probably wouldn't want to have this Lu as a babysitter. The kid fell and would have plunged to his death had he not managed to take a bite of a peach. He instantly became immortal. Usually portrayed with a flute, this boy Immortal is a patron of musicians.

Another unmistakable Immortal you might see in an antique store is Li Tie-guai, literally Li with the iron crutch. You can't miss him because he is dressed in rags and holds a crutch in one hand and a gourd in the other. In fact, Li has not always been a cripple in rags. He was a magician who mastered the out-of-body experience that some late twentieth-century Californians are fervently striving for. While his spirit roamed the universe, he would leave his physical body in the care of his disciple. Once he was gone for a particularly long time. The disciple became impatient; he burned the body and went off, no doubt to follow another guru. When Li came back, he found that his body was gone. Frantically searching for another body, he came upon an old crippled beggar who had just died. And that's how he got to be a cripple in rags.

Yet another Immortal you may have seen sits backwards on a white mule. This guy really has the parking problem licked. When he gets to where he wants to go, he simply folds the mule up and puts it in his pocket. When he wants to travel again, he takes the mule out and sprinkles some water on it and it comes back to life. And so it goes: as I said earlier, the Chinese Immortals are like the gods in Greek mythology, or Santa Claus.

Once, the Eight Immortals had to cross the sea. They each did it in his or her own way, according to their individual magic powers. This incident gave rise to a lovely proverb, "Eight Immortals crossing the sea, each by his (her) power," reminding us that we all have different talents.

Nine: 快 得 利   = Quickly will obtain profit.

Remember the character for "profit" from the phrase for six?

You may wonder why the character for "quickly" contains the compressed heart radical 忄 . In ancient usage, the character means "happy and cheerful" (and is still so used in some contexts). I suppose a cheerful person does things quickly.

What does the number nine have to do with quickness? This is a hard one, and it was by checking with numerous older Chinese that I found the explanation. The character for "nine," 九 , happens to be pronounced the same as the character 久 meaning "taking a long time." Merchants and businessmen do not like this character because it suggests that it would take a long time to turn a profit. Thus they substituted the character "quickly" or "soon" for nine. This sort of folk thinking (avoidance of a disliked character) is related to the sort of thinking that puts bats everywhere (representing a liked character as often as possible). As far as I know, the Chinese obsession with words as omens does not appear, at least to the same extent, in other cultures.

Ten: 全 家 福 = The entire family encounters good fortune.

"Ten," being the largest number expressible with two hands, is associated with fullness and hence with the entire family. The first character expresses the perfection of jade, without any broken parts, and hence it carries the notion of entirety and completeness. You may recognize the second character, meaning "home." Remember the pig under the roof? The third character is once again that character, rhyming with the character for bats, that let loose all those bats.

In summary, the drinking phrases are (0) "Treasured fists facing off!"; (1) "Definitely I'm going to congratulate you!"; (2) "We two are getting along!"; (3) "May the three stars shine on you!" or "May you pass all three exams!"; (4) "May your wealth expand during all four seasons!"; (5) "May you place in the top five in the imperial exam!"; (6) "May you make profit as smoothly as a pair of dice would turn up two sixes!" (7) "May you be united with your love!"; (8) "Let the Eight Immortals cross the sea to help you!"; (9) "Wishing that you will quickly make a profit!"; and (10) "May your entire family enjoy good fortune!"

As may be expected, while the fist-guessing game is known all over China, the actual phrases used vary from region to region. A well-cadenced phrase in one dialect may not sound as good in another. Also, they differ according to the social class of the drinkers. The set I gave you derived apparently from the merchant and scholar classes.

In the days of old, the more refined upper classes, particularly the literati, had more elaborate drinking games. In a particularly literate game, often portrayed in novels, one person would utter a line of poetry and challenge another person to come up with a matching line. If the group felt that your response was not poetic or apt enough, you would have to drink up.

With the vigorous shaking of the fists, it is easy to speculate that the fist guessing game may have a pugilistic origin. It may go back to really primitive times. If you get knocked down, you have to drink up?

And so I was chatting with my father about the fist-guessing game. Well, people don't want to make so much noise anymore, he said. Perhaps it is the Western influence. Quiet and solemnity at dinner. I said there are drinking games the world over. Yes, my father mused, in the West it's the loser who has to pay for a round of drinks for everybody. In the Chinese tradition, it's the loser who drinks. It is a part of the code of hospitality, a way for the host to urge drinks on his guests and to increase the conviviality.

A FEW
RECIPES

My friends who read the manuscript all said, "Ah, come on, you've got to include some recipes." But I protested. I know how to eat but not how to cook. My editors and publisher all urged me on. "At least include a few," they said.

With an abundance of Chinese cookbooks available, there is no point for me to list here recipes contained in every cookbook. Instead, I will give a few recipes that relate to the text in some way. Some were mentioned in passing. I have also opted for recipes that are particularly easy to make. No classic dish involving forty-seven steps here.

I am not a cook, so these are Gretchen's recipes, and her ultimate source is my mother. Thus, the recipes given here represent some everyday dishes that I grew up with and still eat regularly with pleasure. My mother is from the region around Shanghai, and some of the recipes here reflect the flavor of Shanghainese cooking.

A word about ingredients: I have also limited the recipes to those involving fairly simple ingredients that you can get readily in any Oriental grocery store. I have also given the names of some of the less familiar items in Chinese. Having learned some Chinese characters by reading this book, you should have an advantage now when you walk into a Chinese grocery store.

One friend who read the manuscript wrote in the margins that while reading she kept going to the refrigerator to see what she could cook up. Perhaps this book will inspire the same reaction in some of you.

It was fun writing this section. As Gretchen gave me these recipes, she wanted to test them out to make sure. So I had quite a treat.

Serving size is not a particularly meaningful concept in Chinese cuisine. As you know, a Chinese meal typically consists of many dishes. How many persons a dish will serve obviously depends on the number of dishes to be presented during the meal.

RED-COOKED PORK SHOULDER

SERVES 6–10

Pork shoulder, with skin and rind, about 4–5
    pounds
¼ cup cooking oil
2 tablespoons oyster sauce
Dark or "old" soy sauce
1 tablespoon rice wine (optional)
¼ cup brown sugar
3 or 4 slices of fresh ginger, about ⅛-inch thick
1 star anise   八 角
½ Napa cabbage or 4 dried bok choy

Brown the pork shoulder in hot oil on all sides in a wok. Add the oyster sauce and ½ cup dark soy. If you have rice wine on hand, add some to taste. Turn pork in wok until thoroughly coated with sauce. Add the brown sugar, ginger, star anise, ¼ cup dark soy, and enough water to cover the pork. Bring to a boil, then simmer for about 6 hours. Turn pork occasionally. Add water from time to time so that pork is at least half submerged in liquid. After five hours add Napa cabbage leaves to the stew. Instead of Napa cabbage leaves, you can also add dried bok choy. At the end of 6 hours, there should be about two cups of sauce left. The pork should be so tender that it can be broken apart easily with a spoon.

This type of red-cooking (a lawyer would say brown-cooking) is characteristic of the region around Shanghai. People from other regions often find Shanghainese cooking somewhat on the sweet side. In red-cooking, be sure to use a good quality dark soy sauce, known in Chinese as "old" soy sauce. To make sure you have the right thing, check the label for the character for "old" 老 that we discussed in Chapter 16. To make this dish less fattening, you may want to substitute pork loin. We took this robust and satisfying dish to a potluck at the children's school and it was quite a hit.

Star anise, as the name suggests, is shaped like an eight-pointed star. You may recognize its Chinese name 丿乀 角 as literally "eight horns." (Remember the Eight Immortals from the fist-guessing game and the horn hidden in the character meaning "to analyze" in Interlude 4?)

SMOKED FISH

SERVES 4–6

1–1½ pounds fish, any white-fleshed fish with few
    bones
⅓ cup soy sauce
4 tablespoons sugar
2 whole star anise 丿乀 角
3 scallion stalks, chopped
3 or 4 slices ginger, ⅛-inch thick
cooking oil

Cut the fish into ½-inch-thick pieces. Marinate in a small amount of soy sauce for about 15 minutes.

In a pan, heat mixture of soy sauce, sugar, star anise, chopped scallions, and sliced ginger, and bring to a boil. Turn the flame to low.

Heat two cups of oil in a wok on a separate burner. Put in four or five pieces of fish. The oil should cover the fish completely. Do not disturb. When fish browns, turn over gently. When both sides are brown, pick up the pieces of fish with chopsticks and dip them into the simmering soy sauce marinade. Repeat process.

Smoked fish tastes good with lots of sugar. The marinade should be rather sweet to taste.

SMOKED CHICKEN

SERVES 6–8

1 whole chicken, about 3 pounds
1½ tablespoons salt
1 scallion stalk, chopped into 3-inch pieces
2 slices of ginger, ⅛-inch thick
1 tablespoon uncooked rice
2 tablespoons of loose black tea
1 tablespoon brown sugar

Clean chicken and rub inside and out with salt. Set aside for an hour or so. Steam in a large bowl with chopped scallion and sliced ginger for 20 minutes. Do not overcook. (Poke a chopstick into the thigh. If some blood seeps out, the chicken should be steamed a while longer.) Pour out the juice. It can be saved as a soup stock.

Let the chicken cool. Cut in half.

Place a piece of aluminum foil in a wok. On the aluminum foil place a mixture of uncooked rice, tea leaves, and brown sugar. Place the chicken on a bamboo rack over the wok. (A rack can be improvised by tying some bamboo chopsticks together.) Cover and turn on flame. Smoke from 10 to 15 minutes. Turn over and smoke on each side until the chicken is golden brown. Let cool a bit and slice into 1½-inch slices.

This chicken comes out really juicy and tender. One evening when Gretchen made this, my son Peter didn't want to eat anything else. He wanted to concentrate on the chicken.

You can have fun experimenting with different kinds of tea. Gretchen likes jasmine best.

GAN SI

干 絲 *or* 乾 絲

SERVES 4

4 dried Chinese mushrooms
1 package gan si, or dried bean-curd noodles,
    normally 8 ounces
baking soda
1 slice Chinese ham or Smithfield ham 火 腿
½ cup bamboo shoots
2 cups chicken broth

Soak dried mushrooms in hot water for 15–20 minutes. Cut off stems. While mushrooms are soaking, put *gan si* in boiling water. Put in 1 teaspoon of baking soda. Taste one to see if it is soft. If still hard, put in a bit more soda. Avoid putting in too much soda because the *gan si* will disintegrate. When the *gan si* turns soft, turn off flame and drain in cold water.

Slice the Chinese ham, Chinese mushrooms, and bamboo shoots into fine shreds.

Bring the chicken broth to a boil and turn down to a simmer. Add the drained *gan si* together with the shreds of ham, mushroom, and bamboo.

Gan si provides an interesting change from noodles. It is made by cutting pressed dried bean curd into noodlelike strips. You buy it by the package.

Gan si is written 干 絲 *or* 乾 絲 . You already know from Interlude 4 that the character 絲 means "silk." The character 干 is a simplified version of the character 乾 , meaning "dried." Thus, *gan si* is literally "dried silk." This is of course an exaggeration: *gan si* is thinner than linguine, but thicker than angel hair pasta. Well, they exaggerate in the West too.

The etymology of the character for "dry," which we met in Chapter 16 in connection with "dry" and "wet" foods, is rather convoluted. It is even cosmic.

Remember from Chapter 11 that 干 , derived from a pictograph of the pestle, means "to destroy" or "to offend." What has that to do with dry? Well, the character for a drought, obviously an important character for an agrarian economy, is 旱 , showing the punishing effects of the sun 日 .

Meanwhile, another character was developed showing the sun penetrating into a jungle and drawing up the water vapors from the ground. The primitive picture for a jungle or dense vegetation was 朩 , obtained by adding an overhanging branch or a rambling root to the standard picture for a plant 屮 , which you may remember from Chapter 9. Thus, 𠦝 . We see the vapor 乛 low on the ground 一 . Later, for good measure, another wriggle, representing more vapor was added, so that we end up with 乾 .

Imagine yourself lurking around inside a jungle some ten thousand years ago. The sight of shafts of sunlight penetrating through the overhanging jungle canopy and sucking up into the sky the swirling white clouds off the ground must be awe-inspiring. Thus, this character (pronounced *qian*) came to mean "the cosmic essence of the firmaments" and is associated with mystical power. For instance, the emperor Qian Long (the one who ate his way to becoming the longest-lived Chinese emperor) had this character in his official name.

Later, a scribe casting about for a way to write "dry" thought to himself that the concept was already contained in the character 乾 . He also knew the character for "drought" 旱 . So he merged the two to form 乾 , meaning "dry" and pronounced like *gan*. The pronunciation was of course fixed long before the scribe was even a gleam in his parents' eyes.

How these two characters, differing by only one stroke, tormented schoolchildren for millennia! These days, however, even dictionaries have dropped the extra stroke, and you probably won't find one Chinese in a hundred who would know about the missing stroke. What we now have, however, is the confusion of having a single character 乾 pronounced either *qian* or *gan*, and meaning either the "cosmic essence" or "dry." Dry is dry, but dry was cosmic essence.

After this long etymological excursion into the primeval jungle, let us go back to the cooking of *gan si*. There is no secret to this type of Chinese cooking. The procedure is simple and the result tastes only as good as the ingredients.

It so happened that a few days after Gretchen had made *gan si* we went to a Chinese restaurant. Noting that the menu offered it, we ordered some. The children were eager to play food critic. Compare Mommy's *gan si* with the restaurant's. And kids, you have to tell us why you prefer one to the other. There was no contest of course, but the point is not that one cook is necessarily better than another. The restaurant *gan si* had nothing but a few dried shrimp and some pieces of chopped scallion floating in it.

The advantage of making Chinese food at home is that you won't skimp on the ingredients, and the result will in many cases taste better with little effort.

Dried Chinese mushrooms, which are black and gnarly, should not be confused with straw mushrooms.

JELLYFISH SALAD

SERVES 4–6

Jellyfish, 　海　蜇　皮　, *two rounds*
(*jellyfish comes in large round pieces*)
2 tablespoons sesame oil
4 teaspoons soy sauce
¼ teaspoon vinegar
1 teaspoon sugar
1 cucumber
1 white Chinese radish

Soak the jellyfish in a large bowl of cold water. (If you buy dried jellyfish, you will have to wash it thoroughly and soak it for at least two days, changing the water twice.) Cut into very thin strips. Place strips in a heat-proof bowl and pour boiling water over the jellyfish. Drain after about 10 seconds. Run cold water over the jellyfish and drain.

Make a dressing of sesame oil, soy sauce, vinegar, and sugar. Slice the cucumber and the radish into shreds and mix with the jellyfish. Work in the dressing and serve.

The jellyfish, with its chewy texture, is considered an unusual delicacy. Traditionally, this salad is often served as part of a fancy cold appetizer tray at the beginning of a formal banquet. To make sure that you have bought the right thing, you may wish to know the characters for jellyfish 海 蜇 皮 . The first character with its "water" radical means "sea" (Chapter 8). The second character contains the "insect" radical 虫 , often associated with shellfish (Chapter 8). The third character means "skin."

The Chinese radish (also called Chinese turnip) is long and white. In California and in some other parts of the country, they are widely available in supermarkets, sometimes under the Japanese name of daikon.

CELERY AND DRIED SHRIMP SALAD

SERVES 4

3 or 4 celery stalks, cut crosswise
¼ cup dried shrimp 蝦 米
About 2 teaspoons sesame oil

Cut the celery crosswise at an angle into bite-size pieces. Place the celery in a pan of boiling water, then drain immediately. Mix the celery with the dried shrimp and the sesame oil and serve.

As you can see, this salad is rather easy to make. Earlier on the very day I am writing this, we had some American friends over for a casual Chinese meal. They have a six-year-old boy. To everyone's surprise, he really liked this salad and asked for more. He also said he liked the colors, the reddish pink set off against the pale green. (Incidentally, both of his parents are artists.) I included this recipe to remind you, if you don't already know, that Chinese dishes do not always have to be drenched in the gooey dark brown sauce served up by crummy Chinese restaurants.

Dried shrimp are literally called "shrimp rice." See the "insect" radical again in the first character and the grains scattered in four directions in the second? Readily available in Chinese grocery stores, dried shrimp vary enormously in quality. Avoid the really salty kind. Some people eat dried shrimp the way others eat potato chips, popping them in one at a time, perhaps with a beer and some peanuts.

BEEF JERKY

YIELD: ABOUT 40 PIECES

1½ pounds boneless chuck
4 slices ginger, ⅛-inch thick
2 whole scallions, chopped
2 whole star anise   ﾉ丶 角
3 tablespoons brown sugar
Several coriander seeds
1 tablespoon soy sauce
1 teaspoon salt
1 teaspoon rice wine

Place beef in a heavy pot with the ginger, scallions, star anise, 1 tablespoon brown sugar, coriander seeds, and about 3 cups of water. (You can also add hot red pepper, curry, or dried orange peel to your taste.) Bring to a boil. Cover and simmer until tender. Remove beef from pot and retain liquid. Let the beef cool and slice as thinly as possible into bite-size pieces, cutting with the grain of the beef. Return beef to the retained liquid in the pot, add 1 tablespoon soy sauce, 1 teaspoon salt, 2 tablespoons brown sugar, and 1 teaspoon rice wine. Cook uncovered until the liquid has evaporated. Place beef flat on a cookie sheet. Bake in oven for 15 to 20 minutes at 350°. Cool beef on wire rack. Store in a covered jar in the refrigerator.

VEGETARIAN CHICKEN

SERVES 6–8

1 6–8 ounce package dried bean-curd skin,   豆腐衣
    about 10 sheets
⅓ cup dark or "old" soy sauce
3 tablespoons sesame oil
2 teaspoons sugar
4 or 5 dried Chinese mushrooms (optional)
2 or 3 wood ears (optional) 木耳
8 tiger lilies (optional) 金針

Soak the bean-curd skins in hot water until they turn soft. Drain. Mix "old" soy sauce, sesame oil, and sugar in large bowl to taste. Marinate bean-curd skin in mixture for about 20 minutes. Lay the bean-curd skins carefully one on top of each other, smoothing them out as you go along. Tightly roll the layered sheets jelly-roll fashion and secure with toothpicks to keep them from falling apart. One package of bean-curd skins will make 3 rolls. Place the rolls on a deep plate and steam 20 minutes.

That's all there is to it. Slice the rolls into pieces about ¼ inch thick and serve on a plate.

It is optional to make a filling. Soak the mushrooms and the wood ears in hot water until soft. Cut them into thin shreds. Meanwhile, shred the tiger lilies by hand. Sprinkle the shredded mixture on the bean-curd skin and roll.

Many versions of Vegetarian Chicken exist, but this is the version Gretchen likes. This dish is easy to make, but you have to be prepared to make a mess of soy sauce all over the counter and on your hands. Vegetarian chicken is often served as a cold appetizer. For reasons not entirely clear to me, our kids really like this dish. The other day, Gretchen had a plate of Vegetarian Chicken lying around in the kitchen while Peter, age six, was watching cartoons on television. I saw him dash into the kitchen, grab a piece of Vegetarian Chicken, and run back as fast as he could to the TV. The next time I checked in, the whole plate was gone. If you make this dish, you will see that it is not meant to be a mock chicken.

If you have trouble making the man in the grocery store understand that you want bean-curd skin, you can show him that it's 豆 腐 衣 you're talking about. In Chapter 16 I mentioned that the character 衣 , meaning "clothes," looks almost the same as the "divine revelation" radical.

Wood ear 木 耳 is a mushroomlike fungus that grows on trees. Notice how the character for "ear" looks pretty much like an ear. Wood ear comes in black and white. This recipe calls for the black kind.

In Chinese, tiger lilies are called "golden needles." You may remember the character for "gold" 金 , showing the nuggets in the ground. The character for "needle" contains the "gold" character; it's used as a radical for things metallic. Golden needles are the dried buds of the tiger lily. Sometimes they come with stems. You should remove the stems.

Gretchen and I have a running debate about whether to include the filling. Without the filling, the bean-curd skins can be rolled more tightly and somehow taste better. The filling, on the other hand, adds an interesting texture as well as taste.

DIP FOR COLD CRAB

2 tablespoons finely chopped ginger
½ cup good rice-wine vinegar
1 teaspoon sugar

Mix all the ingredients together.

This is how you make the dip I mentioned in Chapter 8 when I talked about eating boiled cold crab. One of the pleasures of living in Seattle is to pass by the Pike Place Market on the way home and pick up boiled Dungeness crab (a poor substitute for fresh live crab, but what can you do?). We'd chop up some ginger and in two minutes we'd be feasting.

NOTES

In these notes, I often list the sources I consulted for the etymology of individual characters. The main references, the books by Wieger, Chang, and Wilder and Ingraham as listed in the bibliography, are abbreviated as W, C, and WI respectively. Well-known folk tales are not referenced.

Chapter 1: Beijing Men Built a Fire

24.   Beijing men were probably the first to use fire to cook. See Tanna-hill.

28.   On lamb and Moslem restaurants, see F. Liu, p. 28.

32.   Scholars have asserted variously that there are 186, 189, 191, 214, 225, 226, or 250 different radicals, but many of these are rarely used and so obscure that the average Chinese reader would not know what they represent. (Just think, entire academic careers rise or fall according to whether one believes that there are 225 or 226 radicals!). See De Francis.

Chapter 2: Slicing Through Water

35.   For the etymology of the character meaning "eternity," see W, p. 289.

36.   Lewis D. Stegink of the University of Iowa believes that the sudden influx of glutamates into the blood triggers "some sort of peripheral vascular response." *New York Times* News Service, 1986. For a discussion of the history and origin of MSG, see McGee.

37. The Japanese usage of 湯 for "hot water" corresponds to ancient Chinese usage. This usage has lingered on in a Chinese idiomatic expression 赴湯蹈火 , which in modern Chinese would mean "going into the soup and stepping through fire." Clearly, at one time, the meaning of "hot water" rather than "soup" was intended.

37. For the etymology of the character meaning urn, see WI, p. 203.

38. I had no idea how soy sauce was actually made before I started writing this book. But I found out. To make soy sauce, you simmer soybeans in water until they form a purée. (The liquid that is drained off is used to make bean curd.) Shape the drained purée into loaves and put away to ferment in a cool dark place. Scrape away the fungoid covering that develops and then soak the loaves in a briny liquid for a few weeks. The result is soy sauce. See Tannahill. For a more precise discussion of how soy sauce is made and of the different methods that are used, see McGee, pp. 252–53.

42. The passage from *The Boy Who Shot the Hawk* also shows how the Chinese love the challenge of trying to discern all the different flavors in a dish. This is in itself of course universal with all haute cuisines. In the original, the author had 獐 , a small Chinese deer. In my translation I just used the simpler term "deer".

INTERLUDE 1: PHONETICS, OR
WHY SOME CHARACTERS LOOK HORRIBLY COMPLICATED

47. According to F. T. Cheng (page 163), the character 烤 was actually invented recently.

48. According to another interpretation, 堯 may describe the piling of a lot of earth 土 on a high place 兀 to make a mound. Perhaps it is the tomb of the ancestor.

CHAPTER 3: SLEEP OF THE TRULY INEBRIATED

55. Story of Du Kang wine, Guo, p. 55.

60. For a description of life in thirteenth-century China, see Gernet.

60.   Prohibitions and repeals of laws on drinking, Aero, p. 243.

60.   For the story on mao-tai liquor, see Shan, p. 221.

62.   One historical chronicle stated (in loose translation): "Grape wine comes from the West and was often offered as tribute in previous dynasties. The emperor Tai-Zong conquered the city Gaochang . . . and thus obtained the method for wine making. . . . The citizens of Chang An then became acquainted with the taste of grape wine."

63.   For some of the words associated with being drunk, see Lin and Lin, p. 32.

64.   For Marco Polo's comment on the quality of the wine he found in China, see Gernet, p. 139.

64.   Yuan emperors and drink, Chang, p. 207.

65.   For a recipe for *jiu nian*, see Claiborne and Lee, p. 398.

CHAPTER 4: SWALLOWING CLOUDS

70.   On the ideal ratio of 3 to 7, Tang, p. 74.

71.   For a theory about the invention of wonton in the Song dynasty, see Liang, p. 81. Liang expressed grave doubts about this theory.

71.   The Chinese word for primeval chaos 混 沌 is also pronounced like "wonton." There is a farfetched theory that somehow the name "wonton" derives from primeval chaos. Hard to believe.

73.   On the folk saying about tastiness and comfort, Liang, p. 199.

73.   According to another theory, the character for "woman" (in one ancient form) shows a woman with her hands folded together on her knees in a respectful pose, such as you may still see in Japan. This theory originated in *Talking about the Written Language and Analyzing the Words* (see Interlude 4) and is repeated in Wieger and Chang.

73.   For the etymology of the character meaning "good," see W, p. 169.

75.   For the folktale about the dumplings in the painting, see Ng, p. 114.

CHAPTER 5: CHINESE PIGS STAND

80.   The passage was cited in Tannahill, p. 140.

83.   Pictograph of "eye," see W, p. 323.

85.   Character for "home," see WI, p. 77.

84.   As may be expected, the God of Wealth is depicted differently in different regions. It is far from clear to me that there is one single God of Wealth. See Yin, p. 13.

85.   For the etymology of the character meaning "guest," see C, p. 226.

86.   According to Wieger (page 55), the roof over the cattle is actually a distortion of a more complicated character indicating a paddock which, in turn, came from a skein of thread or rope tied up at the end.

INTERLUDE 2: THE APPALLING IGNORANCE OF SOME SCRIBES

92.   For the etymology of the character meaning "hand," W, p. 135.

93.   For a description of an ancient Chinese pen, W, p. 7.

CHAPTER 6: A DELICACY FOR AGING MEN

97.   For the many roles played by the chicken in various civilizations, see Smith and Daniel.

99.   For the etymology of the character meaning short-tailed bird, C, p. 819.

99.   On the egg incubator and the Great Wall, Smith and Daniel, pp. 14 and 35.

99.   That Republican campaign pledge of 1928 was originally due to the French king Henry IV, who in the sixteenth century vowed that with Divine help he would make France so prosperous that every peasant would "have a chicken in his pot on Sunday." See Smith and Daniel, p. 262.

100.   On the Fordney-McCumber bill, Smith and Daniel, p. 258.

100.   For the arrival of the Shanghai, Chittagong, and Cochin chicken in England, Smith and Daniel, p. 205.

101.   Duck meat, cut into pieces, may be sautéed with bamboo. For a recipe, see Lin and Lin, p. 98.

101.   History of Long Island ducklings, Brown, p. 118.

102.   For the history of the pressed duck, see Ng, p. 81.

102.   For the folktale about thousand-year-old eggs, see San, p. 143.

106.   There are several versions of the story of Wang the calligrapher and the goose. In one, the literatus is replaced by a Taoist sorcerer, while the goose has magical powers. In other versions, Wang the calligrapher is interested in geese not as a gourmet but as an aesthete. Their shape appealed to him.

106.   One gourmet informs me that squab is best eaten on the seventeenth day after its birth. On the twenty-fourth day, it learns to fly and turns into a regular pigeon.

106.   The alleged sexual potency of squab is discussed in Chan-2, p. 125; Chan-3, p. 6; and Lee, p. 22. If you want to test Dr. Li's theory, you can find many recipes for squab in the last two references.

107.   Kao-tze, see Lau, *Mencius*, book VI, part A, section 4.

108.   F. W. Mote, see K. C. Chang, pp. 248ff.

108.   C. Claiborne, p. 427.

CHAPTER 7: NO CONTEST BETWEEN FISH AND A BEAR WITH EIGHT LEGS

109.   The passage may be found in Lau, *Mencius*, book VI, part A, section 10.

110.   For a discussion of Germans and Russians cooking bear's paw, see Tang, p. 186.

111.   For another interpretation of the etymology of the character meaning fish, see W, p. 56. As an example of the lack of a standard ancient form of any given character, C lists forty different forms of the character for fish.

113.   In China, as elsewhere in the world until quite recently, age is venerated, and in a number of regions, polite terms of address would include a reference to age. In the old days in Kaifeng, a waiter would address you as "Ni lao!" (你 老), literally "You elderly person!" regardless of your

age. He would end every sentence with *ni lao* much as a subservient waiter here would end every sentence with "sir." After you went over to the fish tank to pick out a carp, he would grab the poor creature and suddenly smash it down on the floor with all his might, while yelling "Smash to death, ni lao!" Startled, the visitor from elsewhere, not familiar with the local restaurant way of killing carp, might think for a moment that the waiter was going to smash him, the elderly person, to death! See Tang.

113. The Yellow River got its name from its silt, and so the carp of that region must be kept in a freshwater tank for five or so days before it can be eaten. Some gourmets do not favor the carp for this reason, saying that there is always a residual taste of silt.

114. On Su Tung-po eating fugu, Gao, p. 34.

114. For a further discussion of eating fugu, see Ng, p. 93. For eating fugu in Japan, Steinberg. He reports that fugu was good, but not all that special.

116. Incidentally, etymologists have found an ancient pictographic form for this character explicitly showing the caldron in which the beautifully fat baby lamb was stewed. For the etymology of the character meaning "thick broth," see WI, p. 103.

117. The story about Woman Song was said to have taken place during the Song dynasty. See Ng. Her last name just happened to be the same as the character used for the dynasty; there is no connection between her and the imperial court. In any case, dynasties were not named after the last names of the imperial families.

119. Interestingly, although the German word for leek is Lauch, northern Germans call it Porree, a corruption of the French word.

119. For the etymology of the character meaning "rice," see W, p. 79.

120. The famous doctor Li Shi-Zhen 李 時 珍 wrote an enormous compendium known as 本 草 綱 目 , sometimes translated as *Great Pharmacopoeia*, in which he described about 2,000 drugs and explained how to prepare some 8,000 prescriptions. The work contains details on 1,074 vegetables, 443 animals, and 217 minerals.

120.   For the passage about sashimi, see Yau, p. 21.

121.   There are, of course, numerous characters associated with 生 . See W, p. 79. An unusual one is 星 , meaning "star." It comes from the primitive form 㵘 . Looks like a fancy streetlight to me. The ancients held that the ○ , representing sublimated essence of matter, rose up and crystallized into stars. Later dots were added as in the character for sun. The triplet of stars was then simplified to a single star.

Astronomers don't believe that any more. Amusingly, however, the truth is almost the opposite. Except for simple atoms such as hydrogen and helium, matter is the product of star fires. The simplest nuclei, namely those of hydrogen and helium atoms, were "cooked" into more complicated nuclei by the nuclear reactions in stars. When ancient stars died and exploded, the stuff was tossed out into interstellar space. This interstellar debris later condensed into planets. Incidentally, when physicists talk about the cooking of elements, they are not speaking metaphorically. Nuclear forces are involved instead of chemical forces but the basic processes are similar. Just as a gourmet can tell by taste how a dish was cooked and what spices went in, physicists can tell a great deal about the conditions inside stars and in the early universe by "tasting" the matter around us, that is, by measuring the relative abundances of different elements.

121.   For the etymology of the character meaning "bear," see C, p. 650.

121.   For a discussion on which bear's paw is the tastiest, see Bao.

CHAPTER 8: COURTESANS DO NOT EAT CRABS

123.   For the Jin dynasty poem about crab and wine, see Liang, p. 102.

129.   For the triplet about crab eggs and the famous courtesan, see Tang, p. 118.

131.   A character constructed phonetically is usually simplified by replacing its phonetic element by a simpler one. Thus, in the campaign to simplify the written character, less ravage is done to the etymology of phonetic characters.

134. For the story about the scholar making a soup of fish and lamb, see Shuo, p. 157. The scholar was named Pan, and so this soup is sometimes known as Pan fish.

134. For a recipe for fish and lamb soup, see Lin and Lin, p. 59. They describe the result of mixing up these two flavors as "complex, novel, and amusing."

CHAPTER 9: THE SWEET FRAGRANCE OF CROPS RIPENING

141. For the etymology of the character meaning vegetables, see WI, p. 95.

144. For the list of foods brought back by the Han dynasty envoys, see Chang, p. 80.

145. A more scientific but nerdily literal explanation for the incantation "Open sesame!" is based on the fact that upon maturation, the pod inside which the sesame seed ripens bursts open with a pop. (Thus, in harvesting sesame seeds, timing is of great importance.)

145. In Sir Richard Burton's classic translation, "Open sesame!" was rendered as "Open, O Simsim!" For a reference to cabalistic texts, see the footnote on page 568 of Burton.

146. Stance while eating Mongolian lamb, see Cheng, p. 165.

146. You may have noticed the heart radical in the character for scal-lion 蔥 . It may indicate that often a few wilted outer leaves have to be peeled away. The character sandwiched between the grass radical and the heart radical is purely phonetic.

147. For the etymology of the character meaning "steam," see C, p. 677.

149. For the history of tomatoes, see Tannahill.

150. For the etymology of the character meaning "fragrance," see W, p. 185.

153. Forrest regards the character for "depression" as one of the most poetic characters.

CHAPTER 10: HOW TO AVOID BEING VULGAR

155.   Actually, pandas are omnivores and will eat meat if available. For more on the imminent extinction of the panda, see the article by E. Dolnick in the September 1989 issue of *Discover* magazine.

155.   Depending on the species, the life cycle of the bamboo ranges from 15 to 120 years.

156.   For the etymology of the character "to calculate," see WI, p. 85.

158.   On the relative merits of winter bamboo shoots versus spring bamboo shoots, Liang, p. 167.

160.   Using bamboo as a cooking utensil, Yau, p. 42. See also Zhu.

162.   For the etymology of the character meaning "melon," see W, p. 329.

164.   For the etymology of the character meaning "to cause," see WI, p. 80.

165.   According to C, p. 53, the character for "vulgar" is merely phonetic.

168.   In the Song dynasty, a new form, with uneven lines, emerged.

169.   For the etymology of the character meaning "rock," see W, p. 154.

170.   The Cantonese pronunciation of 雜 is actually more like "cz'ar," combining the *cz* sound in the English word "czar" and the *ar* sound in the English word "harp," but the choice of the word "chop" as a rough phonetic equivalent is brilliant, with its meaning of cutting up into small pieces.

CHAPTER 11: THE POCKMARKED WOMAN AND THE PEARLY EMPRESS

171.   Scholars have puzzled over how the character for "decay" came to be used to describe bean curd. In any case, I can safely bet that it has never even puzzled most Chinese. One scholar I read claims that *fu* is a Chinese corruption of the syllable *kho* in the Mongol word *khorot*, a yogurtlike staple said to be hard and sour by the scholar, who presumably had tasted it.

(Corruption, decay, get it?) Yogurt and cheese and other dairy foods were introduced long ago into China by the surrounding nomadic tribes and were commonly consumed in the Tang dynasty. According to the theory, when the Chinese discovered bean curd, it reminded them of yogurt and they called it "bean yogurt." The character 腐 , being phonetically close to the *kho* in *khorot*, was adopted, so sayeth the scholar. Likely story, eh? While I don't know Mongolian from Greek, I can see, with some stretch of the imagination, how *khorot* sounds not unlike yogurt. But *kho* and *fu* hardly sound the same. Of course, pronunciations shift over time. Who am I to argue with a leading scholar of food history? For further discussion, see Lin, where you can find articles by Chinese, Japanese, and Western scholars on the history of the bean curd. The Japanese record is extensive.

172.   A Han dynasty encyclopedia of food published during the first century B.C. did not mention bean curd. We can imagine scholars perusing ancient texts in gloomy libraries searching for a mention of bean curd. The task is enormous: there are court documents to go through, volumes of poetry, novels, diaries of monks and assorted personages, and so on. So far, not a word about bean curd until the Song, after which bean curd was commonly mentioned. This theory, that bean curd was invented during the Song dynasty, was supported by Japanese records, in which the first reference to it was dated A.D. 1183. Since there was considerable traffic between China and Japan, it was thought that there should have been earlier references if bean curd had been invented in the Han dynasty. The real scholarly task is to prove that every reference to food before the Song dynasty does not describe bean curd under some other name. After all, the names of food and dishes vary from province to province and gradually shift with time. For instance, an early poet mentioned something loosely translatable as "bean cheese." Scholars of the late-invention school then had to come up with learned arguments why that couldn't have been bean curd. The number of doctoral dissertations that can be written is only limited by one's patience. See Lin.

The alleged first reference was in the biographical anecdotes of a local governor who lived a simple and austere life and who urged the populace to have bean curd rather than lamb. The passage went on to say that the people took to calling bean curd "little lamb."

173.   In broad outline, one makes bean curd as follows. Soybeans

are soaked and then ground into a slurry. The slurry is strained and coagulated (with a coagulant like gypsum) to precipitate out the proteins. The result is strained again and pressed into a solid mass. For precise instructions, including a flowchart, see McGee, p. 255.

173.   For a collection of rural folk sayings about bean curd, see Lin, p. 69.

173.   Eating boiled bean curd, see Lin, p. 119.

174.   A study of farm families by J. L. Buck covering 1922–25 concluded that the caloric and nutritional intake was more than sufficient. (Some scholars, however, have questioned the statistical accuracies of the study.) Chang, p. 315.

174.   Bean curd became a common food item only during the Song dynasty (960–1279). It was not until the Ming dynasty (1368–1644) that bean curd entered into the cuisine of the upper class and of the court. See Lin, p. 55.

174.   A cultural history of Chinese food must touch on the conspicuous lack of dairy products in the everyday diet of East Asian people. I have heard of a number of theories. Different races apparently have different amounts of the lactase enzyme needed to digest milk products. East Asians happen to have little of this enzyme. The discomfort of indigestion may have dissuaded many in ancient times. With no dairy products in the diet, the level of lactase may have decreased even more. In Europe, there may even have been some Darwinian selection in historic times, favoring those who could absorb dairy products the best. Yet northern and western China were in contact with nomadic people who relied heavily on dairy products, so why didn't their lifestyle influence the Chinese? One theory is that the Chinese were culturally prejudiced against the nomads, perhaps in the same way that Judaic people developed kosher laws to inculcate a sense of "us" as opposed to "them." Another explanation is environmental. Much of China is not pastureland. The traditional milk-producing breed of cattle in Europe would not do well in the hot and humid climate of East Asia. (The Indians were apparently motivated by religious reasons to have developed special breeds.) I feel that all these factors taken together can probably account for the phenomenon. For a discussion of these points, see Anderson, p. 145.

174.   For a comparison of the populations of Europe and China, see Braudel, p. 39.

174.   For a wealth of details, such as precise names and dates, on the story of Ma-Po Bean Curd, see Lin, p. 85.

180.   Regarding the construction of the character for "man" by combining "field" with "force": in modern physics and in modern movies, there is a concept of the "field of force."

181.   For a discussion of the use of hemp in China, see Aero, p. 136.

181.   For the etymology of the character meaning pestle, see W, p. 102.

181.   I am grateful to T. C. Chen for a discussion of the history of the pepper. For another discussion of the history of the pepper, see Chang.

181.   For the arrival of the pepper in China, see Anderson, p. 131.

181.   The chili pepper 辣椒 is not to be confused with 花椒 and 胡椒, various types of Chinese peppers that had been in China long before the discovery of the New World. The word "chili" comes from the Nahuatl dialect of the Aztec Indians.

182.   For the etymology of the character meaning "thorn," see W, p. 120.

184.   My encyclopedia, a killjoy as such books of facts are apt to be, asserts that pearls are made of the same organic substance that make up the shells of the corresponding mollusk. Now, just tell that to any lady of distinction! But this suggests a less costly experiment: how about simmering some oyster shells in broth for forty-nine days? Or you can always go to some corner drug or health food store and buy pills made of ground-up oyster shells.

185.   For the etymology of the character meaning "old," see W, p. 224.

185.   Recipe for 三鮮百葉捲, see Huang, p. 149.

187.   One of my childhood memories is of a strange form of fermented bean curd known as 臭豆腐, literally "bad-smelling bean curd." It is fermented from a type of dried and hardened bean curd, and it really does smell bad: well, perhaps not so much bad as unusual. In Hong Kong, street vendors would set up a wok full of bubbling hot oil in which pieces of fermented bean curd were fried and sold to passersby. Mirabile

dictu, the stuff smells bad but tastes great, at least to people who like it!

The character for "bad smell" 臭 is another fun character. It is made of two parts, 自 meaning "nose" and 犬 meaning "dog." I am sorry if you are a dog lover but I have always thought that the character got its form because dogs smell bad. Some etymologists, however, presumably dog lovers, felt the character came about because dogs have sensitive noses.

Incidentally, if you think 犬 does not look the least bit like a dog, you are not alone. Generations of scholars have been puzzled by this, particularly because Confucius was supposed to have said that the character looks uncannily like a dog. The etymologist Wieger allowed himself a touch of humor on this point and commented that dogs must have been strange animals in the time of the philosophers. Most likely, Confucius never said any such thing and the quote was invented by some village pedant eager to invoke authority to silence a skeptical pupil.

187.   The etymology of the character meaning "breast" is a matter of some controversy. As a note of scholarship, I may mention that serious scholars dismiss the etymology given in the text as popular nonsense. They claim that 乳 actually refers to the swallow and describes its form as it flies and that the radical on top of the "son" character 爪 does not represent nipples at all, but the foot of the swallow. I don't know, but I like the more popular explanation given in the text better. See W, p. 234.

187.   For the appearance of bean curd in literature, see Lin, p. 77.

INTERLUDE 4: WORDS ARE LIKE OUR CHILDREN

191.   For the etymology of the "silk" or "thread" radical, see W, p. 92.
191.   For the etymology of the character meaning "horn," see W, p. 142.

192.　　　解　　　also appears in the modern expression for liberation as in People's Liberation Army with the obvious sense of freedom from bondage.

CHAPTER 12: BUDDHA JUMPING OVER WALLS

193.　　The relative lack of food taboos in Chinese culture is probably related to the lack of structured and institutionalized religions in China.

194.　　Some Buddhists would actually purchase live fish and put them back into the water.

195fn.　　For the etymology of "Buddha," see W, p. 223.

196.　　Louis Cha, *Eight Parts of the Dragon*.

200.　　For the etymology of the character meaning "white silk," see C, p. 612.

200.　　Interestingly, the nomadic Khitans, who conquered parts of the northern Song, also gave us the word "Cathay," the name used in the West for China.

201.　　The recipe for "the broth of the red glow of the setting sun reflected on the snow" appeared in a cookbook written by one Ling Hung. See W. H. Liu, p. 168.

201.　　Incidentally, the character 電 means "lightning," and is now used to mean "electricity." Thus, the electron and hence electronics, is written as 電 子 , literally, the "son of electricity," but figuratively "the particle of electricity," as the character 子 for child is also used to mean "something small."

202.　　On the first appearance of cookbooks in China, see W. H. Liu, p. 99.

CHAPTER 13: ACT WITHOUT ACTING, TASTE WITHOUT TASTING

205.　　Story about the three sages, see Okakura, p. 24.

208.　　*The Book of the Tao*, see the edition translated by D. C. Lau. I strongly recommend Lau's authoritative translation.

211.	For the etymology of the character meaning "head," see W, p. 160.

211.	For the evolution of head radical, see W, p. 126.

211.	Some scholars feel that *The Book of the Tao* could not have been the work of one man, and that the text in fact dates from about 300 B.C. Others even think that Lao-tze never existed as a single individual.

213.	*The Analects*, see the edition translated by Lau.

219.	Story of the bridge, Blofeld, p. 21.

222.	For the etymology of the character meaning "god" and "divinity," see C, p. 569; and W, p. 29.

226.	For a discussion of the Stove God, see Chi and Yin.

INTERLUDE 5: LIKE EATING POTATO CHIPS

233.	See Paulsen and Kuhn, p. 133, for some Chinese characters related to women; p. 261, for sexism in American school textbooks.

234.	One theory is that in ancient times 姓 was a generic name for "woman" and 氏 for "man"; the combination 姓 氏 is sometimes used as a general term for a human. Eventually, the second character was dropped. According to another theory, 姓 refers to the place where the chief of the clan was born (of a woman). The clan was named after that place. See W, p. 206.

CHAPTER 14: THE SUBLIME FAITH IN ILLUSIONS

237.	Using tea to control the border regions, see Chan, p. 117.

238.	According to a rather charming or gruesome story, depending on your perspective, tea originated with the Indian monk Bodhidharma who introduced a form of Buddhism to China in the sixth century. In order not to fall asleep during meditation, Bodhidharma supposedly cut off his eyelids. When his eyelids fell to the ground, they turned into tea leaves. Because this story is so widely known, many people have the erroneous impression that tea originated in India. In fact, extensive cultivation of tea in India did not start until British colonization.

238.   For a lyrical discussion of the history of tea, see Okakura, on which I relied extensively.

238.   On the amount of tea consumed by the British today, see McGee, p. 216.

240.   On the division of the world's languages into those that call tea "cha" or "tea," see Blofeld, p. 26. In Brazil, tea is called "cha."

242.   According to Blofeld, the Korean tea ceremony is much closer to the ancient Chinese practice than the Japanese tea ceremony.

242.   You may recognize the character for work 工 as a phonetic element in the character for "red" 紅 , as in "red-cooking."

244.   I have retold the story from *The Dream of the Red Chamber* based on a retelling by Blofeld rather than the original text.

245.   Tea contest, Chan, p. 66.

245.   "Small Rounds," see Blofeld, p. 20.

245.   Chopping up antique furniture to brew tea, Gao, p. 146.

246.   The clay around the town of Yee Shing is said to be special in the way it "breathes."

246.   For teacups, the two "good" periods in the Ming dynasty are 正 德 (Cheng-te, or Zheng-de in pinyin) and 萬 曆 (Wan-li). The one period in the Qing dynasty is 嘉 慶 (Chia-Ch'ing or Jia-qing in pinyin).

CHAPTER 15: PIECES OF HER HEART

250.   山 楂 = Crataegus pinnatifolia. See Chang.

250.   For a description of rose candy, see Ng, p. 31.

251.   Dessert and sweets must have a relatively short history in the West since sugar was, until recently, such a luxury there.

251.   Based on their experience at Chinese restaurants in this country, Americans often have the impression that the Chinese have no desserts. For the recipes for some common Chinese snacks, see Huang, *Chinese Snacks*.

253.   For the etymology of the character meaning longevity, see C, p. 185; and W, p. 313.

254.   *The Monkey King,* called *The Westward Journey* in the original, was based loosely on the perilous journeys to India Tang dynasty monks undertook in order to obtain various Buddhist scriptures. The Monkey King accompanied a Tang dynasty monk on the trip and got into all kinds of hilarious adventures.

255.   Porridge in Rome and in Mexico, Tannahill.

255.   For Su Tung-po's quote, see an article by D. G. Yin in *Crown* magazine, 1986.

256.   Recipe for shredded chicken porridge, see Ng.

CHAPTER 16: ELIXIRS AND THE FOOD OF HEALTH

262.   For the etymology of the characters meaning "long" and "hair", see W, p. 268.

262.   Here is a story told in a Chinese joke book of the Ming dynasty. A Han dynasty emperor, at great cost, had actually obtained a potion of immortality, but his minister drank it before the emperor could. Furious, the emperor ordered the minister put to death. The minister, however, argued with the emperor that if the potion were genuine, then he would not die anyway, but if the potion were fake, then he would die, thus causing the emperor embarrassment for having been fooled by charlatans. The emperor decided to spare the minister.

263.   In some stories, the Lady of the Moon goes to various celestial parties and stirs up trouble. See the classic Chinese novel *The Mirror and the Flower.*

264.   All right, I promised you the longevity recipe. Here it is. (I have converted the Chinese weight measures.) Take 2 pounds of 新羅 參 , the juice squeezed from 21 pounds of 生地黃 , 4 pounds of 白茯苓 peeled, 13 pounds of 白沙

蜜 . Mix and seal ingredients in a silver or earthen pot. Then start simmering, et cetera, as described in the text. Don't forget to offer three spoonfuls to the gods before you taste it! See Ng, p. 159.

265.　　The etymology of yin and yang I presented in the text is what is known as arm-chair etymology. One's pictorial imagination can of course easily lead one astray. [Notice that the phonetic element in "yang" is the same as the one in "soup."] See C, pp. 813, 815; and W, p. 220.

268.　　For a history of ginger, see Tannahill.

278.　　For an introduction to tai chi, see Cheng and Smith.

279.　　For the etymology of the character meaning "chi," see W, p. 241.

CHAPTER 17: FROM BANQUETS TO VOYAGES OF DISCOVERY

284.　　Chinese government limits time of official banquets. See *Newsweek*, September 14, 1987, p. 53.

285.　　Ming dynasty official complaint, see the article by Mote in Chang, p. 247.

285.　　Duration of Ming banquets, *ibid.*, 246.

286.　　Grades of Qing banquets, see article by Spence in Chang, p. 282.

286.　　Emperor Kang Xi's proclamation, *ibid.*, 283.

287.　　For the official menu of a Manchu-Han Full Banquet, see Zheng, p. 34.

287.　　Age of the Emperor Qian Long, Zheng, p. 114.

289.　　The episode about Bismarck, Bao, p. 43.

290.　　Strictly speaking, the swallow's nest is the nest of a swift, not a swallow. I thank E. N. Anderson for this remark.

290.　　History of bird's nest, Bao, p. 45.

291.　　Charles Darwin and bird's nest, see Aero, p. 28.

292.　　For the Arab presentation of the giraffe, see Duyvendank.

APPENDIX A: HOW TO EXERCISE YOUR ARM AND THROAT WHILE DRINKING

303.   For the etymology of the character meaning "treasure," see C, p. 237.

303.   For the etymology of the character meaning "jade," see W, p. 215.

305.   For the etymology of the character meaning "joy," see C, p. 160.

306.   For the etymology of the character meaning "mutual," see C, p. 556; W, p. 323. An alternative theory for 相 meaning "to inspect" states that it comes from the carpenter inspecting the wood with his eyes. See C, p. 556.

306.   For the etymology of the character meaning "high," see C, p. 855.

309.   For the etymology of the character meaning "wealth," see W, p. 328.

310.   For the etymology of the character meaning "expand," see W, p. 266.

312.   For the God of Scholarship, see Yin, p. 127, and Williams, p. 207. According to another theory, the association of the God of Scholarship with an ugly monster is due to an absurd error. There was a scholar whose name sounded the same as the character 魅 . By some confusion, in writing the scholar's name, a chronicler mistakenly used the wrong character. Later, people puzzled by the use of a character associated with monsters tried to explain the whole thing away by concocting a story about a monstrously ugly scholar.

312.   For the etymology of the character meaning "gold," see W, p. 49.

313.   For the story of the Weaver Girl and the Cowherd Boy, see Zhan and Chi. In another version of the tale of the Weaver Girl and the Cowherd Boy, it was the Celestial Phoenix who took pity on them, not the Celestial Emperor. The Phoenix commanded her subjects, the magpies, to form the bridge. Incidentally, magpies are known as "birds of joy" in China. In yet another version, the bull rammed into a tree and broke off his horns. The Cowherd Boy ascended to heaven riding on a horn.

319.   For stories about the Eight Immortals, see Zhan, Williams, Aero,

and Christie. The Eight Immortals have changed over the centuries. A less popular Immortal might gradually be replaced by somebody else. The composition of the present group of Eight Immortals dates from the middle of the Ming dynasty (1368–1644). Even the Immortals have to compete for the affection of the people.

There are more stories told about the prankster Lu than any other Immortal, particularly about his exploits in the affairs of the heart. He reputedly entered into liaisons with various historically well-known courtesans. He even dared to fall in love with the chaste Buddhist goddess Guanyin (at whom he threw the gold coin). Rebuffed severely, he fell into the utter dejection of a lover scorned. Ever since, he has been envious of lovers and plays tricks to break them up.

Given Lu's popularity, there are temples devoted to him almost everywhere in China and in Taiwan. His birthday, on the fourteenth day of the fourth month, is a major festival in many regions. In the old days in Suzhou, the leading courtesans would all make a pilgrimage to his temple on that day. In the belief that he might assume human form and mingle with the crowd, people would try to guess who might actually be Lu himself. Incidentally, Lu was an actual person born in A.D. 798. A scholar, he attempted and failed the imperial exam twice. Perhaps that was why he turned into such a prankster.

Not surprisingly, the prankster Immortal Lu also loves to eat and drink, without paying. At one point he frequented a wine pavilion in the city of Yue Yang. Every time the bill came, he would just saunter out. He justified this as a test of the restaurateur's generosity. After six months, he felt that enough was enough. Drawing a picture of a yellow crane on the wall, he told the owner of the wine pavilion that whenever a customer wished it, the crane would come off the wall and do a dance. Naturally, business boomed and the owner became a rich man. One day Lu returned, told the owner that he was rich enough, and rode away on the yellow crane. This wine pavilion, the Yellow Crane, has been immortalized in poetry. Upon visiting the pavilion, a Tang dynasty poet was inspired to write one of the most famous poems in Chinese literature. The poem has in turn given rise to a common saying: "Once the yellow crane is gone, it will never return!"

BIBLIOGRAPHY

BOOKS IN CHINESE

Books in Chinese are referred to in the notes by the transliterated names of authors as given here. The names are transliterated in pinyin except where an author has transliterated his or her own name. The titles in English and the names of the publishers are my translations. The following represents some of the books in my library that I have drawn upon and by no means exhausts the available books on the relevant subjects.

抱殘守缺齋夫, 中國人吃的掌故

Bao Can Sau Que, J. F. *Historical Anecdotes in Chinese Gastronomy.* Taipei: Evergreen Tree Publishing Co., 1980.

陳存仁, 吃的藝術

Chan1. *The Art of Eating.* Hong Kong: Guan Wen Publishing.

陳存仁, 飲食養生法

Chan2. *Longevity and Health Through Drinking and Eating.* Hong Kong: Brightness Publishing.

陳存仁, 飲食養生與補品法專集

Chan3. *Longevity and Health and Body Repair Through Drinking and Eating.* Macao: Three Leaves Publishing.

陳存仁，養生食經

Chan 4. *The Book of Longevity and Health Through Food.* Hong Kong: Brightness Publishing.

陳彬藩，茶經新篇

Chen, B. F. *The New Book of Tea.* Hong Kong: The Mirror Post Cultural Enterprises Co., Ltd., 1986.

齊星，古風民俗

Chi, S. *Ancient Practices and Folk Customs.* Hong Kong: Commercial Press, 1987.

高陽，古今味

Gao, Y. *Tastes Ancient and Modern.* Taipei: Nanjing Publishing Co., 1981.

國榮州，佐餐的典故

Guo, Y. Z. *Stories of Chinese Dishes.* Fujian: Fujian Science and Technology Publishing, 1986.

胡卓及其他，食經

Hu, Z. et al. *The Book of Food.* Hong Kong: Green Harbor Publishing Co., 1983.

李康渝，燉品補品大全

Li, K. Y. *Encyclopedic Collection of Casseroles and Body Repair Dishes.* Hong Kong: Eternal Wind Publishing Co.

梁實秋，雅舍談吃

Liang, S. Q. *Recollection of a Gourmet.* Taipei: Nine Songs Publishing Co., 1985.

林海音，中國豆腐

Lin, H. Y. *The Bean Curd of China.* Taipei: Pure Literature Publishing Co., 1983.

劉枋, 吃的藝術續集

Liu, F. *The Art of Eating,* Volume 2. Taipei: Great Earth Publishing Co., 1986.

劉華康, 中國人吃的歷史

Liu, H. K. *A History of Chinese Food.* Taipei: Evergreen Tree Publishing Co., 1986.

吳瑞卿, 講古講食

Ng, S. H. *Talking about History, Talking about Food.* Hong Kong: Beneficial Publishing Co., 1985.

邱虎同, 古烹飪漫談

Qiu, H. T. *A Discourse on Ancient Cuisine.* Jiangsu: Jiangsu Science and Technology Publishing, 1983.

三一奇, 中國食品傳說

Shan, Y. Q. *Stories About Chinese Food.* Beijing: Bright Light Publishing Co., 1986.

唐魯孫, 中國吃的故事

Tang, L. S. 1. *The Story of Chinese Food.* Taipei: Han Light Cultural Enterprise Co., 1983.

唐魯孫, 說東道西

Tang, L. S. 2. *Talking About This and That.* Taipei: Great Earth Publishing Co., 1983.

陶文台, 江蘇名饌古今談

Tao, W. T. *A Discourse on the Famous Dishes Ancient and Modern of Jiangsu Province.* Jiangsu: Jiangsu People's Publishing Co., 1981.

秀君, 飲食正經

Xiu, J. 1. *The Proper Book of Drinking and Eating.* Hong Kong: Beneficial Publishing Co., 1985.

秀君，飲食奇趣錄

Xiu, J. 2. *The Strange and Interesting in the Annals of Drinking and Eating.* Hong Kong: Beneficial Publishing Co., 1987.

楊永和（馬景海），北京清真菜譜

Yang, Y. H. *Moslem Cuisine in Beijing.* Beijing: Beijing Publishing Co., 1984.

殷登國，中國神的故事

Zhan, D. G. *The Story of Chinese Gods.* Taiwan: New Era Publishing Co.

鄭秀美，中國飲食風俗

Zheng, S. M. *Drinking and Eating Customs in China.* Taipei: Starlight Publishing, 1986.

朱彝尊，食憲鴻秘

Zhu, Y. Z. *Secrets of Eating.* Beijing: China Commercial Press Publishing, 1985.

NOVELS IN CHINESE

The text contains excerpts from these two well-known contemporary Chinese novels. The English titles are my translations.

金庸，射鵰英雄傳

Cha, Louis. *The Boy Who Shot the Hawk.* Taipei: Distant View Publishing, 1979.

金庸，天龍八部

Cha, Louis. *Eight Parts of the Celestial Dragon.* Taipei: Distant View Publishing, 1979.

BOOKS IN ENGLISH

Aero, R. *Things Chinese*. Garden City: Doubleday, 1980.

Anderson, E. N. *The Food of China*. New Haven: Yale University Press, 1988.

Blofeld, J. *The Chinese Art of Tea*. Boston: Shambhala, 1985.

Braudel, F. *The Structures of Everyday Life*. New York: Harper & Row, 1981.

Brown, D. *American Cooking*. New York: Time-Life Books, 1968.

Burton, R., trans. *Arabian Nights*. London: Bracken Books, 1985.

Chang, K. C. *Food in Chinese Culture*. New Haven: Yale University Press, 1977. This book contains articles by E. N. Anderson, M. L. Anderson, M. Freeman, F. L. K. Hsu, V. Y. N. Hsu, F. W. Mote, E. H. Schafer, J. Spence, and Y. S. Yü.

Cheng, F. T. *Musings of a Chinese Gourmet*. London: Hutchinson & Co., 1954.

Cheng, M-c., and R. W. Smith. *Tai Chi*. Rutland, Vermont: Charles E. Tuttle Co., 1967.

Cheng, M-j., annot., and T. C. Gibbs, trans. *Lao-Tzu: "My Words Are Very Easy to Understand"*. Berkeley: North Atlantic Books, 1981.

Christie, A. *Chinese Mythology*. London: Paul Hamlyn, 1968.

Claiborne, C. *The New York Times Food Encyclopedia*. New York: The New York Times Co., 1985.

Claiborne, C., and V. Lee. *The Chinese Cookbook*. Philadelphia: J. B. Lippincott Company, 1972.

De Francis, J. *The Chinese Language: Fact and Fantasy*. Honolulu: University of Hawaii Press, 1984.

Duyvendank, J. J. L. *China's Discovery of Africa*. London: Arthur Probsthian, 1949.

Forrest, R. A. D. *The Chinese Language*. London: Faber and Faber, 1973.

Hahn, E. *The Cooking of China*. New York: Time-Life Books, 1968.

Huang, S. H. *Chinese Cuisine*. Taipei, Taiwan: Wei-chuan Publishing, 1976.

Huang S. H. *Chinese Snacks*. Taipei, Taiwan: Wei-chuan Publishing, 1976.

Lai, T. C. *At the Chinese Table*. Hong Kong: Oxford University Press, 1984.

Lau, D. C., annot. and trans. *Confucius: The Analects*. Penguin Books, Hong Kong: The Chinese University Press, 1979.

Lau, D. C., annot. and trans. *Mencius*. Penguin Books, Hong Kong: The Chinese University Press, 1979.

Lau, D. C., annot. and trans. *Tao Te Ching*. Penguin Books, Hong Kong: The Chinese University Press, 1982.

Lin, H. J., and T. Lin. *Chinese Gastronomy*. New York: G P Putnam, 1982.

McGee, H. *On Food and Cooking*. New York: Macmillan Publishing Co., 1984.

Okakura, K. *The Book of Tea*. New York: Dover, 1964.

Paulsen, K., and R. A. Kuhn, eds. *Woman's Almanac*. Philadelphia: J. B. Lippincott, 1976.

Schwartz, S. *The Perfect Peach*. Illustrated by L. B. Lubin. Boston: Little Brown & Co., 1977.

Smith, P., and C. Daniel. *The Chicken Book*. San Francisco: North Point Press, 1982.

Steinberg, R. *The Cooking of Japan*. New York: Time-Life Books, 1969.

Suen, C. Y. *Computational Studies of the Most Frequent Chinese Words and Sounds*. Singapore: World Scientific, 1986.

Tannahill, L. *Food in History*. New York: Stein & Day, 1981.

Williams, C. A. S. *Outlines of Chinese Symbolism and Art Motives*. New York: Dover, 1976.

BOOKS ON CHINESE ETYMOLOGY

Chang, Hsüan. *The Etymologies of 3,000 Chinese Characters in Common Usage*. Hong Kong: Hong Kong University Press, 1968.

Wieger, L. *Chinese Characters*. New York: Dover, 1965.

Wilder, G. H., and J. H. Ingraham. *Analysis of Chinese Characters*. New York: Dover, 1974.

TABLE OF DYNASTIES

Xia (21st–16th centuries B.C.)

Shang (16th–11th centuries B.C.)

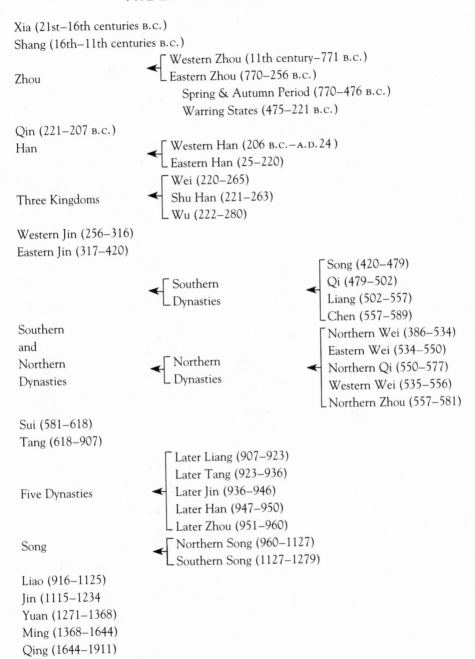

Zhou
  - Western Zhou (11th century–771 B.C.)
  - Eastern Zhou (770–256 B.C.)
      - Spring & Autumn Period (770–476 B.C.)
      - Warring States (475–221 B.C.)

Qin (221–207 B.C.)

Han
  - Western Han (206 B.C.–A.D. 24)
  - Eastern Han (25–220)

Three Kingdoms
  - Wei (220–265)
  - Shu Han (221–263)
  - Wu (222–280)

Western Jin (256–316)

Eastern Jin (317–420)

Southern and Northern Dynasties
  - Southern Dynasties
      - Song (420–479)
      - Qi (479–502)
      - Liang (502–557)
      - Chen (557–589)
  - Northern Dynasties
      - Northern Wei (386–534)
      - Eastern Wei (534–550)
      - Northern Qi (550–577)
      - Western Wei (535–556)
      - Northern Zhou (557–581)

Sui (581–618)

Tang (618–907)

Five Dynasties
  - Later Liang (907–923)
  - Later Tang (923–936)
  - Later Jin (936–946)
  - Later Han (947–950)
  - Later Zhou (951–960)

Song
  - Northern Song (960–1127)
  - Southern Song (1127–1279)

Liao (916–1125)

Jin (1115–1234

Yuan (1271–1368)

Ming (1368–1644)

Qing (1644–1911)

TABLE OF SOME COMMON RADICALS USED IN THIS BOOK

火 ⺍ Fire

水 氵 Water

酉 Fermentation urn

口 Mouth

糸 Silk

亻 Man

雨 Rain *and* weather

女 Woman

食 Eat

辶 Movement *and* transport

宀 Roof

肉 月 Flesh *and* meat

手 扌 又 Hand

鳥 Bird

虫 Insect *and* crawling creature

艹 Grass *and* vegetation

木 Wood

禾 Grain

心 忄 Heart *and* emotion

⺮ Bamboo

力 Force

示 礻 Divine revelation

犭 Animal

囗 Country *or* shape

阝 Cliff *or* hill

衤 Clothing

金 Metal

貝 Money

鬼 Monster

TABLE OF CHARACTERS AND RADICALS
LISTED BY CHAPTER

Characters mentioned in passing are not listed.

CHAPTER 1

火　fire

炒　fry

烤　roast

燒　burn *or* cook

炸　deep-fry

燻　smoke

紅　red

CHAPTER 2

氵　water

酉　urn

口　mouth

水　water

川　brook

湯　soup

油　oil

醬　sauce

醋　vinegar

酸　sour

丁　"ding"

划　oar slicing through water

清　clear

淋　pour

泡　soak *or* pickle

溜　to glide, to marinate lightly

高　high

白　white

色　color

香　fragrance

味　taste

INTERLUDE 1

土 earth

CHAPTER 3

亻 man

山 mountain

仙 immortal

白 white

泉 spring water

醉 drunk

CHAPTER 4

雨 rain

女 woman

子 son

辶 movement

雲 cloud

吞 swallow

好 good

吃 eat

不 no *or* not

過 surpass

食 eat

合 union

吐 exhale

霧 fog

CHAPTER 5

羊	lamb	中	middle
牛	cow	小	small
目	eye	豬	pig
豕	pig	家	home
宀	roof	客	guest
馬	horse	安	peace
肉	flesh	感	feel
大	big	神	god
美	beauty	國	country

INTERLUDE 2

手 才	hand	友	friend

CHAPTER 6

鳥	bird	鴨	duck
佳	bird	鵝	goose
化	transform	鴿	squab
鷄	chicken	叫	call

CHAPTER 7

魚 fish

鯉 carp

先 earlier

生 alive

粥 porridge

米 rice

羔 baby lamb

羹 broth

CHAPTER 8

虫 insect *or* crawling creature

圓 round

尖 sharp

月 month *or* moon

蟹 crab

藝 art

妓 courtesan

龍 dragon

眼 eye

鮮 fresh *or* flavorful

海 sea

參 essence

涼 cool

拌 mixed *or* tossed (salad)

CHAPTER 9

艹 grass

木 wood *or* tree

林 forest

森 jungle

炎 blaze

朵 pick

採 pick

菜 vegetable

爪 paw

出 exit

洋 ocean *or* foreign

蔥 scallion

蒸 steam

冬 winter

菇 mushroom

黑 black

熏 smoke

燻 smoke

五 five

茄 eggplant

甘 sweet

甜 sweet

舌 tongue

香 fragrant

港 harbor

奶 milk

心 heart

忎忑 anxiety

愛 love

感 feel

情 mood

思 thought

想 thought

意 intention

CHAPTER 10

竹 bamboo

竹 bamboo

算 calculate

雙 a pair

双 a pair

冬 winter

炆 braise *or* simmer

筍 bamboo shoot

笋 bamboo shoot

連 connect *or* spread over

覺 perceive

集 collection

雜 miscellaneous

碎 broken bits

無 without

使 cause

俗 vulgar

CHAPTER 11

豆 bean

腐 corrupt *or* curd

婆 old woman

苦 bitter

力 force

田 field

男 male

劣 inferior

加 add

麻 numb, pockmarked *or* hemp

辣 peppery

辛 bitter

束 thorn

棘 thorn

百 hundred

葉 leaves

捲 roll

卷 roll

乾 dry

乳 breast

孚 breast

臭 smell

犬 dog

INTERLUDE 4

言 spoken word

文 written word

糸 silk radical

絲 silk

角 horn

刀 knife

字 words

解 analyze

CHAPTER 12

素 plain *or* vegetarian

雪 snow

CHAPTER 13

仁 interpersonal kindness

道 path *or* Tao

首 head

治 govern

為 (archaic) monkey *or* action

孔 hole

夫 fellow

禪 Zen

神 god

雷 thunder

礻 divine revelation

祈 pray

祭 offer

祝 bless

福 good fortune

蝠 bat

灶 hearth

INTERLUDE 5

呆 idiot

休 to rest

東 east

旦 dawn

早 early *or* morning

莫 evening *or* not

暮 evening

墓 tomb

明 bright

和 harmony *or* and

共 together

音 sound

計 calculate, scheme

犬 dog

狗 dog

獄 jail

樂 music *or* happy

婦 married woman

奸 traitor

姦 rape

眉 eyebrow

媚 flirtatious

姓 family name

CHAPTER 14

茶 tea

經 canonical book

工 work

仿 imitation

CHAPTER 15

點 dot

黑 black

点 dot

團 union

圓 round

壽 longevity

桃 peach

粥 porridge

覺 nap

CHAPTER 16

長 long

髮 hair

陰 yin

陽 yang

太 ultimate

涼 cool

熱 hot

乾 dry

濕 wet

滋 moistening

補 repair

形 shape

氣 *chi or* air

極 extreme

拳 fist

CHAPTER 17

席 banquet

蓆 mat

翅 wing *or* fin

燕 swallow *or* swift

APPENDIX A

宝	treasure	八	eight
玉	jade	零	zero
王	king	季	season
皇	king	貝	money
止	stop	財	wealth
正	proper	發	expand
定	settled *or* definite	鬼	devil
恭	respect	魁	monster
喜	joy	金	gold
兩	couple	順	smooth
相	mutual *or* inspect	利	profit
高	high	快	quickly
六	six	全	entire

APPENDIX B

干	dry	乾	cosmic
旱	drought	耳	ear

ACKNOWLEDGMENTS

FIRST AND FOREMOST, I would like to thank my parents. After all, they were the ones who first introduced me to the Chinese civilization. I thank them for showing me some of the finer things in life and for giving me the education and sophistication to know how to enjoy them. My mother graciously agreed to write the Chinese characters in this book, which has thus become all the more meaningful to me. My father drew upon his experience to tell me about various folk customs, particularly those in connection with the "fist-guessing" game played at banquets.

This is not the place to state in detail how grateful I am to my wife, Gretchen. She plays many roles in my life, not least of which is that she has cooked Chinese food for me for over twenty years. Gretchen is a strong editor and helped me a great deal in organizing the book. She also provided the recipes listed within.

I have had the great fortune and happiness of knowing Sonia Ng. An authority on Chinese food and a television and radio personality in Hong Kong, she is the author of *Talking about History, Talking about Food*, written in Chinese and based on her highly popular radio program. I would like the world to know that not only have I enjoyed discussing food with her over many a fine meal, but I actually have also had the privilege of tasting her cooking! I am grateful to her for reading my manuscript and making numerous useful suggestions. She has been an enormous help to me, patiently answering all my questions.

I am thankful to Louis Cha for kindly permitting me to translate and to use two extended passages from his marvelous novels, *The Boy Who Shot the Hawk* and *Eight Parts of the Celestial Dragon*.

I am pleased to have had Bob Asahina and Belinda Loh as my editors; their encouragement, enthusiasm, and advice did much to improve the book. In particular, Belinda's endless patience had a marvelously soothing effect on me during the later stages, which are often difficult for authors to bear. I thank the people at Simon and Schuster, the copy editor George Wen, the production editor Renée Rabb, and the designers Eve Metz and Barbara Marks for their meticulous and careful work. This book was obviously not easy to design and to produce. They did a terrific job.

Several other friends, Sarah Carr-Prindle, Pat Coakley, and Karen Jacobson, and my son, Andrew Zee, all took time to read the manuscript. Their suggestions and comments really helped me to clarify and to smooth out what I had written. Andrew, who is eleven, read the manuscript to fulfill the reading requirements of his seventh-grade English class.

I would also like to thank Professor Eugene N. Anderson for his careful reading of the manuscript and for several informative and scholarly comments.

Finally, the enthusiastic support of Carol Lalli and Charles Levine was helpful to me in the early stages of this book.

I am grateful to the following for providing the various illustrations: Sonia Ng, Gretchen Zee, Stella Zee, and Peter Zee. Photographs on page 81 are by James Chen.

ABOUT THE AUTHOR

Born in China, reared in Brazil, and educated at Princeton and Harvard, A. Zee has traveled and lectured around the world. *Publishers Weekly* called him "an extraordinary writer: playful, inspired, and brilliant," while *The New York Times* praised his "wry, poetic humor." His previous book, *An Old Man's Toy,* was nominated for a Pulitzer Prize in nonfiction.